Mad Men & Bad Men

Sam Delaney is an award-winning writer and broadcaster. He is the author of two previous books: *Get Smashed: The Story of the Men Who Made the Adverts that Changed Our Lives* and *Night of the Living Dad: Confessions of a Shabby Father*. He has made documentaries for the BBC and Channel Four, and his writing has appeared in the *Guardian*, the *Telegraph*, the *Big Issue* and the *Observer*. He is the former editor of *Heat* magazine.

Further praise for *Mad Men & Bad Men*:

'Fresh and spiced with surprises . . . Describes the incestuous, sometimes disingenuous world of London advertising with authority and clarity.' Andy Beckett, *Guardian*

'With his first-hand knowledge of both sides, Sam Delaney shows how the love-in between the ad men and Westminster that began in the seventies has rewritten the rules of political persuasion. Would they lie to you? Oh, yes . . .' John Crace

'Legendary Saatchi ad men . . . loom large on these pages and add many laughs to Delaney's balanced and thoughtful account of the power of advertising in m ... The livelines ... ial

idea of the ad man as champagne-fuelled, colourful and full of mischief . . . *Mad Men & Bad Men* makes an eloquent and entertaining case for letting the ad men open the champagne and do their worst.' Olivia Cole, *GQ*

'Thorough and intelligent.' Brian Appleyard, *New Statesman*

'Delaney's breezily readable history, charting the recent alliance of politics and advertising, asks whether the millions spent on election adverts are worth it.' Nicholas Blincoe, *Sunday Telegraph*

'It is a common prejudice about modern politics that it is all focus groups and spin, all public relations and advertising. The rather heartening conclusion from Sam Delaney's history of advertising in politics is that this is a calumny on the political trade . . . Delaney is an entertaining guide.' Philip Collins, *Spectator*

---

by the same author

GET SMASHED
NIGHT OF THE LIVING DAD

SAM DELANEY

MAD MEN & BAD MEN

WHEN BRITISH POLITICS MET ADVERTISING

ff
FABER & FABER

First published in 2015
by Faber & Faber Ltd
Bloomsbury House
74–77 Great Russell Street
London WC1B 3DA

This paperback edition published in 2016

Typeset by Ian Bahrami
Printed in England by CPI Group (UK) Ltd, Croydon, CR0 4YY

Photos pp. x, 34 and 266: courtesy of M&C Saatchi; pp. 2, 76, 124, 162 and 184: Getty Images/The Conservative Party Archive; pp. 20, 94 and 144: People's History Museum; p. 58: Garnet Edwards; p. 206: Victoria and Albert Museum, London; p. 232: Saatchi & Saatchi; p. 250: Rex Features/NTI Media Ltd

A CIP record for this book
is available from the British Library

ISBN 978-0-571-31240-5

FSC
www.fsc.org
MIX
Paper from responsible sources
FSC® C101712

10 9 8 7 6 5 4 3 2 1

For
Baz and Lenny

CONTENTS

Introduction

A FOOTNOTE IN HER HISTORY

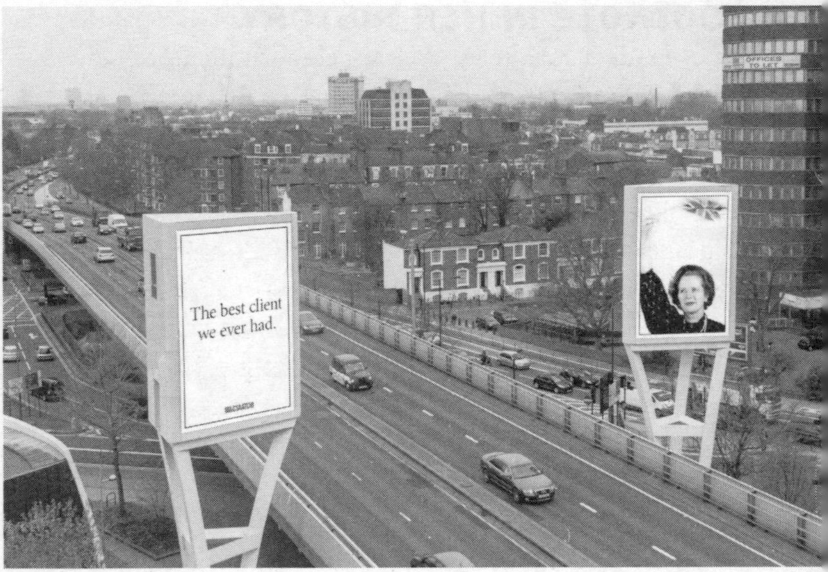
OFFICES
TO LET
The best client
we ever had.

When Margaret Thatcher died, the ad executive Maurice Saatchi made a rare television appearance on *Channel 4 News* to talk about his time working with her. The presenter, Jon Snow, wanted to know exactly how Saatchi had used the dark arts of adland to transform Thatcher from political outsider to iconic leader. But Saatchi surprised Snow by insisting that he really hadn't done much at all. He said that it was Thatcher's ideas and leadership style alone that won her success and acclaim. The presentation techniques devised by him and the ad agency he ran with his brother Charles were neither here nor there. 'On a good day we would be a footnote in her history, but that's all,' he said.

'Well, you can't simply say that she was such a great philosopher and politician that [you] didn't need to do anything,' insisted Snow.

'That's exactly what I'm saying,' said Saatchi.

'Are you saying that presentation isn't important in politics?' asked Snow.

'Yes, I am,' responded Saatchi firmly. Which was a bit strange.

Saatchi & Saatchi has been synonymous with the Conservative Party, and Mrs Thatcher in particular, since the late seventies. In fact, the agency made its name by working for the party, creating iconic campaigns that heralded a whole new approach to political communications. Its association with Thatcher put it on the map, helping it win more acclaim, awards and business than it knew what to do with and, in no time at all, grow into the world's biggest ad firm. Even today, Saatchi & Saatchi remains the only ad agency ever to have become a household name. Some might say Maurice Saatchi owed it all to Mrs Thatcher. And here he was suggesting she owed him nothing.

Perhaps he thought it was inappropriate to take any credit for her success in the immediate aftermath of her death. Maybe he felt he had little to lose in admitting after all this time that advertising was, just as so many businesses and politicians had always suspected, a complete waste of time and money. Saatchi was now rich enough to never have to make another ad for anyone ever again. But most probably he was, like any good adman, continuing to loyally serve his client – even after she had stopped breathing. A great adman will never take credit for a client's success. The emphasis must always be on the quality of the product.

I wanted to find out if Saatchi was telling the truth when he said all of his well-paid work for the Conservative Party had been totally pointless. If that turned out to be true, it would make for a brilliant story. Now I don't want to ruin the ending of this book, but I can tell you that Maurice Saatchi was, at the very least, exaggerating to make a point. I spent the next six months or so speaking with all sorts of admen, politicians, academics and commentators. Some of them said that the Saatchis had too much influence, others that their influence has been wildly exaggerated. But the only person who said Maurice Saatchi was irrelevant to the Tories' success was Maurice Saatchi himself.

The role that he, and numerous other admen, played in political combat between the late seventies and late nineties was unprecedented. This was a period in which politicians became besotted with admen, spin doctors and image makers, convinced as they were that the acceleration of mass communication made an award-winning adman as crucial to their political armoury as a decent policy advisor.

Admen would eventually enter the very heart of the political hierarchies within both the Labour and Conservative parties. In many cases they went beyond just communicating policies; they were also involved in devising the policies themselves. That they were involved is a matter of fact; whether their involvement had any practical impact is difficult to determine. But that was broadly what I set out to do – simply talk to the individuals involved, both politicians and admen, and ask them what difference they thought advertising made to election outcomes.

But I wanted other questions answered too, questions like: what happens when stuffy politicians and swishy admen collide? I'll be honest, this was one I was particularly keen to resolve. My first book, *Get Smashed*, was about the rise and rise of the British ad industry from the sixties through to the eighties. It was the story of how a rag-tag band of scruffs and smart-arses staged a coup in adland, rising from the post rooms to the boardrooms of agencies and revolutionising the industry for ever. They were young, usually uneducated, mostly working-class and uniformly wild and reckless in their behaviour. Irreverent, long-haired, cocksure and drunk more often than not, they made London the advertising capital of the world, earning the sort of money and having the kind of adventures that usually only pop stars could dream of. This was the world that Maurice Saatchi and his brother Charles grew up in, a world that seemed far removed from the one occupied by politicians.

I had had my own experiences of the ad industry. When I was a kid I used to sometimes go and visit my dad at work. I lived in the suburbs of west London with my mum, who worked as a secretary in a local building firm. My impressions of the grown-up working world were mostly based on her office, which was a bit dreary – the sort of place where everyone had one eye on the clock all day. So when I first got the Tube to the West End to visit my dad at the ad agency he had started with his brother, I was astonished. Their building was in Covent Garden, surrounded by Italian cafes and trendy clothes shops. His office was painted in bright colours; it smelt of fresh coffee; it was full of really attractive women and flashy blokes who just seemed to sit around drawing and taking the piss out of each other all day. They always went out to restaurants for lunch and drank wine. It didn't seem like work; it seemed like a ludicrous Shangri-La where people got paid for pissing about.

That said, I didn't fancy it as a career. My dad taught me that advertising might be a lot of fun, but it was basically pointless. He was with Maurice Saatchi on that one. The only time he seemed to take his work at all seriously was when he worked pro bono for the Labour Party. It was ironic that he worked for free because trying to make the Labour Party popular in the eighties was probably one of the toughest briefs in the history of British advertising.

Politics, by comparison to the ad game, seemed both exciting and important. When I was a kid I devoured shows like *Yes Minister*, *Spitting Image* and *House of Cards* (the original one, with Ian Richardson). The latter depicted Westminster as a seductive and mysterious world where silvery-haired gents struck shadowy deals over large glasses of whisky in oak-panelled rooms. I liked the look of it. So after I'd finished my A-levels and before I went off to study politics at university, I got a work-experience placement as a researcher at the House of Commons. For six months I worked in the parliamentary office of Harriet Harman, the MP for Peckham and a member of Labour's shadow cabinet. I did a lot of photocopying and tea-making but very little to justify my admittedly ostentatious use of the title 'researcher'. There was certainly not much in the way of silvery-haired gents striking shadowy deals. I occasionally entered an oak-panelled room but was never once offered any whisky. All in all, I found it a bit of a let-down. The offices were more akin to those of my mum's building firm than my dad's ad agency. There was the occasional errand to be run in the Commons itself, but the MPs' offices were all based in buildings dotted around Westminster that were significantly less imposing. There were a lot of worn-out carpet tiles and cold, dimly lit Victorian corridors that smelt of bleach. At lunchtime we all ate sandwiches from Boots at our desks and drank watery coffee from a vending machine. There wasn't much in the way of horsing around. This was the biggest difference between politics and advertising: in advertising, no one seemed to take anything seriously; in politics (especially Labour politics) everyone took everything seriously. And why shouldn't they? They were trying to work out how best to run the country, not just dreaming up a new slogan for a brand of fabric conditioner. Daily restaurant lunches accompanied by wine probably helped my dad and his colleagues fan the flames of creative whimsy, but that sort of carry-on would have been unlikely to have helped the minions in Harriet Harman's office devise a new VAT policy.

The point is, these were radically contrasting worlds, and I was fascinated by what happened when they collided. Of course, my curiosity stretched beyond just wanting to know what happened when grumpy politicians hung out with crazy admen; I also wanted to examine the widely held view that advertising was somehow bad for politics. People are cynical about advertising because they think it is inherently manipulative; it uses cheap tricks and artful hoodwinkery to convince us ordinary schmucks to do, think and buy stuff we don't actually like. Which is bad enough when it's being used to flog us breakfast cereal but even worse when it's used to shape our political choices. But could it be that finding more effective ways of communicating politicians' ideas and intentions to a wider audience might actually be good for democracy? Might the adman's skill in taking complicated and boring ideas and turning them into snappy, engaging propositions help us make more informed decisions about how we vote?

For the average Joe who votes every few years but isn't a committed daily viewer of *Newsnight*, the story of politics is the story of elections. Real politics – the stuff that happens in draughty church halls, Commons committee rooms, parliamentary chambers and those cold corridors smelling of bleach in Westminster where I once worked – is too boring for most of us to pay much attention to. But elections are like World Cups: they come round periodically and dominate the media with a short burst of high-stakes brinkmanship, bloody public battles and captivating drama in which the winner takes it all. Much of the election narrative is spelt out by admen: the posters, political broadcasts, slogans and stunts they dream up on behalf of politicians are often what define our memories of those barmy circuses that erupt once every four or five years and somehow dictate our national destiny. 'Labour isn't working', 'Double whammy', 'Demon eyes', 'Things can only get better': these are the phrases that spell out electoral history in the modern age. Elections are the sexy part of politics, and the ads are the sexiest part of elections.

The first person I spoke to was Norman Tebbit, the man in charge of the Conservative campaign in 1987 – the dark apex of British politicians' love affair with advertising. I remembered his *Spitting Image* caricature better than I did him: a Gestapo-type thug in a leather trench coat wielding a truncheon in the direction of his party's enemies at the behest of the prime minister. With his bald head, imposing gait and cold, booming delivery he was characterised as the Chingford Skinhead by the press. When I was a kid, I was shit-scared of him.

Now, he lives in Bury St Edmunds, the very epitome of the Tory heartland. It's rural but smart; neat, tidy, charming and posh. 'You get a real mix here,' Tebbit says as he welcomes me into his home, an impressive converted B&B right in the centre of town. 'In Waitrose the staff call me Lord Tebbit. In M&S they call me just plain Norman. And at the market on a Saturday morning it's Norm!'

He's a bit frail but perfectly pleasant as he ushers me into his study and offers me coffee. The Estuary growl is still there to remind you of the truncheon-wielding days but all in all he could be best described as kindly. His life still revolves around his wheelchair-bound wife, Margaret.

Although he is a member of the House of Lords, his trips to London are infrequent as he prefers to stay with her as much as possible. In his study, where a Harold Wilson biography sits on the shelf and a well-thumbed copy of George Orwell's *Nineteen Eighty-Four* leans against a framed picture of a Thatcher cabinet from that same year, he explains to me the philosophical logistics of an election campaign. 'Imagine we're both political parties,' he says. 'You're sat there three feet away from me and I decide to move into the centre ground.' He actually shuffles his chair about a foot closer to me. 'Now the centre ground has moved even closer to you, hasn't it? Mathematically, I mean.' I nod. 'Now if I keep chasing that middle ground, then where do I end up? On your lap!' We are now so close we can feel each other's breath. I've been in Norman Tebbit's house just twenty minutes and things are not transpiring in a way I could ever have imagined. 'Of course, the person laughing all the way to the bank in all of this is Nigel Farage!' he continues. I'm still nodding and smiling. 'Because by moving all the way onto your lap I have vacated that huge amount of space behind me, which UKIP can claim for themselves!'

Tebbit might look less frightening than he once did but his passion for politics is clearly undimmed. Because of his commitment to his wife he gets fewer opportunities to vent to journalists than he once did. Which evidently means that when someone like me comes to visit, he's got a great deal of vent in reserve.

Tebbit, like Thatcher, was a thoroughly modern Tory: a state-educated boy from the lower middle classes, self-made and ambitious. He had grown up in a political culture that still seemed to be more about politics and less about spin. Politicians were very often men with experience of the real world who had neither the need nor the inclination to seek advice from admen about how to do their job. But by the time he became Conservative Party chairman in the mid-eighties, the world around him was changing fast. Tebbit would have to learn to work with professional image-makers, whose influence was growing rapidly. But he was a pragmatist who quickly saw how such men could help him. 'I remember attending the 1985 party conference and thinking it was a mess,' says Tebbit. 'There were no themes, no consistent messages, it looked devoid of ideas, and the press seemed to be writing what it wanted. I knew that I'd be in charge the following year and vowed that things would be very different.'

Shortly afterwards, Thatcher appointed Tebbit party chairman, and his first aim was to plan a conference for 1986 that would be a springboard for a general election the following year. The party machinery at Conservative central office in Smith Square was vast and it would take Tebbit a while to harness it. In the meantime, he decided he would lean heavily on the party's ad agency, Saatchi & Saatchi.

The Conservatives went into the conference in third place in the opinion polls, sitting behind both Labour and the SDP–Liberal Alliance. The repercussions of the miners' strike were rumbling on; Britain's assistance in the US bombing of Libya in April of that year had attracted much negative attention; and an internal government dispute over the fate of a struggling helicopter company, Westland, had rocked the government and led to the resignations of two senior ministers. In addition, Thatcher's personal ratings were at a low. 'She was rightly admired for being strong and passionate, but there was a sense among the public that we had run out of ideas and direction,' says Tebbit. 'And a strong leader with no direction is regarded as a dangerous thing.'

The world's flashiest admen and the Chingford Skinhead might have seemed an unlikely pairing but it was with the Saatchi team that Tebbit and his right-hand man, Michael Dobbs, conceived the 'Next Steps Forward' strategy for the 1986 conference. Saatchis' extensive research showed that after two terms in power the Conservatives were perceived as having run out of ideas. They advised Tebbit that it was vital the Tories used that year's conference to re-establish a sense of momentum. Together with Tebbit's team at central office, Saatchis supplied cabinet ministers with bullet-pointed lists of the 'next steps' their ministries would take during a third term in office. Then, as each of them finished delivering their speeches, those bullet points would go up on posters all around the conference centre. Journalists were effectively spoon-fed their stories. It was the sort of succinct thinking that politicians often struggle with but admen specialise in. 'It was clear and focused and it worked brilliantly,' says Tebbit. 'It was the first thing Saatchis had done for me and I was hugely impressed.'

The strategy worked. By the autumn the Conservatives were back on top in the opinion polls, establishing a lead they would maintain right up to polling day. When Margaret Thatcher called the election in the summer, Tebbit's message to his campaign team was clear and succinct: 'Let's not have a fuck-up! Because on day one we've won this election!'

The subsequent campaign might have ended in victory but it was hardly the uneventful process Tebbit had hoped for. His relationship with Thatcher was already under strain. She was reported to have become paranoid about Tebbit's growing media profile; he was disgruntled that she had not consulted him over Britain's role in the US bombing of Libya. Tebbit was ensconced in party HQ at Smith Square, surrounded by his own team of campaign advisors, including senior figures from Saatchi & Saatchi. Across Westminster in Downing Street, Thatcher was forming her own alternative team, led by her favoured adman, Tim Bell.

Bell had been the frontman for Saatchi & Saatchi during the Conservative election campaigns of 1979 and 1983. During that time he had forged an extremely close relationship with the prime minister, who, a former cabinet colleague explains, 'thought Tim Bell *was* Saatchi & Saatchi'. But by 1987 Bell had gone through an acrimonious split from the Saatchis. The brothers were now anxious that their former colleague would seek to steal their biggest clients for his new agency, and they supposed that the Conservative account would be Bell's prime target. When the campaign began in April 1987, battle lines were drawn between Bell and the agency he once worked for.

Bell had been regarded as such an integral part of the Saatchi story that he was widely known in the business as 'the third brother'. But he had become increasingly close to Margaret Thatcher, and the Conservative account seemed to be his priority; meanwhile, the brothers were preoccupied with growing the agency globally via a series of acquisitions. A distance had grown between the three men and, eventually, it was decided that Bell should leave. 'They never actually told me why,' he maintains. The Saatchis suggested one condition to his departure: he would remain a consultant on the Conservative Party account in return for a £24,000-per-year retainer. This was an acknowledgement of the close relationship he shared with the prime minister and a safety measure against Bell attempting to poach the Tory business. But it soon turned out to be nothing more than a gesture: despite their £24,000 outlay, the Saatchis would fiercely resist Bell having any involvement with the Conservative election campaign whatsoever.

The stereotypical adman of the time was wild, working-class and fashionably left-wing. Tim Bell was quite different. Handsome, smart and public-school-educated, people in advertising described him as 'so charming that dogs would cross the street just to be kicked by him'. Thatcher had been smitten since they first met in 1978. 'I was her favourite and people didn't like it,' says Bell. 'I would be invited into cabinet meetings to give presentations and you could see them rolling their eyes while she beamed enthusiastically.'

Bell's desire to help was personal. 'I never wanted to take the Conservative account from Saatchis for business reasons,' he says. 'I just wanted to help Mrs Thatcher because I believed in what she was doing. The Saatchis weren't Conservative supporters. Charlie [Saatchi] used to say that he'd be just as happy to do Labour's ads, if they paid him the same.'

In April 1986 Saatchi & Saatchi was invited to give a presentation to the prime minister at Chequers, outlining its strategy for the following year's election. Michael Dobbs had been a young researcher for the Conservatives at the 1979 election, and was subsequently hired by Tim Bell to work at Saatchi & Saatchi. By 1986 he had been seconded by the agency back to Conservative central office to work alongside Tebbit. The task of delivering some unflattering research to the prime minister fell to him. He remembers rising to his feet in front of the entire cabinet, as Thatcher furrowed her brow. 'Negative opinions on Thatcher came up again and again when we spoke to the public,' says Dobbs. 'The phrase that stuck was "that bloody woman", which became known as "TBW". The public were sick of her, and I was the person who had to give her the bad news.'

Dobbs's audacious plan was to limit Thatcher's role in any campaign and push her senior cabinet colleagues, such as Tebbit and the chancellor, Nigel Lawson, forward as the prominent faces of the party. Tebbit backed the idea. 'The public had originally liked the fact that she was strong and determined,' he says. 'But by 1987 they thought she lacked any real focus. And a determined leader with no real focus is perceived as a dangerous thing – like a bull in a china shop.'

'It was the hardest presentation of my life,' says Dobbs. 'But I knew I had Norman's backing, so I told her our findings and even used the "that bloody woman" phrase. Her face was like thunder.' On her return to London, she immediately asked Tim Bell to visit her at Downing Street to express her concerns. 'The first thing she said was, "I need you back on the team,"' says Bell. 'Then she asked why everyone at Saatchis was so hostile to the idea. I started to explain that they were paranoid about me stealing their business. Then I stopped myself and thought, "What am I telling her all this shit for? She's the prime minister!"'

Bell agreed with Thatcher that she could not force the party to move its business to his new agency. 'Maurice Saatchi and Michael Dobbs had successfully crawled up Tebbit's arse by then and there was no way he'd agree to let them go. Plus, he hated me,' says Bell. Instead, Bell agreed that he would meet Thatcher regularly as her personal campaign advisor. 'We had to meet in secret because Tebbit and the Saatchis would have hit the roof if they knew I was critiquing their work for her!' says Bell. 'But as far as I was concerned they had welched on their consultancy deal with me and, worse, they had welched on their deal with her. She asked for me to be involved and they point-blank refused. She's the fucking prime minister! If she asks for something, then you give it to her. The Saatchis have a very different idea of loyalty to me. I would do anything for people I respect. They just think anyone who doesn't agree with them is an idiot who needs to be shouted into submission.'

With Bell operating behind the scenes at Downing Street and Thatcher still furious about the presentation at Chequers, her relationship with Tebbit soured even further. She became convinced that he was planning a challenge for the party leadership – and took the 'that bloody woman' presentation as conclusive evidence of the fact. 'Negative stories started to come out in the press about Norman throughout the early part of the year,' says Dobbs. 'It was well known that Number 10 was leaking them. We were in a situation where we were heading towards a general election with the leader and the party chairman engaged in open warfare.'

Thatcher had spent Saturday 9 May at Chequers, the prime ministerial retreat in Buckinghamshire, setting down the final plans for the election. During the day she had finessed the Conservative manifesto with Norman Tebbit and Professor Brian Griffiths. But by the time their work was concluded in the early evening, Tim Bell had been ushered through the security gates in a chauffeur-driven car, accompanied by his fiancée, Virginia Hornbrook. The pair were hidden in a back room until Tebbit left Chequers, at which point the prime minister greeted them as guests at her husband Denis's seventy-second birthday party. Her party colleagues might have been able to stop Bell contacting her professionally, but not socially: he was a friend of the family. Nevertheless, as the birthday dinner proceeded, conversation naturally turned to election matters, with Thatcher grilling Bell for his thoughts on the Saatchi strategy. This set the tone for how the whole campaign would proceed: the PM taking advice from Tebbit and Saatchis, before consulting Tim Bell through back channels. It would inevitably make for a confused, tense and disjointed few weeks, and would end with punches being thrown in Number 10. Could it be true that a government was rocked so badly by the petty squabbles of admen?

When I asked Tebbit this question, he smiled. 'You have to understand the different points of view Margaret and I were coming from in 1987,' he said. 'My own forensic research had pinpointed a few marginal seats that I thought were crucial to winning the election. Margaret, on the other hand, was far more interested in the national campaign by that stage. She liked the flashy posters and the election broadcasts. She thought that was the key to winning. I think she was enthralled by advertising.'

1

YESTERDAY'S MEN

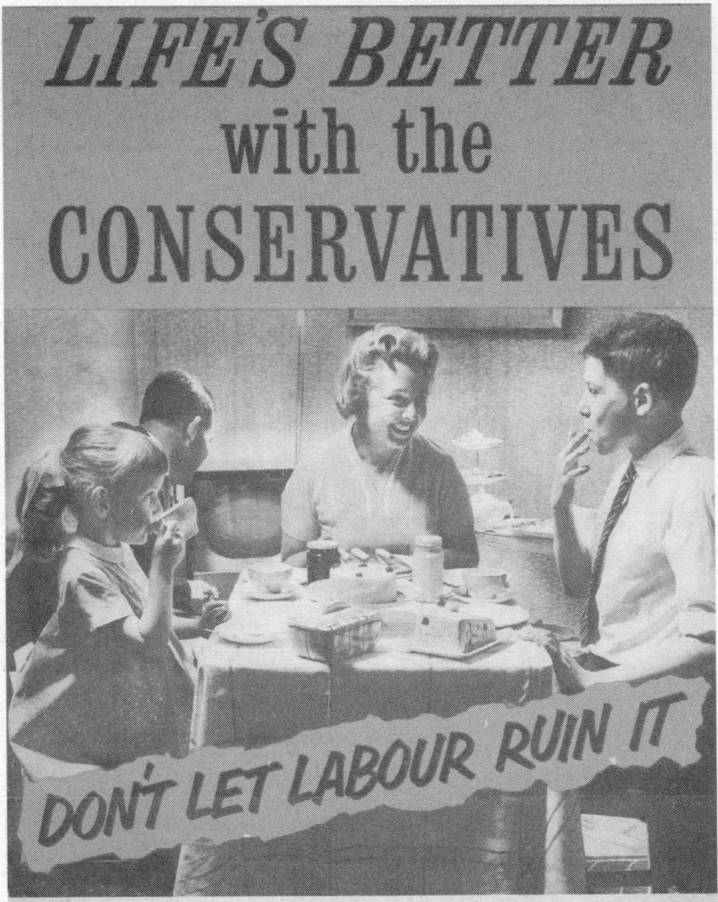
LIFE'S BETTER
with the
CONSERVATIVES
DON'T LET LABOUR RUIN IT
VOTE
CONSERVATIVE

Television advertising arrived in Britain on 22 September 1955. The first commercial was for Gibbs SR toothpaste. It featured a tube of toothpaste and a block of ice, accompanied by a voiceover espousing the product's 'tingling fresh qualities'. It was all a bit stilted and uncertain. The following day journalist Bernard Levin wrote in the *Manchester Guardian*: 'I feel neither depraved nor uplifted by what I have seen . . . certainly the advertising has been entirely innocuous. I have already forgotten the name of the toothpaste.'

Consumerism was in its fledgling stages in Britain, where people were generally suspicious of salespeople – especially those who invited themselves into their living rooms via the television set. While advertising was already booming in the US, the dictates of British society in the fifties remained: to make something is noble; to sell it is crass.

But before advertising agencies were even allowed to make TV commercials, politicians were having a shot at it. There is a fantastic election broadcast you can watch on YouTube featuring the then foreign secretary, Harold Macmillan, shuffling awkwardly around his office explaining how much better things had got under the Conservatives since 1951. It plays like a Harry Enfield parody of early British TV: Macmillan actually feigns surprise at the start of the film, leaning casually against a mantelpiece for a second before turning to face the camera. He is unsure about where to put his hands, cannot stop moving clumsily around the room and, having eventually settled himself in an armchair, spends several seconds delivering his stilted monologue to the wrong camera.

It's easy to laugh, but how was Macmillan, a man born in 1894, supposed to adapt his well-honed rhetorical skills, nurtured at the hustings and the despatch box, to a newfangled medium that necessitated speaking into a giant mechanical box? He had no chance. That said, the filmmakers did show some imagination: the broadcast cut away to an insert demonstrating the improved living standards of post-war Britain. Tax cuts were illustrated with images of scissors cutting through flowers; a waste-paper bin was filled with screwed-up documents to signify the assault on bureaucracy; footage of women and children burning their ration books painted a convincing picture of a society on the up. These were the fledgling days of TV: politicians and filmmakers were learning how to illustrate ideas with moving images – and to do so in a way that might be engaging, convincing, perhaps even a little charming.

The early years of TV advertising delivered little creative progress, with many commercials simply adapting ideas from posters for the same product. The first Persil ads showed dancers and sailors in different shades of white, with a voiceover declaring: 'Persil washes whiter. That means cleaner.' Another popular format was to use a presenter – very often a celebrity of the time – to deliver an endorsement of a particular product, usually laced with a faux-scientific demonstration.

The business was yet to be professionalised. The only people allowed by union laws to direct TV commercials were existing TV or film directors. Ad agencies would usually rely on out-of-work practitioners from these fields, who would make ads between jobs with some reluctance. In short, there were no specialists seeking to innovate.

But that would quickly change. The growth of consumerism and the rise of a new generation of young spenders encouraged big business and their ad agencies to seek fresh ideas from a new generation of admen. Soon, a tribe of ambitious young men would infiltrate the industry and try to elevate the art of advertising. 'Suddenly one day the plates moved,' said David Abbott, who started as a copywriter in the fifties and went on to become one of the pre-eminent admen of the twentieth century. 'The only criterion that mattered in the industry was producing great work. And the people who created that great work became the new stars.'

The seeds of this revolution had been sown a decade earlier in New York. The US ad industry had started to embrace a new style of creativity that eschewed the formal, corporate tone of traditional marketing in favour of a fun, engaging and colloquial approach. The catalyst was a quiet New Yorker of Jewish descent called Bill Bernbach, who had worked as a political speechwriter for the Democratic Party prior to cutting his teeth in Madison Avenue. He was the first to explicitly endorse the idea of addressing the consumer society with grace, charm and humour. 'Bob suggested that once you'd worked out what you wanted to say, it was just as important to work out how you wanted to say it,' recalled one of his former colleagues, Bob Cooperman. Bernbach was the first adman to boldly oppose the research-driven methodology of traditional advertising. 'I warn you against believing that advertising is a science,' he said. 'Rules are what the artist breaks. The memorable never emerged from a formula.'

Bernbach formed an agency called Doyle Dane Bernbach, which chose to adopt a more creative and intelligent approach. DDB was an immediate success, winning numerous clients such as Avis car hire and Volkswagen. For Levy's Rye Bread it created a campaign in which a variety of ethnic faces – from a Native American chief to an Afro-Caribbean to a Chinese American – all announced: 'You don't have to be Jewish to eat Levy's.' For Avis, Bernbach made a virtue of being second to Hertz in the car-hire market by creating the slogan 'We try harder', and he wrote a press ad for the Volkswagen Beetle under the headline 'Think small'; the accompanying copy breezily encouraged the American car buyer – traditionally preoccupied with size and power – to purchase this oddly shaped German car on the basis of its low fuel consumption. Such ideas ran counter to all of advertising's received wisdom, but consumers responded in droves.

The ads also inspired a generation of young British admen to start their own revolution in London. It was all about emulating the work of Bernbach: discarding the hard sell in favour of wit, eloquence and warmth. There was a new breed of suave admen who had no time for traditional agencies like J. Walter Thompson; they wanted to make great ads and have fun doing it. Soon, they would turn their attentions to selling politics.

Part of that generation was Jeremy Scott, a partner at Garrett's, London's leading commercials production company of the era. With his rakish demeanour, E-Type Jag and seemingly ever-present entourage of beautiful models,

Scott appeared to have lived the archetypal swinging-sixties lifestyle. I had devoured his raucous memoir, *Fast and Louche*, some years ago, in which he recounted his experiences working for Edward Heath's 1970 election campaign team. This was exactly the sort of incongruous meeting of minds that fascinated me: a proto-Austin Powers type in a fast car helping the post-war generation's most strait-laced would-be prime minister get his hands on the keys to Number 10.

I arranged to meet Scott in his local pub off the King's Road in Chelsea. The man I discovered when I got there did nothing to confound my preconceptions: Scott is impossibly suave, with a sartorial elegance and cut-glass delivery that's two parts David Niven, one part Roger Moore.

Over several half-pints of Italian lager, Scott dissected his adventures in adland, politics and beyond with captivating candour and a pathological tendency for wondrous tangents. His tales of fast times and high rolling were offset by laments about how it all ended in bankruptcy and ill health for many of his contemporaries. 'An old adland friend of mine has got pancreatic cancer,' he told me. 'It's terrible because he's in hospital on nil by mouth. And this chap has got used to drinking about two bottles of decent red a day for the past forty years.' Keen to relieve just a little of his friend's pain, Scott conjured up an idea. 'I remembered reading about how some of these rock stars in the seventies liked to pop cocaine up their bottoms when their noses gave up on them. So I called a doctor friend and asked him if the same thing might be possible with booze. He said he didn't see why not but that I should probably try it out on myself before imposing it on a friend. So I bought a syringe from the chemist, went home and shot about fifteen milligrams of cooking brandy up my anus. I've never been a big drinker myself but I can honestly say it felt wonderful! I went straight to the hospital and did the same thing to my friend, and he felt the same way.'

I wondered how a man given to such imaginative high jinks might have helped mastermind Edward Heath's unexpected electoral victory all those years ago. 'I had been working with James Garrett, whose company had been producing ads for all the top agencies of the time,' he says. 'But I'd got bored and quit to write a screenplay. Until one day James called to say that the Conservatives were coming in to talk about the election campaign. He knew nothing about politics and wondered if I might help out.' Scott saw it as a fresh opportunity for just the sort of unusual and unexpected work that had defined his career thus far. 'Willie Whitelaw was the chairman and came in with a team of rather dull pinstriped youngsters from central office. We tried our best to enthuse them about our credentials but they sat there stony-faced. Nevertheless, they said they'd like to have a second meeting and invite Heath along.'

Garrett instructed Scott to pull out all the stops to make the second meeting rather more lively than the first. 'I knew exactly what to do,' says Scott. 'First I went to Fortnum and Mason and ordered some canapés and decent wine for everyone, which I thought might help loosen them all up. Then, for safety, I visited my former nanny's home, where I stashed my box of contraband.' Inside the box was a bottle of Methedrine that Scott had stockpiled just before the drug went out of production in 1966. Prior to the meeting, Scott ground several of the amphetamine tablets to a fine powder and sprinkled them over the expensive canapés.

'It wasn't much, just enough to make them slightly more enthusiastic,' he told me. 'But what I didn't account for was the appetite of Heath and Whitelaw. They couldn't stop scoffing the food! By the end of the meeting we couldn't get rid of them, they were so animated. I was actually rather worried about Heath, who was very flushed in the face, with speckles of saliva forming at the corners of his mouth. Still, he seemed ready for the battle ahead.'

Scott hired his friend, the celebrity photographer Terence Donovan, to direct an election broadcast. The brief was to portray ordinary working people, outside of the traditional Conservative demographic, expressing approval of Heath. 'Terry was a cockney who had made good. He picked me up in his Rolls-Royce and took me to an estate in south London to film a friend of his,' says Scott. 'Her name was Tracy. Terry promised me she was "proper common" and could "talk your fucking head off". He was right, she could, and she had all the right sort of views that our client wanted to hear. She and her husband were aspirational working class. She said a great bit about her husband working hard and not feeling rewarded properly. I asked her what he did, and she glanced at Terry as if to say, "Doesn't he know?" Then she turned back to me and said, "Well, he's a . . . right Jack the Lad, ain't he?"'

When the Conservatives won the election on 18 June it was deemed one of the biggest electoral surprises of the century. The unfancied Heath had tapped into the aspirational working-class vote just enough to earn a 4.5 per cent swing in his favour and an unlikely forty-two-seat majority in the Commons. It was a small victory for a freewheeling new breed of London admen: James Garrett, the convivial maestro who had pulled together a gang of adland's best and brightest talent; Terry Donovan, who had not only been congratulated by Ted Heath for the best broadcast of the whole campaign but also rewarded with a set of new Rolls-Royce tyres by Tracy's Jack the Lad husband; and Jeremy Scott, who celebrated in style when he was invited to Number 10 for the victory party. 'I'd been overdoing the cocaine at the time,' says Scott. 'But I decided to finish off the last I had at the victory party. I excused myself halfway through and snorted a line in the Downing Street toilets!'

The admen had lent more than just colour and creativity to the Conservative Party campaign; they had applied consumer-research strategies too. Ever since Colman, Prentis and Varley – the biggest British ad agency of the time – had been appointed by the Conservatives in the fifties, these creatives had helped identify a new breed of Tory voter. 'The Labour Party had always assumed that all they need do was mobilise their natural support and they could win any election,' says Professor Ivor Crewe, master of University College, Oxford, and former editor of the *British Journal of Political Science*. 'But in the fifties and sixties the Conservatives had realised that there was a new working class who aspired to upward mobility – and they targeted them quite successfully.' In 1959 they ran a series of posters featuring a slogan that would be reused and rehashed by the party for decades to come: 'Life's better with the Conservatives – don't let Labour ruin it'.

Labour only began to catch up after the election of Harold Wilson as party leader in 1963. Dynamic and forward-thinking, Wilson had already written a report in the fifties on the need to modernise the Labour Party organisation, which he had described as a 'penny-farthing machine'. He understood that calculated use of the mass media was crucial to electoral success.

In 1963 Wilson addressed his first party conference as leader, dramatically illustrating his vision of a modern Britain forged in the 'white heat' of technology. This was the first sign of Labour gradually discarding its 'cloth cap' image and trying to cultivate a more modern one that might appeal to a changing society. It would emerge only later that a key figure behind Wilson's bold party rebrand was the young adman David Kingsley, who would soon emerge as the first moderniser in British politics. He was, perhaps, Labour's first spin doctor, more than two decades before the term was applied to Peter Mandelson.

Kingsley and Wilson were both hugely influenced by a social study published in 1960 entitled *Must Labour Lose?* The book, written by academics Mark Abrams and Richard Rose, examined the same shift that the Tories had got wise to some years previously: what they called a 'bourgeoisification' of the working class. Abrams and Rose's studies identified a narrowing gap between the aspirations of the affluent and non-affluent working classes. They suggested that the Labour Party needed more middle-class-friendly policies, which should include a commitment to both public and private business and services. It was in many ways a foundation for what would become known many years later as New Labour. Unsurprisingly, ad execs like Kingsley – men with socialist values who had made good by virtue of rampant capitalism – were enamoured by the study.

David Kingsley was the embodiment of the modern British adman: educated in a state school, his sharp wit and intelligence had helped earn him a degree at the London School of Economics before he began making his way in advertising. Overt socialism was still a relatively rare thing in the ad industry, and the fact that Kingsley wore his left-wing leanings on his sleeve naturally brought him to the attention of John Harris, Labour's director of publicity, and, in turn, Wilson. 'I was a rare thing in that I was politically motivated and I had spent a great deal of effort establishing a reputation in advertising,' said Kingsley. 'There weren't many of us about at that time.'

Along with media-management expert Peter Lovell-Davis and PR man Denis Lyons, Kingsley became one of Wilson's so-called Three Wise Men, the unpaid advisors who would help guide communications strategy throughout the decade. They were responsible for the campaign slogans 'Let's go with Labour and we'll get things done' in 1964 and 'You know Labour government works' in 1966. They pushed Wilson to make the party more appealing to emerging social classes and imbued the party with a sense of optimism to counter the austerity of the post-war years, all of which helped Labour end thirteen years out of power by winning the election of 1964.

After Wilson's historic victory, Kingsley became a significant figure at Number 10. Considered the most talented of the Three Wise Men, he visited the prime minister every fortnight. It was Kingsley who convinced Wilson to bring in the American pollster Bob Worcester to look at the reasons behind the voting intentions of the electorate. Polling of this sort was rare in British politics at the time, but Kingsley had seen the good it did his commercial clients and believed it could do the same for Labour.

Worcester now lives in a thirteenth-century castle in Kent surrounded by a moat and numerous acres of woodland occupied by rabbits and an assortment of other wildlife, which is where I went to visit him. Labour had been one of his first clients when he arrived in the UK in 1969. It was Kingsley who invited him to meet Wilson, but, says Worcester, there was scepticism within the party towards his business.

'There was a general sense among the people who controlled the party that they didn't need outsiders telling them what their supporters thought,' he says. Worcester positioned himself as a non-political consultant: he offered to present a thorough and rigorous reflection of the public's views, not policy guidance or solutions. He quickly discovered that working with Labour's 'penny-farthing machine' was not easy for any sort of consultant. 'Tony Benn was the chair of the communications subcommittee, whom I had to report to,' he says. 'He specifically told me that I was not to include any questions in my polling about MPs' personalities. He said it was irrelevant and they were not interested. Clearly, this was the sort of information that was crucial to people like David Kingsley when they were deciding which ministers featured in political broadcasts. But officially I was answerable to Benn and his committee.' As many advertisers and consultants would discover in subsequent years, the party leader's office was usually more compliant than the officials and committee members inside Labour's HQ. 'I went to Wilson and asked, "What should I do?"' says Worcester. 'He told me, "Ask whatever questions you like. Just bring the answers to me."'

But while officials at Labour's Transport House HQ wanted to minimise his remit, some cabinet ministers would ask him for more than he was willing to deliver. 'I sat in a cabinet meeting at Downing Street giving a presentation, and Jim Callaghan, who was foreign secretary at the time, turned to me and said, "I've got three questions I want you to answer for me, Bob!" And he fired three very specific policy questions. I turned to Wilson and said, "Prime Minister, you don't pay me to make political judgements." And he said, "Quite right, Bob!" and the meeting continued.'

Wilson called an election in 1970, one that Labour was widely expected to win. 'He decided to go to the polls in June that year because he'd had some positive local election results and most of the polls in the press had them in the lead,' Worcester says. 'But my private polling in the final week of the campaign showed the Tories ahead by 3 per cent. His special advisor warned him of this, and Wilson said, "Well, Bob has only been in the country a short while and he doesn't quite understand these things yet." But by the Friday he was asking around for a spare room to lay his head!'

After the defeat, Wilson lost faith in Kingsley. The adman had devised a campaign poster depicting the Tory shadow cabinet as puppets, under the headline 'Yesterday's men'. The intention was to portray the opposition as tired throwbacks to a bygone political era. Kingsley had intended to follow this up closer to an anticipated October election with a separate poster depicting Labour's cabinet by contrast as young, thrusting and dynamic. But when Wilson unexpectedly called an early election there was no time, and after the Tories won by a narrow margin Wilson blamed Kingsley's poster, which he deemed to be overly negative. Like most prime ministers before and since, he was convinced that celebrating government achievements was a more effective strategy than attacking the opposition.

Wilson's disappointment with the campaign was compounded a year later when a BBC documentary about how former cabinet members were adapting to life in opposition was titled, with no little irony, *Yesterday's Men*. Kingsley was now ejected from Wilson's circle of trust. He remained adamant that if Wilson had paid closer attention to Worcester's polling studies, then defeat could have been averted in 1970.

By 1976 Jim Callaghan had replaced Wilson as leader. He had called upon Worcester to provide private polling to the party during the European referendum in 1975 and had been so impressed by his work that he asked him to occupy the same role in the build-up to his first general election campaign as prime minister, originally scheduled for October 1978. 'He had come to understand more about what I could and couldn't provide him with by then,' says Worcester of Callaghan. 'I would provide daily poll information to him and he would test me by asking, "Are you sure?" To which I would always reply, "I am not forecasting here. I am telling you what people were thinking yesterday. It could change. Events are unfolding all the time that could alter their views."'

Worcester had worked hard to focus the minds of Labour's often unwieldy election team on the job in hand. To do so, he had developed his '4 per cent theory': 'I came up with the conclusion that 4 per cent of the British electorate would choose who would be prime minister and by how much. Labour has a core support of 30 per cent. The Tories have 30 per cent. And the Liberal Democrats and the other odds and sods were 20 per cent. That leaves 20 per cent of those who vote to determine what the election result is going to be. But only 20 per cent of them live in marginal constituencies. So really it's just 4 per cent of people you've got to worry about. Now the problem with it is that those 4 per cent are the least likely to watch party election broadcasts. They don't read party manifestos. They are not strongly political in any way but they do have an almost religious belief that it's their duty to vote in the general election. So they've got to somehow figure out who to vote for.'

Worcester's theory effectively rendered the notion of national advertising campaigns pointless. The votes that mattered were in very specific places among a very small group of people. The posters that plastered big cities up and down the land and the broadcasts that filled the national airwaves in the build-up to elections were nothing but expensive white noise. So did he advise politicians against persisting with their costly advertising campaigns? 'No, I didn't,' he tells me. 'My job was to give them the information that allowed them to draw their own conclusions, not to draw those conclusions for them.'

In the autumn of 1978 Worcester had informed James Callaghan that the best he could hope for if he went to the polls in October was a hung parliament. Callaghan had sweated over the prospect and eventually decided to postpone the election until the new year, convinced that an uplift in the economy would boost the government's popularity over Christmas. But as Worcester had warned him previously, events are always able to cause unpredictable fluctuations in public opinion. Pay disputes with the trade unions reached breaking point towards the end of 1978, leading to mass strike action and the infamous winter of discontent. With new Conservative leader Margaret

Thatcher exploiting the chaos, Callaghan faced the almost impossible task of retaining the keys to Number 10 in the spring of 1979. Worcester continued to undertake daily polls for the Labour Party, which by now was thirteen points behind the Conservatives. 'I thought it was unwinnable by then and I think Callaghan did too, but he fought on,' says Worcester.

The election was announced on 7 April, allowing an extended five-week campaign. The official campaign team in Transport House was being run by Percy Clarke, Labour's director of communications. Clarke was cautious of Worcester's polling and concerned about the political direction it might encourage. 'He was very old-school,' says Worcester. 'He told me in no uncertain terms not to present a finding that showed that the public wanted a party that represented all classes. He said, "We are the party of the working class! We don't need the middle class."' It was an exchange indicative of the attitude of Labour officials towards all kinds of outside advice: if the research didn't fit in with their prejudices, they weren't interested.

Clarke would oversee Worcester's polling as well as Labour's PR activities and advertising in 1979. But to the frustration of most of the parties concerned, he chose not to co-ordinate the three different elements of the campaign. 'I was never allowed to deliver my research to the ad people directly,' says Worcester. 'It all had to go through Clarke. I think he was paranoid about people, especially ad people. He thought they were all going to steal their information and take it to the opposition!'

Labour's advertising team consisted of a gang of various sympathisers from the business, assembled in secret. Over the spring of 1979 they devised work that has since been completely overshadowed by the iconic Conservative ads produced in the same period. 'The truth is, the Labour ads were great and the polls showed that they made a bigger impact on Labour popularity than Saatchi ads did for the Tories,' says Worcester.

I was surprised by this. The archives reveal very little of Labour's 1979 election ads. It was an election that became defined by a single Saatchi poster, but Worcester was adamant that the long-forgotten Labour campaign had the greater impact. I asked him who had been responsible for the ads. 'It was a young guy from an agency called BBDO,' he told me. 'His name was Tim Delaney. Do you know him?'

I did know him. Tim Delaney is my uncle.

2

THE LAST RITES

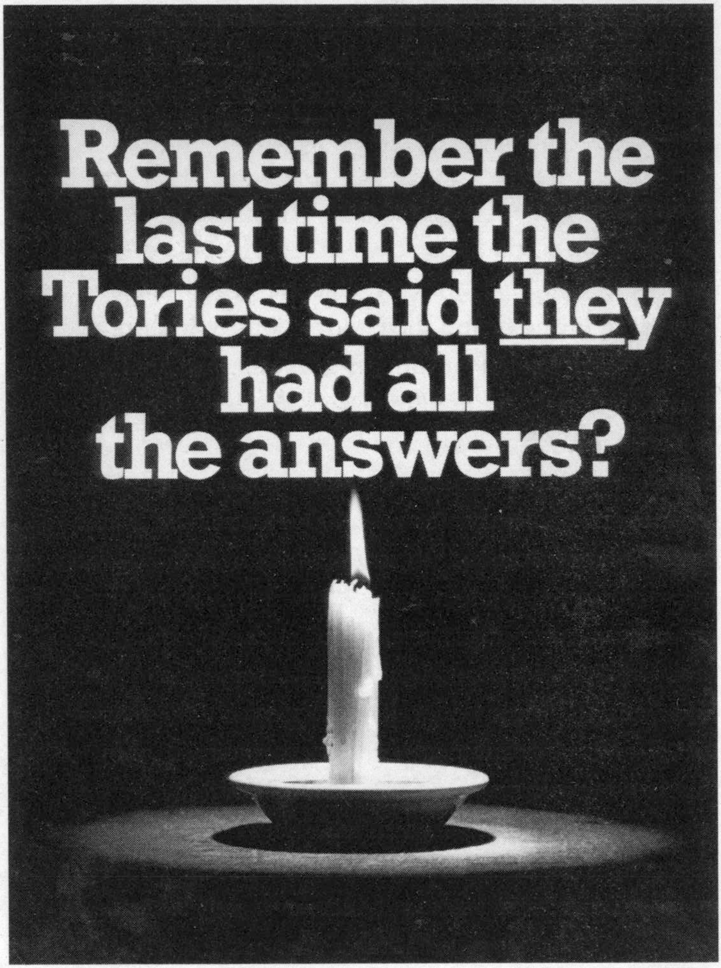
Remember the
last time the
Tories said they
had all
the answers?

Tim Delaney is my dad's younger brother, the third of eight children. They grew up together in a council house in Stanmore in the fifties, the children of my Irish immigrant grandfather and Liverpudlian grandma. The oldest three sons all left school at fifteen and hustled a living as best they could (they ran a rock 'n' roll club together in Harrow in the early sixties), before stumbling into advertising. In adland at that time qualifications and connections weren't necessary, only ideas. Tim Delaney had a large amount of those and soon worked his way up through the industry. By the time he was thirty-two he was creative director in the London office of one of the US's most respected ad agencies, BBDO. That was when he found himself at the helm of the prime minister's 1979 general election campaign.

My family is huge and very close but, of all my numerous uncles and aunts, Tim is the one I know least well. He is renowned for his almost obsessive devotion to work, and this is the reason why he rarely attends family events. It's also why, even after some months of research for this book, I had failed to discover that he was responsible for making all of James Callaghan's ads in 1979.

Despite the fact that he is a blood relative, Tim's continued devotion to his life as an adman makes him an extremely difficult person to pin down. While I was successfully scheduling interviews with current government ministers, former prime ministers and some of the world's foremost spin doctors, Tim seemed strangely – almost wilfully – elusive. Eventually I got hold of his mobile number and called him one afternoon. 'Is now a good time?' I asked. 'No,' he deadpanned. 'Now is a fucking shit time.' Tim is also renowned for his bad temper and bad language.

We arranged to speak on the phone the following evening. I didn't expect him to answer when I called, but he did. I told him that Bob Worcester had informed me he was responsible for Labour's ad campaign in 1979 and that it was, despite its relegation to historical insignificance, rather brilliant. 'Yes,' said Tim. 'It was.'

His involvement with the campaign had started by chance. Tim had been on a rare break from work in Paris when he had bumped into Edward Booth-Clibborn, chairman of the Design and Art Directors Association, the most prestigious industry body in British advertising. 'He mentioned he was working with Callaghan,' Tim says. 'I said that I'd always wanted to help Labour out but that I'd heard they were a complete mess. Booth-Clibborn told me they were shaping up and invited me to get involved.'

On his return to London, Tim visited Labour HQ at Transport House in Westminster, where he met with Percy Clarke, head of communications. 'I wasn't very impressed,' says Tim. 'His deputy was his wife and they both seemed pretty old-fashioned and unprofessional. I couldn't see myself working with them.' But he soon discovered that there was another, more competent campaign team working behind the scenes. 'I was invited by Booth-Clibborn to Number 10, where I met Callaghan's inner circle: Bernard Donoghue, David Lipsey and Tom McNally. They realised that Transport House was hopeless and had decided to run their own campaign secretly from Number 10. We got on and they quickly invited me to what was called the White Room meeting.'

At the secretive White Room meetings the real campaign strategy for the election was mapped out by a wider team of Callaghan's closest advisors, including his son Michael, *Daily Mirror* editor Mike Malloy, cabinet member Michael Foot and the chancellor, Denis Healey. 'At this young age I suddenly found myself sat on a sofa opposite the PM and a bunch of senior politicians who were asking me my opinion on things. Merlyn Rees, who was home secretary at the time, asked me, "Why is it that the majority of Western incumbent governments do not get re-elected for a second term?" I more or less looked over my shoulder as if to say, "Are you addressing that question to me?" I mean, he was the fucking politician! I told him it was because incumbent governments were often complacent and seen as aloof and devoid of new ideas. It was too easy for the opposition to say, "This lot are crap. It's time for something new." But, I mean, this was self-evident. I didn't see why he needed me to tell him.'

Tim quickly found himself elevated to insider status. His forays from his West End offices to Whitehall encapsulated the contrasting cultures of the two worlds. 'In those days there were no gates at the top of Downing Street and I would be able to drive in and park my Porsche right outside Number 10,' he tells me. 'They used to call it the Batmobile.'

Callaghan called him to an emergency meeting in the autumn of 1978 to announce that he was going to delay the election until the new year. On his way out, Tim found himself alone with the prime minister on the staircase of Number 10. 'He asked me what I thought of the decision,'

Tim says. 'I told him the truth: "I don't agree with your decision." He was putting all his confidence in the economy reviving and winning a Scottish devolution vote in March. I told him, "Events can take over – stuff is happening every day that could influence the public mood and your support. You need new ideas and you're leaving yourself open to accusations of complacency."'

His thoughts tallied with those expressed by Bob Worcester. In later years politicians learnt to seek the advice of admen and pollsters before they made decisions, not afterwards, but in 1978 Callaghan still thought it was the politicians who were best placed to predict how the public would react to events.

Nonetheless, Tim was retained on the White Room team and his advice on the timing of the 1979 election campaign was taken more seriously. 'I persuaded them to extend the campaign period to five weeks rather than the usual three in order for us to pull back the Tory lead.'

Tim then set about the creative work, producing a confrontational poster that showed a melting candle and the knowing headline: 'Remember the last time the Tories said they had all the answers?' Printed underneath was the campaign slogan: 'Keep Britain Labour'. The line was a reference to the three-day week presided over by the Heath government in 1974 in response to industrial action by coal workers. 'The team at Transport House were furious,' says Tim. 'They hadn't been consulted on the poster and they thought it was far too negative. There was a hostility towards ads that knocked the opposition. It wasn't the done thing. But I had clearance from Number 10, so I ignored them and put the posters up all over the country.'

Next he set about producing Labour's election broadcasts.

‘Many of them were the classic politician talking to camera,’ he tells me. ‘But the difference was I used the top ad directors of the time. Transport House came back after they saw the first film with Callaghan and said, “This is ridiculous! You can only see half of Jim’s face!” I told them, “That’s because he’s been lit properly for once. This way makes him look cool and interesting.”’

For a key broadcast featuring the chancellor, Denis Healey, Tim hired firebrand commercials director Sid Roberson, a fellow lifelong Labour man. Roberson was a bodybuilder from Tottenham and a former fitness trainer to the Kray twins. Handsome and charismatic, his first taste of advertising success had come when his friend Ridley Scott had cast him as the muscular hero in a series of commercials for Strongbow cider. His gruff demeanour and often combustible temperament were renowned in the ad business, but his work as a director had also earned him professional fame. ‘I think I was approached by Tim because I was one of the few people in the business who was vocally left-wing,’ he says. Roberson had seen many admen like him ditch their socialist principles once they achieved success. ‘They might have started out [Labour supporters], but by this stage they were all making money and telling me, “What are you still banging on about that left-wing bullshit for, Sid?” They were all worried about getting taxed 70 per cent by a Labour government. But there is more to life than the amount of tax you have to pay. I was making more than enough out of making silly adverts anyway. My morals were still in the same place and I didn’t see myself as anything special just because I’d had some success in the ad business. I was still a common, chippy little fucker.’

In fact, Tim Delaney and Sid Roberson were probably the two worst-tempered people in advertising at that time. The combination of the two could have been catastrophic for the campaign, but they found a way of muddling through. 'Tim was more difficult to pin down than the fucking prime minister anyway,' says Roberson. 'So we didn't have to see much of each other face to face. Plus, when he told me I was doing something wrong, I could tell him to fuck off because I wasn't being paid anyway.'

Tim devised a script in which several different cabinet ministers would read out the same speech from behind their desks. Roberson would shoot each one, then make a film which cut between them. 'They were mostly unimpressive on camera, apart from Denis Healey,' Roberson reflects. 'To be honest, they came across as a bunch of losers.'

His first port of call was the energy minister, Tony Benn. 'He's just going on about the amount of oil produced per second and all this technical mumbo-jumbo, so I stopped him and said, "Look, I'm just a punter, mate. I'm here to direct the film and it's not my place to tell you what to say, but I am a voter. And you're talking about a lot of shit that nobody cares about, let me tell you. People know about their kids, their jobs, their health, but all this shit you're talking about is completely wasted on them. I know you've got your head up in it, but I haven't and nor has anybody else. If I were you, I wouldn't say all that." And he goes, "You're right."'

Not all ministers were so quick to comply. Fellow adman Dave Trott was part of the team behind the broadcast and he accompanied Roberson to Number 11 Downing Street to film the chancellor, Denis Healey. 'The script was written in relaxed, colloquial language in order to make it a bit more accessible to punters,' says Trott. 'But Healey wasn't used to reading stuff like that. One of his aides came down all panicked, saying, "Mr Healey doesn't like the script and says he won't read it." None of us were particularly keen to go and argue the toss with him about it. So we sent Sid in.'

Roberson walked upstairs to the chancellor's office, where Healey repeated his dissatisfaction with the script. 'I told him, "You'll have to excuse me for saying so, but I didn't write the speech,"' says Roberson. '"I'm just a dumb director. I point the camera and you just say the words. If you don't like them, then you don't have to say them." So Healey says, "Well, I don't want to do it." And I says to him, "Mr Healey, you do what you like, all I can say is that the next-door neighbour has approved the script. If you want to change it, you'd better tell him." So he said, "I'll tell you what I'm going to do: I'm going to rewrite it, and I'm going to tell your script girl to come up here and take notes."'

Once Healey was satisfied with the reworked script, Roberson readied his crew. 'I had already told them all that if they had any political objections to what we were doing, they should speak up,' he tells me. 'But to them it was a day's work. I wasn't being paid, but they were. And none of them raised any concerns.'

But things soon changed once the cameras rolled in Healey's office. As the chancellor began to recite his pledges to the nation, Roberson heard the continuity girl muttering disapproving remarks under her breath. 'She was a bit posh with pearls and all the rest of it and I didn't have her down as much of a socialist,' says Roberson. 'Every time Healey said something about rebuilding the economy, I could hear her tutting or laughing sarcastically off-mic. Eventually he said something about inflation, and I heard her say quite clearly, "Bloody hypocrite!" I stopped the cameras and confronted her. I said, "What the fuck are you doing? I told you before we came if you didn't want to do this you didn't have to."'

When it came to cutting the various ministerial interviews together, Roberson painstakingly went through the footage with his editor, marking every twenty-fourth frame in chinagraph pencil with an 'X'. This was standard procedure in the analogue era and was invisible to the viewer unless viewed in ultra-slow motion. Clearly, someone took the trouble to do just that – freeze-framing the entire broadcast and identifying the marks, which, claimed a story in the *Daily Express*, were a devious subliminal trick to lure people into voting Labour. 'It was ridiculous,' says Tim. 'We later heard a rumour that it had been the team at Transport House who had leaked the story to the press. They were effectively briefing against their own side, which pretty much summed Labour up in those days.'

Compounding the impact of disunity within the party was a lack of funds. The Conservatives, backed by big business, were able to outspend Labour in every area of the campaign. Meanwhile, Tim was sent out to woo union bosses into contributing more funds. 'I used to have to go and have lunch with union officials, explaining to them what they would get for their money if they paid for the next broadcast,' he says.

At the same time, an inherent mistrust of advertising within Transport House continually hindered his efforts. 'I wanted to run a poster featuring a head shot of Jim Callaghan but it was vetoed because Transport House thought it focused too much on the personality, something they were very adverse to.'

With almost universal hostility to Labour from the press, the winter of discontent still fresh in the public's mind and a leader who was popularly portrayed as being at the mercy of union bosses, it was increasingly apparent to the campaign team that they were fighting a losing battle. But in the final week of the campaign, public opinion polls showed that the Tory lead of thirteen points had narrowed to just a single point. However, it was just a brief glimpse of hope. The Conservatives swept Labour aside on 3 May 1979 with a 5.2 per cent swing in their favour – the biggest since 1945. Margaret Thatcher was elected prime minister with a parliamentary majority of 44 seats.

The impression that Labour had narrowed the Tory lead was synthetic, the result of a rogue poll. Bob Worcester suggested that City traders had been conspiring to leak these inaccurate polls, manipulating the figures in the final week of the campaign to indicate a probable Labour victory. The subsequent fall in share prices this provoked could then be exploited as traders bought low, then made huge profits by selling high the day after a Conservative triumph. 'I wrote about it and talked about it as much as possible and I tried to publicise it whenever I could, but the Stock Exchange's attitude seemed to be, "Oh well, boys will be boys!"' says Worcester.

It wasn't just financial traders manipulating the polls. 'An editor of a right-wing paper once told me during this era that if he saw a poll he didn't like, he would quietly screw it up and throw it in the bin so it would never see the light of day,' says Worcester. 'The Tory press would always want a poll in the final stages that showed Labour gaining on the Tories. That would motivate Conservative voters to get out and vote.'

Perhaps this is why Tim Delaney was convinced that his campaign had helped build more support than it actually did: he had only been aware of carefully selected public polling. Worcester's private polling – which painted a far more realistic picture of voting intentions – was never seen by Tim or any of the Downing Street campaign team. 'It was crazy,' says Worcester. 'We rarely met or shared information. The campaign was completely disjointed, with party officials actively looking to divide us.'

Irrespective of the winter of discontent and the economic turmoil that engulfed Callaghan's government in 1979, the Labour Party was in no fit state to fight an election. I was forming a picture of an utterly dysfunctional party machine, hamstrung by internal strife, suspicion and paranoia. They were underfunded and completely disorganised. The only surprise is that, under such circumstances, the Labour Party had managed to survive at all. Future deputy leader Roy Hattersley would later remark that 1979 represented 'the last rites of Old Labour'.

Many senior party officials had an overblown sense of their own ideological superiority: they believed that they would win elections by virtue of intellectual debate, not vulgar salesmanship. 'The poster with the melting candle was the best of the campaign on either side,' says Dave Trott. 'But the party didn't like the direction it took because they thought it was cheap to attack the opposition. They thought they could fight on the basis of their own record. It was a complete mistake.'

Conservative Party headquarters, situated just across from Transport House in Smith Square, couldn't have provided more of a contrast. With ample funding from a sympathetic business community, the campaign team had purred like a well-oiled machine. While Delaney, Trott and Roberson were struggling to get the tiniest of decisions through the convoluted Labour Party procedures, the Saatchi & Saatchi team were churning out bold and brilliant ads with cavalier abandon.

'One thing they [Saatchis] did in that election was bring everyday language into political advertising and assimilate it with popular culture,' concedes Tim Delaney. 'But the impact it had on the actual results has been wildly exaggerated – mostly by the Saatchis themselves.'

Thirty-five years later Tim still seems annoyed that Labour's own weaknesses prevented him from doing a more effective job and that the Tory campaign has received greater recognition than it deserved. 'It was all PR, which Maurice and Charlie [Saatchi] have always been great at, and Tim [Bell] too,' he says. 'But the truth is that the posters had no impact whatsoever on the result. The election was decided, as always, by C2 women, the sort of people who don't engage with political posters at all.'

Tim told me that he had been in constant contact with the leading academic and one-time Labour pollster Ivor Crewe throughout the 1979 campaign and that his figures had categorically proven the irrelevance of the Tory posters. I noted that he was more willing to accept poll findings when they suggested a positive impact had been made by his own posters. I also thought it strange that Tim still seemed so angry, frustrated and competitive about the effectively unwinnable election of 1979. But this, as I was to discover in all of my encounters with admen who dabbled in election campaigns, was inevitable. There is a meaning, an intensity and an immersive nature to election campaigns that admen simply don't experience with any other client. The experience seems to live with them for ever. Not that many of them wish to experience it again.

'Callaghan offered me a safe Labour seat once the election was over,' Tim tells me. 'But I dismissed it in an instant. I told him that I couldn't join a party that said it was for the masses but didn't believe in mass communication.'

More than that, once the votes are counted and the victory parties are over, it is the politicians who get back to the hard work of constituency surgeries in draughty church halls and late-night votes in the house. Tim Delaney was a young man on the up in 1979, earning good money for a job that was exciting and glamorous. Why would he have given it up for life as a poorly paid MP? As he says, 'I was in the gents at the Commons once and in walked one of the most prominent cabinet ministers of the time. I glanced over and saw his fat arse hanging out of a cheap, shiny suit that looked like it was from Burton's. And he was considered one of the most sophisticated politicians in the country. I thought to myself at that moment, "Fuck it, that life's not for me."'

3

LAUGHING BOYS

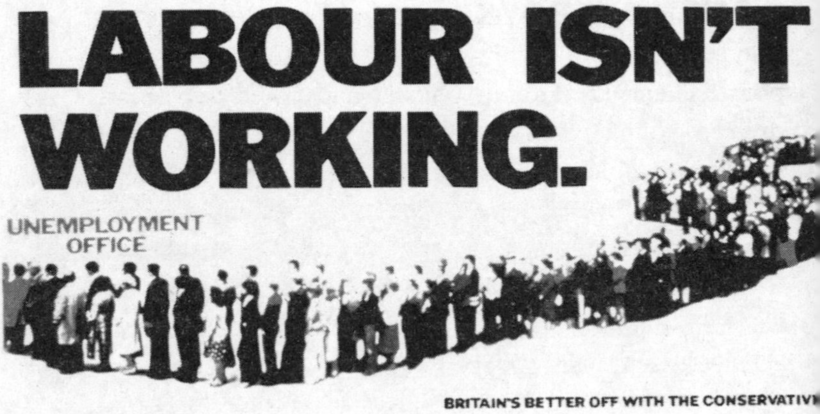
LABOUR ISN'T
WORKING.
UNEMPLOYMENT
OFFICE
BRITAIN'S BETTER OFF WITH THE CONSERVATIV

Bob Worcester had caught a telling glimpse of the opposition team in 1978. Sitting in a Soho restaurant with a corporate client, the Labour pollster had noted two smartly dressed young execs enjoying an extravagantly lengthy lunch on a table opposite. He recognised them as Tim Bell and Gordon Reece. 'They were drinking endless champagne and eating nothing but caviar,' Worcester recalls. 'Huge spoonfuls of the stuff.' Reece was the Conservative Party's communications boss; Bell was chairman of the agency he had just hired to deliver the party's advertising. Together they were about to change the face of political advertising. But first, lunch. 'I don't know if this was the sort of thing they did every day,' says Worcester. 'But it was certainly different from the Labour team, sat at their desks eating sandwiches.'

While for much of British society the seventies had been defined by economic hardship, the advertising industry was thriving. It was during this decade that the young lions who had joined the business a decade earlier, evangelising about Bill Bernbach's new brand of creativity, had ascended to the vanguard. British advertising agencies had replaced their American counterparts as the most admired and successful in the world. Now Americans were coming to London to work with fabled creatives from hot British agencies such as Collett Dickenson Pearce and Boase Massimi Pollitt. And Saatchi & Saatchi.

While Heath, Wilson and Callaghan rotated the reins of power and the country lurched from one economic crisis to another, Soho's adland was incubated inside a bubble of success and extravagance that seemed to be never-ending. At the heart of it all was Tim Bell, the high-profile chairman of Saatchi & Saatchi. The agency had been formed in 1970 by the two sons of Iraqi immigrants: Charles, the mysterious creative firebrand; and Maurice, the impossibly young account exec. They had brought Bell in for his experience, charm and credibility: 'They were Iraqi Jews at a time when there was still quite a lot of anti-Semitism around,' Bell told me when I first met him. 'They might have hired me because I had a reasonably posh background. My father was a professional and I had spent most of my upbringing in Norfolk, which is a fantastically grand county. I might have seemed more palatable to the outside world. But everyone at the agency was engaged in a revolution. We were a bunch of young men fighting the establishment.'

The Saatchis had set out to create the number-one agency in the world. It was quite an ambition for a pair of brothers with no experience of running a business. But they saw the advertising establishment as the old-school agencies from America such as J. Walter Thompson and Grey – already a century old and built upon long-standing relationships with big business. The Saatchis were part of a generation determined to shake things up and succeed on the basis of their creativity and effectiveness rather than 'Martinis with the client at the eighteenth hole'.

The Saatchis and many of their contemporaries were driven by a sense of being on the outside: they resented the old-boy network and wanted to prove that they could thrive without the same connections or educational backgrounds of their rivals. Charles Saatchi had made his name at the most credible agency of the era, CDP. It too had been a scruffy, anti-establishment agency that had cultivated the early creative careers of Ridley Scott, Alan Parker and David Puttnam, among numerous other luminaries of British culture. Each was from an ordinary background and had made millions from the ad business while still in their twenties. This was the culture that Bell became embroiled in at Saatchis. There was a spirit of endeavour and aspiration that permeated adland and chimed with a new brand of Conservatism. 'The key thing we brought to the Conservatives in the seventies was aspiration,' Bell told me through a fog of cigarette smoke in his Mayfair offices. 'The advertising industry at that time was living proof that anyone could get on and do better for themselves. We didn't hide it – we celebrated it by buying nice cars and eating in great restaurants. Why wouldn't we? They [the Conservatives] have lost that now. They've become the party of the strivers and hard-working family. But that doesn't mean anything. What you have to do is position something so people want to be a part of that brand. People want to be aspirational. They don't want to be strivers.'

This was the birth of Thatcherism: a moment in history when the post-war One Nation consensus had reached its death throes. As governments of each hue failed to control inflation and the unions seemed to tighten their grip on the mechanics of state, the fresh, dynamic and altogether exciting culture of adland seemed the perfect antidote. Most of the country didn't know about it yet. But they soon would.

Tim Bell's quaffing partner, Gordon Reece, had been

appointed as personal advisor to Margaret Thatcher after her election as party leader in 1975 and given the task of communicating her new vision for Britain in a fresh way. In Bell he was to find a kindred spirit: they were both the sort of energetic, can-do characters Thatcher liked to surround herself with. In time, she would come to call the pair 'the Laughing Boys' for their constant optimism. She would record in her memoirs: '[Reece] jollied me along to accept things I would have rejected from other people.'

Gordon Reece was born in Liverpool in 1930, the son of a car salesman. After an education at a Catholic public school, he became a reporter for local newspapers before finding his true vocation in television, working first in entertainment (as a producer on *This Is Your Life* with Eamonn Andrews and then for the comedians Spike Milligan and Dave Allen) and later covering elections for ITN. In 1970 he had been hired on a freelance basis to help produce some of the Conservative Party's election broadcasts, working alongside Jeremy Scott and James Garrett. He had encountered a young Mrs Thatcher, then shadow education secretary, and the two had stayed in touch.

Thatcher had asked for Reece's help in her bid to become party leader, and it was he who had suggested she allow herself to be filmed doing the dishes at her London flat in order to cast her as an ordinary woman whom voters could relate to. The strategy worked, and once she was elected she asked for him to be seconded to her office (he was by now the managing director of a video cassette production wing at EMI) to advise her on image and presentation. While she was naturally awkward in front of the camera, she was the first Conservative leader to truly embrace the importance of professional communications. 'If you have a good thing to sell,' she would later say, 'use every single capacity you can to sell it. It is no earthly use having a good thing and no-one hearing about it.'

Reece helped her transform her image from that of a provincial housewife to that of a stateswoman. She embraced his advice, allowing him to critique everything from her hairstyle and choice of jewellery to her tone of voice. She had taken elocution lessons in her youth, which, Reece felt, had resulted in a contrived upper-class accent that might alienate parts of the electorate. He helped her soften her delivery while retaining her authority and even recruited Sir Laurence Olivier to advise her on how to do so.

In 1976 Reece visited the US to observe the presidential election campaigns of Jimmy Carter and Gerald Ford. He was impressed by the forensic way in which their public appearances were stage-managed to assure appropriate backdrops for the candidates, which helped communicate a positive image even when they weren't speaking. 'He came back convinced that the next general election would be the first one in Britain that was fought through advertising,' Bell says. 'What he didn't point out to Margaret was that it was TV advertising he had in mind. And that in this country we weren't allowed to do it!' While the main political parties in the UK had free broadcast slots allocated to them, buying space to advertise in was – and remains – against the rules.

In March 1978 Reece was moved from Margaret Thatcher's office to Conservative HQ in Smith Square in his new role as director of communications. As Jeremy Scott had discovered in 1970, the staff at Tory central office were a traditional and stuffy bunch. Many of them were unused to someone like Reece, who sashayed into

Smith Square every day puffing on an enormous Cuban cigar, resplendent in hand-made pink shirts and silk ties. Even more alarming was his taste for vintage champagne, which he drank frequently and charged to expenses. Janet Young, the then deputy party chairman, was quoted in the *Observer* in 1983 recalling her concerns about the media executive's extravagance. 'I did question it,' she said. 'He seemed to breakfast on champagne and gulls' eggs and I didn't think it was a good image for the party. It made fund-raising more difficult because it undermined our efforts to attract donations. How could we approach companies and individuals on the basis that we needed the money if our own money was being spent in this way?' She explained that she had eventually approached the party treasurer, Lord McAlpine, with her concerns. 'Something should be done,' she told him.

'Do you have a car, Janet?' McAlpine had asked her in response.

'Yes, a small one,' she replied.

'But you have to buy petrol for it, don't you? You see, if you have a Gordon Reece you have to run him on champagne.'

It's a tale that reveals how modern media culture was encroaching upon the relatively austere world of politics. But more than that it reveals a key difference between Labour and Conservative attitudes towards fighting elections: while Labour were still warring with each other over the moral ambiguities of using communications professionals, the Tories were employing a blunt pragmatism to the matter. They were convinced that Reece could help them win over the British electorate and were unconcerned by moral dilemmas, not to mention scrutinising the minutiae of his working practices. In short, the Conservatives were concerned only with winning.

Reece was unhappy with the communications policy at central office. Until then, the Conservatives had used a collection of admen, PR people and production experts to deliver their communications around election time. But Reece saw this collective as difficult to manage: all too often there were warring factions and egos at play. 'I've always thought a committee approach to running a political campaign was a very bad idea,' he said. 'One of the reasons is that they're all chiefs and there isn't a single Indian there.'

With an election expected in the autumn of 1978, he had no time to lose and resolved that the Conservative Party should appoint an ad agency to run its campaign full-time. He convinced Margaret Thatcher that this was the correct policy and set about appointing the right agency. 'I was looking for an agency with a rising reputation but not too big,' he said. 'One that was hungry, with creative people. Large enough for the media clout we required but not a giant corporation . . . I wanted somebody who would say "God, we could get really famous if we did this properly."'

In Saatchi & Saatchi he would find the perfect match. This, after all, was an agency that was as preoccupied with its own promotion as with that of its clients. It had launched in September 1970 with a splash on the cover of the industry magazine *Campaign*, under the headline 'Saatchi starts agency with £1m'. Charles was already an industry star and was pictured at his desk in a flashy white suit, his unknown younger brother Maurice emerging over his shoulder. In truth, their clients at launch had committed far less than the reported £1 million to the agency, but the brothers had artfully managed the story to convey a compelling largesse. Next they paid for a full-page advertisement in *The Times*, under the headline 'Why I think it's time for a new type of advertising', followed by a detailed mission statement by the agency's lead copywriter, Jeremy Sinclair. Many of their contemporaries dismiss the success of the Saatchis as being built on such spin and bluster, but it's hard not to be impressed by the sheer bravado with which they announced themselves to the world. Prospective clients were immediately alerted to the agency's knack for generating a buzz. When prospective clients from sewing-machine manufacturer Singer visited their offices in Soho, the staff paid tourists and passers-by £5 each to pose as Saatchi employees, thus filling the place and lending it an appealing air of success. The account was won. It might have been trickery but it was informed by the sort of smart thinking that big business – and eventually prime ministers – could use to their own advantage.

Terence Donovan, the Rolls-Royce-driving veteran of Heath's 1970 campaign, had recommended Saatchis to Reece. Reece was impressed by an initial meeting at their offices in Charlotte Street. Maurice Saatchi had assured him that they were all Conservative supporters, but Reece was less concerned with their political leanings than with their working practices. 'There was a dynamism about the place,' he said. 'It was the coiled spring, the kettle bubbling. I felt I had to get them appointed.'

In actual fact, the Saatchis were, if anything, apolitical. The agency had worked for the Labour administration a few years previously, when they were commissioned by Michael Foot to communicate the government's concern about the vicious circle of unemployment. They had devised a poster featuring an unemployed youth, under the headline 'I can't get a job without experience and I can't get experience without a job. Vicious, isn't it?' They had even approached Labour communications director Percy Clarke in 1976 with a request to pitch for their advertising. 'We had to explain that our principles were that we did not use agencies to project our image,' Clarke had told them.

Jeremy Sinclair was eventually to become the key creative figure at Saatchi & Saatchi. Later, when the brothers were forced out of the company by shareholders in the mid-nineties, Sinclair would leave with them to set up a new agency called M&C Saatchi. Today, their imposing headquarters sits on the north side of Soho's Golden Square. On the top floor of the building is a large open-plan office occupied by the agency generals: Sinclair, executive director Bill Muirhead and Maurice Saatchi. As their persistently thriving empire buzzes beneath them, administered by a younger generation of executives, it is difficult to ascertain exactly what these advertising veterans actually do all day in their lofty sanctum.

I was first granted access to the top floor in 2006, while researching a book about the creative revolution in British advertising. Maurice Saatchi had agreed to meet and talk to me off-record. Jeremy Sinclair joined us. They were both charming and affable: we sat on sofas and talked over the old days for about an hour. But when I said my goodbyes, Maurice made it clear that he was unwilling for any of the things he had just told me – as innocuous as they were – to go on the record. Instead, he proposed that I email over a few questions, which he then responded to with strangely brief answers. About his relationship with Margaret Thatcher and the Conservative Party he wrote simply: 'Our job was to précis her philosophy.' Other questions were addressed in a similarly terse manner. It appeared that a man with such a keen sense of publicity management felt uncomfortable appearing in a book over which he had little control. Or maybe he just didn't like me.

Jeremy Sinclair had been a much warmer interviewee. Less fame-hungry than the Saatchis, less garrulous than Bell, he was credited by many as being the real talent behind the agency's success. He spoke thoughtfully and softly. Tall, slim and bald, many had commented on his resemblance to Norman Tebbit, although there was a chumminess about him that distinguished him from the former cabinet secretary. When I returned to the penthouse suite at M&C Saatchi in 2013, Sinclair showed me a newspaper ad the agency had taken out in the aftermath of Margaret Thatcher's death, describing her as 'the best client we ever had'.

'I was always interested in politics,' says Sinclair. 'I was instinctively a Conservative supporter. Maurice and Charles weren't right-wing by any means. That would come later. But Charlie had an eye for publicity. And he saw in the Conservative account something that would help put his agency on the map. We knew from experience that government accounts were creatively the best, because you were fighting on the side of the angels. Here again, you had complicated issues that you had to make simple. Above all, you had to get the public's attention.'

But not everyone in the agency was as positive about the new account. Tim Bell was on holiday in Jamaica when he received a call from Maurice Saatchi informing him that he would manage the campaign. 'I said it was a huge mistake and that we shouldn't do it,' Bell tells me. 'I had worked at Colman, Prentis and Varley in the fifties when they had handled the Tory campaign, and it caused havoc. It takes up the time of all your best people and you end up neglecting other clients, who soon get disgruntled. Plus, the money is never as good as a commercial client.'

But the brothers were adamant and knew that Bell was the man to manage the job. Charlie was resistant to dealing with clients, let alone those as formal as the Conservatives, and Maurice was impossibly young, so Bell was the closest the agency had to a respectable face who knew how to conduct himself around old-fashioned Westminster types. But on his first visit to Smith Square his demeanour provided a sharp contrast to the strait-laced inhabitants of Tory HQ. Lady Young noted his shoulder-length hair, silver necklace and open-necked shirt. This, she thought, was going to cost the party a great deal of money.

Things were truly being shaken up in the Conservative Party as Reece, backed by Thatcher, attempted to drag the party machine into the modern era. The key man that needed convincing was party chairman Lord Thorneycroft: while the embodiment of the old-fashioned Conservative on the outside, he had a mischievous sense of humour which helped his relationship with the brash young admen. On one visit to their offices at Charlotte Street, he noted an array of expensive cars in the underground car park. 'Whose car is that?' he asked, pointing out a Jeep Cherokee with bull bars affixed to the front bumper. 'That belongs to Charles Saatchi,' he was told by an agency executive. 'Get a lot of trouble with cattle in Hampstead, does he?' Thorneycroft replied with a smile.

Bell's legendary charm soon won over the chairman. 'We would be extremely deferential to him whenever we visited central office,' he says. 'We said "Yes, sir" and

"No, sir" and snapped to attention whenever he entered the room. That sort of thing went down very well with these old-fashioned men with military backgrounds. The other key trick was to give them a little nugget of information to take away. For instance, we'd say something like, "The reason we are using that particular font, Lord Thorneycroft, is because it is the oldest font in existence and has a certain gravitas about it." That would give him something to regurgitate to other people within the party. Clients like that.'

Despite Margaret Thatcher's secretary greeting him outside the Tory leader's parliamentary office with the dismissive remark 'Oh yes, you're the man from Starsky and Hutch,' Bell's attitude towards the account brightened once he had met Thatcher. She told Bell that she insisted on being told the truth at all times, assuring him that she would not take offence at any negative appraisal of her performance or image. Bell began to see that she might be easier to work with than the average politician, and a clear strategy for the campaign began to take shape in his mind. 'It was clear we had three huge advantages over Labour,' he tells me. 'Firstly, Thatcher might not have been the best speaker in the world but she was miles better than Callaghan or anyone else they had. Secondly, the Tories had more money to spend than Labour and it's always nice to fight the enemy with a weapon they can't afford. Thirdly, she believed in the power of advertising. She knew we were professionals and put her faith in us. Meanwhile, Labour were still morally hostile to the very idea of using ads.'

It was Sinclair's job to devise the creative strategy that might exploit these practical advantages. 'The country was in trouble,' he says. 'The unions were taking over and

Callaghan was weak. There was much to exploit. We were convinced that attacking was the way to go.' The Saatchi team decided upon a campaigning policy that would serve them and the Conservatives well for decades to come. 'We weren't scared to be negative. We relished it. We welcomed a row. Our approach became "Hit first, hit hard and keep on hitting",' says Sinclair.

Labour's cautious and disorganised campaign team on the other side of Smith Square had no idea what lay in store for them. First came a political broadcast in which the agency cast Michael Heseltine as the star: he was young, dynamic and carried himself with a statesmanlike gravitas. 'Party political broadcasts were usually stuffy politicians behind a desk reading deadly prose,' says Sinclair. 'We treated broadcasts like any other ad. We tried to treat the audience as adults. We employed humour, ordinary language and compelling images. We took everything we had learnt from serving our commercial clients and applied it to politics.'

Rather than focus solely on Heseltine, the broadcast used captivating imagery of Britain in a high-speed state of reverse: from Big Ben to a fleet of Spitfires, iconic national symbols were depicted going backwards. The pace and vigour with which the film was delivered felt fresh and unusual for a political broadcast. It ended with the dashing Heseltine declaring to camera: 'Backwards or forwards, because we can't go on as we are. Don't hope for a better life, vote for one.'

Saatchis had taken the bold step of limiting politicians' appearances. 'They were dull on camera,' says Sinclair. 'Everyone knew it. We decided that images combined with a voiceover could best demonstrate economic arguments and explain the Conservative position. The film would then cut to a politician who would give a short, punchy summary or interjection. We limited their appearances to twenty seconds at a time.'

It was a complete break with the traditions of political broadcasts, an admission that politicians themselves didn't make for captivating TV. Thankfully the agency's thinking was shared by their key client, Gordon Reece. 'He was an open door for that sort of idea,' says Sinclair. 'He was a TV producer by trade and understood that viewers glazed over if an MP was on screen for too long.' But not everyone was as easily corralled to the agency's cause. 'One of the problems we had was finding actors to provide the voiceover,' recalls Sinclair. 'Acting was a very lefty and lovey profession and they were all worried about upsetting their union. In the end, one of the few we could find who was willing was Robert Powell, who had recently played Jesus Christ. A lovely, intelligent voice.'

The media were beginning to sit up and listen. Newspapers reacted to the broadcast with enthusiasm. 'There was an appetite for something new,' Tim Bell says. 'It was so unusual to break away from the convention of a boring politician sat behind his desk. Being admen we always thought it was better to convince people by entertaining rather than lecturing them. We wanted to use wit and charm to address the audience, not bore them to death.'

James Callaghan was widely expected to call an election in the autumn of 1978, and Saatchi & Saatchi had been instructed to prepare for a long and bloody campaign. They assigned a fleet of their top creatives to the cause, overseen by Sinclair. A key moment arrived one Sunday when Sinclair instructed a team of writers and art directors to assemble at Saatchis' offices on a Sunday afternoon for an emergency ideas session. The Conservatives were demanding a presentation of potential campaign ideas that evening. One of the creatives was Andrew Rutherford, a young copywriter. He sat at his desk hastily scribbling ideas, one of which featured a queue snaking out of a dole office under the headline 'Labour isn't working'. Rutherford presented his draft to Sinclair and Tim Bell, who expressed mild enthusiasm but wanted to see his other efforts. Rutherford refused to show them, knowing that none of his other ideas was as strong. He knew Sinclair and Bell were wrong to overlook the strength of 'Labour isn't working' and wanted to force them into presenting the poster to Thatcher that evening.

Bell eventually included Rutherford's idea in a file marked 'possibles' and took it with him to Thatcher's flat in Flood Street, Chelsea. After the material he and Sinclair had deemed to be the best had been rejected, Bell resorted to producing Rutherford's draft poster. But the Conservative leader was initially unimpressed. 'No!' she said. 'You know perfectly well that you should never have the other side's name in your own poster!' Bell smiled reassuringly. 'It's a double entendre, Mrs Thatcher. They are using the word "Labour" in both senses.' Thatcher snorted. 'Well, it can't be very good because I don't get it.' There was a frosty silence for a few moments before Gordon Reece, ever capable of allaying Thatcher's concerns, concurred with Bell that the poster was 'brilliant'. Thatcher relented. 'Although I don't much like having the other man's name on it, I must admit there's something very compelling about the whole thing.'

The poster was soon displayed on sites across Britain, attracting yet more newspaper column inches. There was a brutal simplicity to the headline and imagery that captivated the passing voter in the street, fascinated the newspaper columnist and struck at the heart of a nervy Labour government. Chancellor of the exchequer Denis Healey reacted furiously when it was discovered that the unemployed masses depicted in the poster were in fact members of Hendon's Young Conservative Association. He decried the ad as 'fraud', sparking yet more discussion of the poster in the wider media. Tim Bell estimated that the continuing furore over the poster earned the party £5 million of free publicity. The ad had cost £50,000 to make. 'I remember Gordon Reece running down the corridor clutching the "Labour isn't working" poster, laughing, shouting, "Labour are going to hate this!"' says Jeremy Sinclair. 'He knew that if they complained, the poster would be reproduced in the papers. And the more they complained, the more it was reproduced.'

As the team at Saatchis geared up for the start of the campaign, James Callaghan wobbled in the face of negative opinion polls and delayed the election. While there was a sense of anticlimax in their Charlotte Street offices, the fuss surrounding 'Labour isn't working' had helped the agency's reputation skyrocket. To this day, the poster is still credited by some as being a crucial factor in Callaghan's decision to stall. It had cut through the complexities of the argument with rapier sharpness and communicated a key weakness in the government's record. It's unlikely that Callaghan stewed over the impact of the poster as much as some people had supposed (after all, he and his party were still sceptical about the impact of advertising), but one thing is certain: the poster was crucial to the rise of Saatchi & Saatchi. But, by the time of the next election in 1983, the man who had created it would have left the agency and would never have any involvement with the Conservatives again.

I met Andrew Rutherford in the winter of 2013. He spoke with fondness about his formative years at Saatchi & Saatchi and the aggressive ambition that surrounded the agency at the time. 'We had something about us in that we all wanted to be the best at what we did,' he told me. 'Because of that, we bucked the trend of the advertising wild man. We were young but we were serious and more studious than the people at rival agencies.'

The young Rutherford was politically ambivalent but had a tendency to fall in love with any client he worked for. 'I tended to immerse myself in the product and develop a real passion for it, which helped the quality of the work I produced,' he said. 'It was no different with the Conservatives. My mother had been a champagne socialist and I had been indifferent to the Tories until I started working on the account. After that I think we all became devoted to the cause.'

But thirty-five years after he had scribbled out his notorious poster, Rutherford was still aggrieved about the way it was remembered by most. 'Whenever it is written about it is either credited to Maurice Saatchi, Charles Saatchi or Tim Bell,' he said. 'I've had to call so many newspapers over the years to set them straight about it. But most journalists are lazy and just name the more famous adman. I don't know how much impact it had on the election in 1979, but I know for a fact that it had a huge impact on the success of the agency. After that poster came out, they had clients flying through the door.'

But the Saatchis weren't likely to look back. By the time the election was finally called the following year, the country had watched the shocking depiction of the winter of discontent on the television news, with rubbish piled up on the streets and, according to the enduring legend, the dead going unburied due to industrial action by the gravediggers' union. The facts and myths of the winter of 1978 are still a matter of debate but politics was now being fought out on TV news bulletins, where high-impact visuals and soundbites trumped complex analysis every time. This was a gift for admen, especially those at Saatchis, who had resolved to fight a campaign of attack against a crisis-ridden government. As Rutherford pointed out, 'The floating voter isn't sat down poring over the party manifesto. He's making his mind up on the basis of broad impressions. And we were experts at creating broad impressions.'

While Labour's volunteer admen engaged in counterproductive struggles with their own party machine, Conservative central office was providing the Saatchi team with invaluable support. The Conservative research department was headed up by the young Chris Patten, later a party chairman, whose job was to provide the facts that admen could use to attack the government. 'I had been director of the research department since 1974, so had worked with other agencies, but our relationship with Saatchis was unique,' says Patten. 'I spent a lot of time at their offices working closely with them. They wanted more and more material with which to attack Labour. Our job was to find it for them.' An early example was another high-impact election poster bearing the headline 'Tax. The facts.' Further down the copy read: 'In the last 30 years, every Labour government has increased income tax. Every Conservative government has cut income tax.' It was a striking précis of a major issue – expressed with an adman's gift for artful exaggeration. 'Chris Patten gave us the angle and we would dream up the lines,' says Tim Bell. 'But I remember he'd get frustrated when we played fast and loose with the facts. When he saw that tax poster for the first time he said, "That is not entirely true." And I told him, "Well, it's *almost* true, Chris!"'

But not everyone in the Conservative Party scrutinised the Saatchi output as much as Patten. When Andrew Rutherford was asked to write a script for a broadcast starring deputy leader Willie Whitelaw, he expected his own words to be embellished by the minister. 'He arrived at the shoot, read the script, declared it brilliant and regurgitated it verbatim in front of the camera,' Rutherford recalls. 'I said, "Don't you want to change anything?" But he just said, "No, it all seems fine to me!" I found it all rather surprising that these government ministers were happy to make statements that a bunch of admen had written.'

The key broadcast in the campaign was taken out of Saatchis' hands by Chris Patten and Thatcher's chief speechwriter, the playwright Ronald Millar. They had seen a film that Saatchis had shot on a windswept rooftop in London's Tottenham Court Road. Millar asserted that it had 'no theme, no passion and no relation to a country in turmoil', so he and Patten wrote a new script: a rousing, patriotic speech which Thatcher would use to position herself as the only leader with an empathy with the British people. Lord Thorneycroft and Tim Bell agreed to the changes and arranged for a reshoot in Thatcher's House of Commons office. She had previously been criticised for her stiff, hectoring demeanour on camera, but Bell had developed a close relationship with her that allowed him to diffuse this. He would sit behind the camera and smile in order to relax Thatcher; if that didn't work, he would pull faces and make her laugh. The strategy worked, and Thatcher delivered her nine-minute speech with assurance and gusto. No longer was she an ambitious party politician; she was now a potential national leader. The script might not have come from Saatchi & Saatchi, but the execution and finesse of the production was down to Bell. 'The Labour government had been caught in a position where they had to pretend that nothing was going wrong at all,' Bell later surmised. 'The Conservatives could therefore present themselves as the party of the nation.'

By 2013 Bell was still convinced that Saatchis' first campaign for the Conservatives had been close to perfect, but less sure about the practical impact it had on the result. 'The fact is that Callaghan was avuncular and dull,' he says. 'Margaret didn't need to do much to be better than him. The country was in crisis and nobody wanted to be British any more. What we learnt as admen that year was that governments lost elections, oppositions didn't win them. But we could at least help the government along the way.'

When Thatcher swept into Number 10 on 3 May 1979, party chairman Lord Thorneycroft gushingly told the press that Saatchis had won the election for the Conservatives. Jeremy Sinclair certainly saw it as the moment that the agency got started on the road to world domination: 'That election made Saatchi & Saatchi famous. Within a few years it was the biggest agency in the world and a household name.'

The country was about to change for ever too, much like Tim Bell's life. He was now one of the prime minister's most trusted friends and allies. His relationship with her would guide his future career entirely, eventually contributing to the complete breakdown of his relationship with Charles and Maurice Saatchi. On the night of the victory party at Number 10, Charles – the founder and lynchpin of the agency – arrived enigmatically at Downing Street, handed in a congratulatory card and left immediately without even stopping for a drink. In contrast, Bell partied with the new prime minister and her closest colleagues late into the night. It was indicative of the schism that lay ahead. But while there were those who still queried how much real influence the Saatchis had on the eventual result, they had set a new template for political advertising.

This seismic shift was encapsulated by Rutherford's 'Labour isn't working' poster. Funny, aggressive, bold and concise, it marked a new creative approach that applied commercial advertising techniques to politics. Strategically, it squarely targeted the floating voter and the vulnerable or 'soft' Labour supporter. It also heralded the moment when the gloves came off: from 1979 onwards an atmosphere of antagonism would develop between Labour and Conservative advertising. The principal aim of every ad would be to provoke the opposition into a response. It was the poster that changed everything.

In 2000 a group of ad industry peers voted it the greatest of the twentieth century. For once its author, Andrew Rutherford, received the credit he deserved. 'The first I heard of it was when I received this ugly little statue in the post from Saatchis,' he told me mournfully. 'At least they gave me that.'

4

COLLECTIVE NERVOUS BREAKDOWN

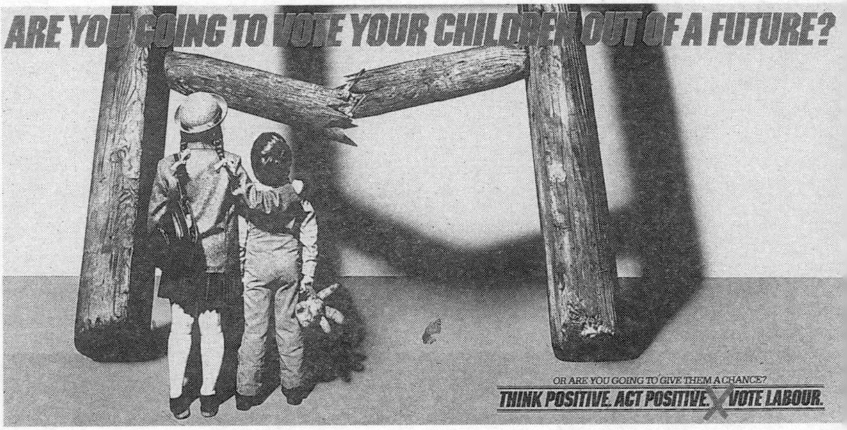
ARE YOU GOING TO VOTE YOUR CHILDREN OUT OF A FUTURE?
OR ARE YOU GOING TO GIVE THEM A CHANCE?
THINK POSITIVE. ACT POSITIVE. VOTE LABOUR.

'I've never voted or thought of voting anything other than Labour. Though I'm sort of middle-class, public-school and so on, that's just where my political heart has always been. And yonks ago I set up my own advertising agency. It wasn't very successful. Until the Labour Party asked me to run their election campaign in 1983. It changed my life for ever really.'

Johnny Wright was like most Labour admen: he worked out of conviction, belief and passion. But ultimately this was to be his downfall. Like so many other admen who have tried and failed to sell Labour's message to the British public before and since, Wright lacked the cold-eyed detachment that Saatchis was able to apply to its work for the Conservatives. Labour's advertisers perennially suffered from a syndrome whereby they simply couldn't understand why anyone wouldn't want to support their party.

These days, Johnny Wright lives in retired tranquillity on a houseboat in Chiswick, west London. He is jolly and contented. The vessel is crammed with books and archives from the days when, briefly, he was the talk of the London ad scene. 'Nobody really knew who I was in the business before that election,' he says. 'I'd left my job at a big agency called Grey's to set up my own thing with three colleagues. We called it Johnny Wright and Partners. We'd done some work for Crown Paints and Angel Delight but we weren't really on the map for the first couple of years.'

All that was about to change. A journalist from the industry magazine *Campaign* decided to write a profile of Wright. In it, he mentioned that he was a lifelong Labour Party supporter, one of a dying breed in the industry. Since defeat at the 1979 election, Labour had fallen victim to ugly internal disputes. Militant and radical groups were at war with the party leadership, while Labour's 'March for Jobs' campaign in 1981 had provided news cameras with startling images of a party driven mad by civil war.

In the same year senior MPs David Owen, Shirley Williams, Roy Jenkins and Bill Rodgers had left the party to form the Social Democratic Party. There was a sense that Labour's position as the main party of opposition was under threat. Future foreign secretary Jack Straw said of the period: 'You could almost describe the years between 1981 and 1983 as a very important political institution having a collective nervous breakdown.'

Labour's new leader, Michael Foot, was in his late sixties and was portrayed by much of the press as elderly, out of touch and incapable of controlling the warring factions within his party. The party manifesto was so radical that it stood comparison with that of the Soviet Union's Communist Party. For advertising agencies, associating with Labour had become too dangerous. 'They had several policies that were very anti-business,' says Wright. 'Corporate tax proposals were astronomical and they were particularly hard on multinational companies. All the big agencies had clients just like that, and they would stand to lose them if they were linked to the Labour Party.'

Just as in 1979, the party was still reliant on a collective of freelance sympathisers to manage their communications. An advisory committee comprised of admen and journalists had been established to devise a strategy and recruit creative talent. Foremost among them was Chris Powell, of Boase Massimi Pollitt.

Powell had looked at the relationship between the Conservatives and Saatchi & Saatchi with admiration. He saw the benefits of employing an agency full-time to handle all party communications: it allowed for strategic focus and consistency. But he was unwilling to put his own agency forward for the Labour account. 'I sidestepped it because, frankly, I could see it was a disaster waiting to happen,' says Powell. 'But I knew Johnny Wright was a good Labour man, and he seemed to think that the publicity would do his agency some good, just like it had done for Saatchis. From my point of view, I knew Johnny would give it his heart and soul. But he was walking into a campaign that turned out to be a complete mess. He partly has me to blame for that.'

Powell approached Wright after reading the *Campaign* profile. Wright was immediately enthusiastic about working with Labour. 'I was mostly motivated by my belief in the party,' he says. 'But, to be honest, the agency needed the business too. Labour were willing to pay us £600,000, which was a huge amount at the time. I thought the publicity of working on an election could help us just like it had done the Saatchis in 1979.'

The difference, of course, was that the Saatchis had backed a winner. Wright approached his partners in the agency, most of whom were fellow Labour supporters. Creative director Garnet Edwards was from the mining heartlands of Wales, a traditional Labour stronghold. He had seen the damage that Conservative policies were doing to such areas but was objective enough to see the attraction of some of them. 'I had friends back home who had been allowed to buy their council house for £5,000,' he says. 'That policy was very appealing to working-class people who would usually have voted Labour. I could see the challenge we had on our hands when we took the account on.'

Wright and Edwards were introduced to the party's communications chief, Nick Grant, by Chris Powell. What they expected to be a pitch for the business was rather more straightforward: they were offered the account on the spot. 'I don't think they could believe that they'd found an agency willing to take them on,' says Edwards.

Edwards saw it as a gamble: however much money they made out of Labour was likely to be offset by bad publicity. It was an account that could stigmatise the agency. But Wright was defiant. 'We had hardly any clients to upset in the first place!' he says. 'Our main one was Crown Paints. And their chief executive was a lifelong Labour supporter. He was only too happy for us to take on the business.'

Wright and Partners delivered some work for the party in 1982 but weren't given the green light to commence work for the 1983 campaign until just six weeks before polling day. 'Labour HQ was utterly disorganised,' says Wright. 'They had no strategy and it was chaotic. They were asking us to turn around ads for them in a couple of days. This sort of stuff would ordinarily take a matter of months to get right. Plus, we had to have every piece of work we produced examined and signed off by about forty different people on the campaign committee. It was like advertising hell.'

While the committee members argued exhaustively along sectarian lines, they were generally hostile to Wright and his creed. 'In their heart of hearts, the party as a whole didn't really believe in advertising as a discipline and mistrusted admen as flash Harrys,' says Wright. 'But they knew the other side were investing loads into it and so they felt they had to tick the box.' It was with a sense of begrudging obligation that an already under-resourced Labour Party gave £600,000 to men they vaguely mistrusted for ads they suspected were pointless in an election many of them knew was unwinnable.

Gerald Kaufman was the shadow environment secretary in 1983 and had written off the party's chances of victory three years beforehand, when Michael Foot had been elected leader. 'I remember leaving the committee room after the results had been called, turning to a couple of my colleagues and saying, "We have just voted to lose the next election."' In 2013, aged eighty, Kaufman was still a serving MP, and his reflections on the disastrous campaign of 1983 remain heavy with regret and frustration. He had been angered by what had happened after the disaster of 1979 and, it seemed, was still unable to forgive those responsible three decades later. 'Foot was a highly intelligent man and one of the greatest speakers I've ever seen,' he says. 'But as a leader he was an absolute disaster. He had only narrowly beaten Denis Healey in the leadership election and the decisive votes had been cast by MPs who left to join the SDP shortly afterwards. They later told me they had voted for Foot specifically to hamper our chances.'

Famously, Kaufman had described the Labour Party manifesto going into the 1983 election as 'the longest suicide note in history'. It advocated abolition of the House of Lords, immediate withdrawal from the European Community and unilateral nuclear disarmament at a time when cold war paranoia was at its height.

'The job those admen had on their hands wasn't just difficult, it was impossible,' says Kaufman. 'Just before the election was called I was in the Commons tea room looking around at all the colleagues who I knew were destined to lose their jobs. I couldn't sleep that night. The next day I went to see Michael Foot and urged him to resign. I said that he would be responsible for all those Labour MPs losing their seats. He told me it was too late. He wouldn't listen.'

Foot's image was a fatal turn-off for voters. His professorial demeanour was alienating to many; when he arrived at the Cenotaph on Armistice Day he looked distracted and was dressed in a short dark overcoat which the tabloid press chose to describe as a 'donkey jacket'. It was taken to be a mark of disrespect to the memory of the dead and the royals in attendance. He embodied one of the public's deepest suspicions about Labour: that they were militants without patriotism or pride whose principles were more aligned to those of Moscow than Britain. The press relished characterising him as a doddery old man. As speculation about his leadership intensified, *Private Eye* ran a cover featuring a white-haired geriatric in a wheelchair who bore a striking resemblance to Foot. A nurse leant into his ear and asked, 'Nod your head if you want to stay on.'

Foot was, at best, indifferent to campaign strategy. The then shadow environment secretary Roy Hattersley recounts: 'Right at the beginning of the 1983 election – with polling date already announced – Labour's campaign was found to be in such chaos that Larry Whitty and I were drafted in to pull it all together. Michael Foot insisted that I talk to him before we began work. At supper at his house, it turned out that his only concern was to have Neil Kinnock associated with our efforts. After I agreed – knowing Neil would play no active part – Michael would only talk about books and writing. How he introduced Arnold Bennett to Lord Beaverbrook. Did I know that Blake wrote "Jerusalem" as a hymn to free love? Fascinating stuff but . . . So eventually I asked for instructions, and Michael just replied, "Do your best."'

Meanwhile, Johnny Wright and Garnet Edwards were busy trying to pull together a plan of attack to redress Labour's nineteen-point deficit in the opinion polls. They had a matter of weeks to do so. There was certainly vulnerability in the Conservative record: unemployment had rocketed beyond three million since 1979 and a generation of young people found themselves out of work. Their frustrations had spilled over into violent rioting in some of the country's worst-affected areas: from Brixton to Toxteth and Moss Side. 'The Tories had sort of breezed through it all by saying, "We'd love to care but we simply can't afford to,"' says Edwards. 'We thought that was a pretty negative way of looking at our problems. We decided we wanted the whole campaign to push a more positive approach, with big ideas about how to create jobs.'

They conjured the line 'Think positive, vote Labour' and brought a selection of creative ideas based on this sentiment to present to the shadow cabinet at the start of the campaign. It was an intimidating encounter, even for Garnet Edwards, the adman who looked and sounded rather more like a Welsh international prop forward. 'Some of the people in the room outwardly disliked us and everything we stood for,' he says. 'When we started to talk [left-wing MP] Eric Heffer got up and said, "Who the hell are these fucking idiots?"'

The pair had been told by the party's communications chief Nick Grant that they should treat Labour like they would any other commercial client. But the admen knew this was impossible. 'If they'd been an ordinary client, we'd have told them they shouldn't be advertising at all because their product wasn't right,' says Edwards. 'But that wasn't really an option with an election six weeks away, so we had to do the best with what we had.'

Johnny Wright decided to take two separate campaign ideas with him to present to the committee in order to give them the illusion of choice. He felt sure that one was stronger than the other. By this time Labour HQ had moved from Smith Square in Westminster to Walworth Road in the south London borough of Lambeth. The meeting room they entered in the ramshackle headquarters was filled with twenty politicians sat round a table, each with advisors stood behind them. Foot passed each piece of work around the table, asking each individual for their point of view. After this lengthy process, the leader delivered an eloquent summary of the opinions before declaring the winning campaign. But he chose the wrong one. 'Somehow he came down in favour of the one we'd chucked together just for show,' says Wright. 'So I intervened and said, "Excuse me, Michael, but I think the consensus of opinion was in favour of the other campaign." Without hesitation he delivered a new summary, expressing the opposite view! It was like the verdict was guilty, then not guilty. I think they just all wanted the meeting to end by that point.'

The agency was thrust into a whirlwind of activity over the subsequent six weeks. Wright formally announced to his staff that they had been appointed by the Labour Party and that anyone with political objections wasn't obliged to work on the campaign. 'Hardly anyone refused, which was handy, because the amount of work we were required to do was incredible,' he says. 'The party political broadcasts alone amounted to about 105 minutes of airtime – which was equivalent to an entire year's output for most of our clients.'

The agency began to commission research groups to refine its strategy but was met with resistance at Walworth Road. 'We were told that there was no point in paying for research when they could just ask party members for their opinions,' says Wright. 'Which rather missed the point.'

Edwards was responsible for devising the scripts for the broadcasts but had no say in which politicians he could feature. Whereas Saatchis had put huge amounts of thought into which Conservative MPs were the most telegenic, Labour had a characteristically democratic approach. Each shadow minister would be given equal screen time. The agency was instructed to make a series of films on a variety of policy areas, with the relevant spokesperson starring in each.

Kaufman was called in to feature in a broadcast about housing. His voice, slightly stilted and ominous, narrated a long, slow, panning shot across a derelict street of houses surrounded by wasteland. He spoke of the urban degradation and spiralling unemployment that Margaret Thatcher had presided over since 1979. Eventually the camera found him standing awkwardly amidst this bleak scene of social decay, earnestly explaining how a Labour government might remedy the situation.

The film then cut to Kaufman in a studio, where he spelt out Labour's economic and social strategy in some detail. He shifted blocks around representing each element of government activity to demonstrate the Labour approach. His words were then endorsed by Maurice Peston, a professor of economics (and father of BBC journalist Robert Peston). 'It was what we were calling "Labour's new deal",' says Edwards. 'We were trying to demonstrate that all policy areas were linked and that once government invested in one area it would have a positive knock-on effect on all the others. A lot of people responded well to it.'

The ads had rigour and substance but were dry and overly forensic in their explanation of policy. As the Conservatives successfully took their own advertising in a more emotional direction, playing to the preconceptions of the electorate with bold, simple messages, Labour seemed to be going the opposite way: preaching to the public about Keynesian economic theory, which the average voter had little interest in. Numerous broadcasts followed the same structure: a bleak monologue from an uncomfortable MP followed by a baffling show-and-tell on economic theory.

Edwards and director Brian Wiseman would take their footage directly from the shoot to the edit, working up a rough cut overnight that Edwards would then deliver through Johnny Wright's letterbox in the early hours of the morning. Wright would take the film to Walworth Road to present to the campaign committee. 'There wasn't a tightly defined approval process and we were still having to get dozens of people to sign everything off,' he says. 'One day Arthur Scargill of all people stood up in the middle of a meeting and said, "This is ridiculous, they're never going to get anything done if we all keep sticking our oars in!" He proposed a smaller approval committee made up of Nick Grant, Michael Foot, Denis Healey and a couple of others. Things started to speed up after that.'

As soon as that day's broadcast had been signed off, the agency was instructed on what topic to tackle next. 'They seemed to be choosing at random,' says Edwards. 'Someone would say, "I think we should focus on the nuclear issue next," and everyone would nod. And then we'd have to go off and make a broadcast about nuclear disarmament in half a day!' The agency men knew defence was Labour's weak spot but felt in no position to argue. 'We could have told them that we should avoid the nuclear issue like the plague,' says Edwards, 'but our opinions really didn't matter.'

Chris Powell's vision of a single agency able to communicate the party's entire message soon transpired to be a fantasy. 'Even if we got one message across through the broadcasts, we never knew what an MP was going to turn up and say on TV next,' says Edwards. While Saatchi & Saatchi was maintaining a united front by orchestrating every public utterance by government ministers, Labour's PR machine was in disarray. Shadow minister Neil Kinnock was well aware of the party's presentational problems. 'I tried to run most of my campaign myself,' he says. 'I knew that if I gave the campaign material to the people at Walworth Road, they'd make a mess of it.' The lack of professionalism at Labour HQ meant Michael Foot was hung out to dry, says Kinnock. 'They sent him round the country, and he was then sixty-eight years of age. He did over eighty meetings and all the television interviews, he wrote articles, he did the whole bloody thing with only a couple of chums to help him. He was crucified. It was bloody terrible.'

Meanwhile, Wright and Edwards were finding it marginally easier to get work approved under the stewardship of Denis Healey's smaller campaign committee. 'Healey insisted on inserting a line into our slogan,' says Edwards. 'What was "Think positive, vote Labour" became "Think positive, act positive, vote Labour". He said our version had sounded too passive.'

Wright would often find himself summoned to the Commons rather than Walworth Road for approval meetings. 'In long meetings I noticed that Healey and the rest would get up and disappear at about six-ish, then come back half an hour later looking rather flushed and sounding more willing to sign off our work!' he says. 'I must admit that was a period in which I briefly gave consideration to working full-time in politics. It was one area where advertising culture overlapped with theirs.'

Edwards created a series of posters that tried to attack the government's record by using literal imagery. One poster depicted a traumatised pensioner being squashed in a gigantic metal clamp, above the headline 'Are you going to vote pensioners into 5 more years of the pinch?' Another showed a collection of miserable-looking teenagers slumped on an actual scrapheap: 'Are you going to vote for retirement at 16?' Each of these was accompanied by several paragraphs of text outlining the specifics of Labour's policy solutions. It was a far cry from the succinct vigour used by Saatchis. One poster was rather more on the nose: it depicted a sinister red and black portrait of Margaret Thatcher, under the headline 'Are you going to vote for Mag the Knife?' The portrait was annotated with a series of knife-related puns, such as 'She's carved up our children's education,' 'She's slashed the jobs of 2,000,000 people' and 'She's filleted British industry.' It was hardly subtle but it at least showed some of the bold, combative spirit that the Tories had been using so successfully. But it didn't go down well with the Labour leadership. 'Michael Foot disapproved of it for being too negative,' says Wright.

As polling day loomed, polls showed the Conservative lead still solid at nineteen points. Six weeks of intensive work by Johnny Wright and Partners had made zero difference to Labour's popularity. 'From day one I had told my people, "You know we don't stand a chance. There is no way we can win. We'll do our best,"' admits Wright. 'If you were a brand of shampoo and you trailed the market leader by 19 per cent, you wouldn't bother advertising. You could spend millions just to gain a single point on them.' Foot remained upbeat to the last, refusing to accept the bleak prospects spelt out by every published opinion poll. 'He would attend Labour rallies where everyone would cheer him, and that convinced him that they had a chance of victory,' says Chris Powell. 'But he was only getting a very narrow view of the country.'

Polling day arrived on 9 June. It was one of the greatest electoral disasters in the history of the Labour Party: their share of the vote shrank by more than 9 per cent, they lost sixty parliamentary seats nationwide and they received only 700,000 more votes than the newly formed SDP–Liberal Alliance. Wright was disappointed but not surprised. Plus, his experience of working with the party had left him hugely sceptical about their ability to govern. 'I had a severe concern that if they were elected, it would be worrying,' he admits. 'They were a shambles. They couldn't make decisions. They would have had a committee of forty-five people running the government and it would have been unworkable.'

But Wright was pleased with the impact the campaign had on his own profile and his agency's prospects. 'I went from being a nobody to briefly being one of the most famous admen in London,' he says. 'A TV company came to make a film about us at the agency. The day after it aired I was in a restaurant and I heard a young boy say, "Look, it's that man off the telly." I realised that my profile had benefited. The agency had been struggling and a few years later another company bought us out.'

Garnet Edwards has less positive memories about the campaign. 'It was the most stressful but the most exciting time of my career,' he says. 'But while I was up all night editing a broadcast, I always knew we were fighting a losing battle.' He and Wright remain close friends but the two differ about the impact it had on their agency's fortunes. 'We were very young and we needed the money; the Labour Party were willing to pay, so I agreed it was a good project to take on at the time,' says Edwards. 'But it did for us in the end. Potential clients wouldn't go near us because of our associations with Labour. We had a meeting lined up with the guy from Lindt chocolates in Switzerland. It would have been a big account. But he read in the newspaper about us doing the Labour campaign and told us he couldn't be seen doing business with us.'

As the journalist Michael White noted in the *Guardian* at the time, 'There was something magnificently brave about Michael Foot's campaign – but it was like the Battle of the Somme.' To many of the Labour insiders I spoke to during the course of writing this book, the efforts of Johnny Wright and Partners in 1983 remain the very model of how not to run a successful campaign. But Wright, Edwards and their colleagues worked hard for a cause they believed in, despite a certain knowledge that it would end in failure. There was something heroic about their efforts, which

Edwards remains very proud of. 'There were loads of Labour sympathisers in the ad industry in 1983,' he says. 'The only difference between us and them was that we had the balls to take the job on. We worked for the party we supported when it wasn't fashionable and nobody wanted to touch them. Ten years later the same ad people were falling over themselves to get involved.'

There's something very calming about being in the company of Johnny Wright; sitting on his boat he chuckles even as he recalls the bleakest of mishaps from that summer of 1983. Perhaps he really was the only sort of man who could have handled the Labour Party campaign back then. He even refuses to see the catastrophic electoral results as any reflection on his own endeavours. 'Our ads didn't lose Labour that election, just like that "Labour isn't working" poster didn't win it for Thatcher in 1979,' he says. 'What role can advertising play? None. It sometimes, at the most, gives the press and the public something to talk about – but where is the evidence for its mind-changing abilities? There is none. What it can do is help to boost the morale of the party's supporters, politicians and leaders during the campaign. They see a poster with a strong message in their favour and it gives them a boost. But that's all.'

It's hard to see where the blame lies for Labour's disarray in 1983. The admen were victims of what they called a bad product. The Labour Party was riddled with infighting, shambolic organisation and a deep philosophical suspicion of any modern form of communication. It seemed preoccupied by an internal struggle for decision-making power: between Tony Benn's left-wing hardliners, union bosses, the leader's office and the national executive. An unworkable brand of democracy had been installed that meant decision-making was almost impossible. In the eye of the storm was Michael Foot, a man out of time – too old and perhaps a little too cerebral to navigate his way successfully through the slings and arrows of a campaign fought in the unforgiving glare of the modern media. But to Wright and Edwards, he was the best client they ever worked for. 'He was deeply intelligent but never overly earnest about what we were doing,' says Wright. 'I'm not sure he had complete faith in advertising but he treated us with respect and interest. Towards the end of the campaign I was called to his home to present some work. It was just him, his wife, Denis Healey and a couple of others. I laid the posters out on the sitting-room floor and his dog, Disraeli, walked in. He walked all over the work and started sniffing one of the ads. Foot said, "Well, perhaps we might as well go with Disraeli's comments." Then he put on his coat and went out for dinner.'

5

LIKE YOUR MANIFESTO, COMRADE

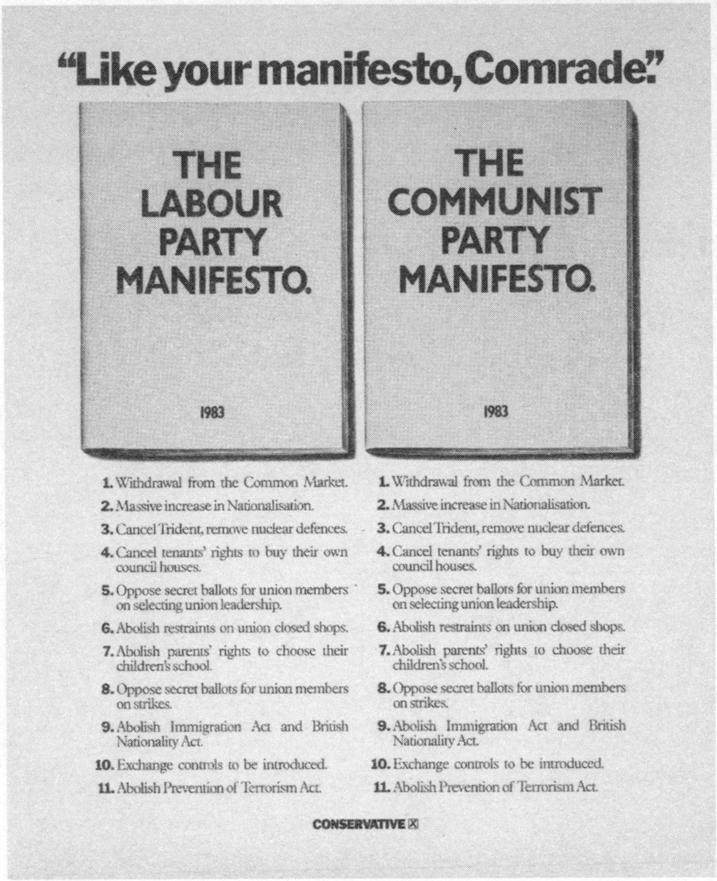
"Like your manifesto, Comrade."
THE LABOUR PARTY MANIFESTO.
1983
THE COMMUNIST PARTY MANIFESTO.
1983
1. Withdrawal from the Common Market.
2. Massive increase in Nationalisation.
3. Cancel Trident, remove nuclear defences.
4. Cancel tenants' rights to buy their own council houses.
5. Oppose secret ballots for union members on selecting union leadership.
6. Abolish restraints on union closed shops.
7. Abolish parents' rights to choose their children's school.
8. Oppose secret ballots for union members on strikes.
9. Abolish Immigration Act and British Nationality Act.
10. Exchange controls to be introduced.
11. Abolish Prevention of Terrorism Act.
1. Withdrawal from the Common Market.
2. Massive increase in Nationalisation.
3. Cancel Trident, remove nuclear defences.
4. Cancel tenants' rights to buy their own council houses.
5. Oppose secret ballots for union members on selecting union leadership.
6. Abolish restraints on union closed shops.
7. Abolish parents' rights to choose their children's school.
8. Oppose secret ballots for union members on strikes.
9. Abolish Immigration Act and British Nationality Act.
10. Exchange controls to be introduced.
11. Abolish Prevention of Terrorism Act.
CONSERVATIVE

On the night of the 1979 general election, Conservative Party chairman Lord Thorneycroft had publicly credited Saatchi & Saatchi for masterminding Margaret Thatcher's landslide victory. Since then, the agency had become a household name. The company had gone on a buying spree, led by their dynamic young finance boss, Martin Sorrell, and had acquired a number of smaller agencies and PR companies. By the early eighties it had overtaken prestigious rivals such as J. Walter Thompson to become the UK's number-one ad firm. Soon, it would become the biggest in the world. 'Our relationship with the Conservatives had been the springboard for all of that,' Jeremy Sinclair told me. 'And Tim Bell had become the key man in the relationship.'

Bell had been running the agency since 1979, first as managing director and later as chairman, while devoting a huge amount of his time to advising the new prime minister. Many observed that he was stretching himself too thinly and wondered how long he could sustain the workload. But he seemed to relish the profile, success and influence that his dual roles afforded him. His relationship with Thatcher had been growing ever closer and he enjoyed people knowing it. Not only was it good for his ego, it was good for business too. One of his most prized clients was British Leyland, and he had developed a particularly close relationship with its chief executive, Michael

Edwardes. In late 1979 Edwardes ordered a review of his company's advertising business, inviting both Saatchis and the joint holders of the account, Leo Burnett, to deliver presentations. The stakes were high: both agencies knew they were in danger of losing their half of the lucrative account to the other side. Leo Burnett's chief executive, Roger Edwards, spent days preparing for the presentation. 'I was immensely confident,' he recalled. 'I knew he [Bell] couldn't beat me. Then when Tim walked in he walked over and said, "Hello, Michael, Margaret sends you her best regards." I was completely floored.'

Saatchi & Saatchi had by now moved to Charlotte Street in London's West End, a road renowned for its expensive restaurants. The Saatchi execs held most of their important meetings over lunch and dinner, wining and dining their key clients lavishly. The Conservative Party was treated no differently – government ministers were frequently invited to 'brain-storming sessions' over dinner in smart private dining rooms. Essentially, it was an excuse to drink several bottles of fine wine at the agency's expense. 'They weren't used to doing their business like that but they certainly enjoyed it,' says Bell. At one dinner, attended by Willie Whitelaw and Michael Heseltine, melon was served as a starter to the assembled group. Copywriter Andrew Rutherford recalls seeing the politicians pouring an entire boat of salad dressing onto the fruit. 'We didn't want them to feel embarrassed, so we all did the same thing,' he told me. 'Then we just left it there, covered in vinegar, untouched.'

British ad agencies were growing at lightning speed in the eighties, raising millions overnight through public share offerings. Displays of excess were encouraged in the flashy, increasingly competitive industry. Bell had once proudly told me that he would take a chauffeur-driven car from the front door of his office to his favourite restaurant two hundred yards down Charlotte Street. 'Why?' he'd said. 'Because I'm lazy, that's why!' Rutherford claims that Bell had even employed a bodyguard during this period – a decision fuelled by a heady mixture of ego and paranoia. 'I remember coming back from a meeting with Tim, Willie Whitelaw and Tim's bodyguard,' Rutherford says. 'When we passed Whitehall, Willie casually got out of the car and strolled back to his office. He was the deputy prime minister. Meanwhile, there's me and Tim, a couple of admen, heading back to Charlotte Street with a bodyguard looking after us!'

Government ministers, many of whom were from aristocratic backgrounds, were often taken aback by the opulence of their admen. 'Lord Carrington was coming over for breakfast and, because he was the 14th Marquis of something or other, Maurice and I thought we'd better treat him right,' Bell says. 'We decked out the boardroom with silver trays filled with bacon and kidneys and kedgeree. We even had a butler in full uniform. Carrington took one look at the spread and said, "Bloody Christ, you admen live well!" Then he sat down and had some toast and scrambled eggs.'

Bell was pulling out all the stops to nurture the agency's relationship with the government, but there was a schism developing between him and the Saatchi brothers. Maurice and Charles were growing the company globally and felt Bell was too preoccupied with his political profile. A storm was brewing, and their senior colleagues were caught in the middle.

Bill Muirhead, like Jeremy Sinclair, is another long-term Saatchi exec. In the eighties he worked and lived with Bell.

The two were close friends but Muirhead could see Bell heading for a fall as his career and profile reached dizzying heights. 'Tim is a brilliant combination of a lot of things,' he says. 'He will say things that are patently bullshit. But he'll say them in such a way that you think, "Oh, that must be right." But he never exaggerated how close he was to Thatcher. I saw it with my own eyes.'

Muirhead and Bell were the very epitome of thrusting young admen: barely into their thirties and running the most successful agency in the country. Often, says Muirhead, their lives seemed beyond fiction. 'One morning we woke up with nothing to do and Tim said, "Let's go and see the prime minister,"' he recalls. 'And the next thing I know we're at 10 Downing Street. We go upstairs, and the PM comes to me and says, "Tim needs a haircut." And I thought, "Why are you telling me this?" She clearly loved him in a way. Maybe he was the son she wanted to have, I don't know. Or maybe the lover.'

The pair whiled the day away over a series of gin and tonics with Margaret and her husband Denis. 'Denis offered me another drink and I told him I'd had enough,' says Muirhead. 'He said, "Don't be stupid! There's never enough in this house!"'

In the eyes of the prime minister, Bell had gone from being a trusted adman to a trusted friend. However good that might have been for the agency's reputation, the Saatchis were beginning to query the amount of time he spent with the PM. 'I think a bit of jealousy might have crept in,' says Muirhead.

The brothers had appointed a new managing director in 1979, making Bell chairman of the company. His profile in the industry was extremely high and he had received numerous offers to leave and set up on his own. But he had stayed loyal – and was keen for something in return. He had always told clients that he was effectively the 'third brother' or the ampersand in Saatchi & Saatchi. But by the early eighties he was pushing for his name to be officially incorporated into the company title. The brothers refused, and Bell began to feel increasingly left out.

Soon he would begin to feel the same way about his relationship with the Conservatives. His old ally Gordon Reece had moved to California, remaining only a part-time advisor on communications. His replacement at Conservative central office was David Boddy, who was more interested in building relationships with the press than with ad agencies. The former marketing director of Mars, Charles Lawson, was now the man in charge of advertising. He was the latest recruit to Mrs Thatcher's inner circle of advisors from outside of politics and was a former corporate client of Bob Worcester. 'I was working for him at Mars and we were on our way home from a conference in Chicago,' Worcester says. 'Charles turned to me and said, "I'm going to tell you something that might come as a surprise. I'm quitting Mars to work as marketing director for the Conservatives." I said, "Charles, why?" And he told me, "Because Mrs Thatcher asked me to and I believe in the cause. I'm not even going to take a salary."' Thatcherism was becoming an established dogma, attracting its own breed of acolytes.

One of Lawson's first acts was to inform Tim Bell in January 1982 that Saatchis was no longer the party's ad agency and that it must re-pitch for the business. Bell was astonished. In reality, Lawson had no intention of dropping the agency but was merely guarding against complacency.

Life was becoming harder for Bell. Gone were the days

when Lord Thorneycroft, who had been replaced as party chairman by Cecil Parkinson in 1981, would welcome their presentations with gushing enthusiasm ('He used to say it was like being in a sweet shop as a child, not knowing which of our ideas he wanted most!' says Bell) and party treasurer Lord McAlpine sign off their fees with gleeful abandon ('It's better to be a bankrupt party in power than a cash-rich party in opposition!' he would rationalise).

No matter what the hierarchy at central office thought of him, Bell had always been able to depend on his close friendship with the prime minister to help maintain the Tory account. But he even contrived to put that relationship at risk on a couple of occasions. In 1981 British Leyland's marketing director, Tony Cummings, had enquired about the possibility of being introduced to Thatcher. With characteristic largesse, Bell had promised his valued client that he could easily arrange a social meeting. The opportunity to do so arose a few months later, at a charity performance of *Anyone for Denis?*, the satirical stage play that poked fun at Denis Thatcher. Bell had advised the prime minister that it would be wise for her to attend the show in order to display a sense of humour. She agreed, and Bell arranged for Cummings to attend the play on the same night, followed by a drinks reception at Downing Street. But the plan backfired. The prime minister disliked the play and found the characterisation of her husband – as a casually racist little Englander – deeply offensive. When Cummings finally got to meet the prime minister that night, she was filled with anger and resentment at the play. Bell would later describe the evening as 'one of the greatest mistakes of his life'.

The fast-paced, high-flying nature of Bell's life appeared to have clouded his judgement, and he was finding it harder to sustain the business relationship with central office. New party chairman Cecil Parkinson was sceptical about the effectiveness of advertising and wanted to run a tighter ship than his predecessor. I went to meet Parkinson at the House of Lords on an autumn afternoon in 2013, recalling on my journey his racy eighties caricature. While a cabinet member he became embroiled in a scandal after fathering a child with his mistress and saw his skyrocketing political career curtailed as a consequence. From then on *Private Eye* and *Spitting Image* would incessantly portray him as a rakish scoundrel with a voracious sexual appetite. It probably didn't help matters that Parkinson was a handsome, suave sort of a fellow with matinee looks not entirely dissimilar to those of Tim Bell's. In 1981 he was one of Margaret Thatcher's favoured ministers, earmarked for the very top. Clearly, she had a type.

In 2013 Cecil Parkinson was the healthiest-looking octogenarian I had ever set eyes on. He was tanned, slim, athletic-looking and sharply dressed. It wasn't just sickening, it was a bit scary, putting me in mind of those conspiracy theories about aristocrats who replace their blood supply with that of children every few years to maintain eternal youth. It was an unlikely theory, mind you. Probably more to do with genetics.

'I was astonished at how much credit the Saatchis had got for the victory in 1979,' he tells me. 'I think that perhaps the "Labour isn't working" poster had helped convince Callaghan not to call an election in 1978. But, beyond that, the country just went with the tide of things. The ads went along with the national feeling that it was time for a change. To put it in stark business terms: you can't give away a bad product. And there is little point in giving the hard sell to a good one. We were always going to win those elections because we were the better product.'

It was with this attitude that Parkinson entered the 1983 general election campaign, which Margaret Thatcher called on 13 May. In the early years of her premiership, polls had shown Thatcher to be one of the least popular prime ministers in British history. Unemployment had doubled since 1979 and social unrest was rife in the inner cities. Her character was considered by many to be overly hectoring and unsympathetic to the plight of ordinary people. But by the time the election was called, the Conservatives were looking in much better shape – thanks partly to Thatcher's successful response in 1982 to the Argentinian invasion of the Falkland Islands. 'That is one of the biggest myths of the time,' Parkinson tells me. 'When I became chairman in September 1981 we were in third place behind the Alliance and Labour in the opinion polls. The Argentinians invaded on 2 April, but on 31 March we'd gone into the lead in the polls for the first time. We had overtaken Labour and the SDP, and I was elated. The reason was that the economic policy was beginning to work, and people were beginning to say, "Well, maybe this woman's right."'

Rather than the informal chats with the party hierarchy that Tim Bell and Gordon Reece had enjoyed in 1979, the admen were now marginalised. Parkinson and his inner circle worked on the strategy, and the agency would follow a strict brief. 'Was Saatchi & Saatchi involved in developing the manifesto? Answer: no,' says Parkinson. 'They were told what the manifesto contained when it was produced. They played no part in building up the policies or in the development of the programme for the prime minister's press conferences every day. We mapped out the ideal scenario for us, what we would love to happen, and by an extraordinary fluke – because the Labour Party were so incompetent – we never had to change a thing.'

Parkinson saw the PR operation as far more important than the advertising. He focused his attentions on strategising where and when the prime minister would appear on television news. A series of carefully choreographed public appearances were arranged to coincide with each day's major policy announcement. The natural advantage of being the incumbent, married with the patent disorganisation of Labour's campaign, allowed the Conservatives to drive the agenda.

The Tories even had the bravado to start their campaign three days after Labour. 'We thought it would lend us an air of gravitas,' says Parkinson. 'By the time Margaret actually did start campaigning, the media were mad with anticipation.' For the first time since the thirties, unemployment in the UK had risen to three million. The Conservatives' monetarist policies had also failed to keep inflation under control. Key promises from their general election campaign had been broken – and Parkinson expected Labour to attack them on that basis. But he decided the best policy was to confront such issues head-on. 'We knew Labour would focus on unemployment, and so we thought we'd get the first punch in,' he says. 'We said, "We will accept that the government has presided over an increase in unemployment. Will they accept their share of responsibility for the fact that the steel industry was chronically overmanned and we had to deal with it, that shipbuilding was chronically overmanned and we had to deal with it?" We questioned who had caused the unemployment in the first place. The people who presided over it or the people who left it? By the time we'd finished, we were seen as the party with the better answers on unemployment. Unemployment became a strong issue for us.'

This strategy ran counter to the prevailing wisdom at Saatchi & Saatchi. Tim Bell, Jeremy Sinclair and the Saatchi brothers wanted to continue with the combative style that had worked in 1979. They considered Parkinson's complex arguments over unemployment to be advertising suicide. They favoured simple, blunt messages that attacked the opposition. 'I happen to think negative advertising works,' Bell says. 'People vote out of fear. Fear of change, mostly. So if you're in government you need to scare people about what change might bring about.'

Bell began to bring posters to present to Parkinson and Thatcher. The first pandered to the party's desire for positive messages. A midwife was pictured slapping the bottom of a newborn baby; the headline read: '48,000 new midwives since we came to power. Children are better off under the Conservatives.' At the presentation meeting, Thatcher and Parkinson were joined by junior minister Ian Gow, a trusted confidant of the prime minister. He was also the MP for Eastbourne, a constituency with a large population of pensioners. 'We can't show childbirth on our posters!' Gow exclaimed. 'The elderly will be completely disgusted!' Parkinson was in agreement. Thatcher leaned in towards Bell and smiled: 'I think you better come back when they're not around, Tim, I don't think they like it!'

She was not always so easy to win over. 'She disliked our tendency towards oversimplification at times,' says Bell. 'And she would occasionally veto ads just to remind us who was boss.' One such occasion came in 1983, when Bell arrived at Downing Street with a mocked-up poster of sixty-eight-year-old Michael Foot hobbling across Hampstead Heath with a walking stick. The headline read: 'As a pensioner, he'd be better off under the Conservatives.' Thatcher was furious. 'She practically threw me out of the room,' says Bell. 'She said it wasn't right to make personal attacks on politicians. I said, "But Prime Minister, he is a pensioner!" And she said, "Yes, but you're trying to make a joke out of the fact that he has a disability and wears bad clothes!" To which I replied, "That's exactly what we're doing." And she said, "Well, you can't!"'

This was to be the central clash between party and agency in 1983: Saatchis was salivating at the opportunity to demolish one of the weakest opposition parties in memory; Thatcher and her colleagues were determined to win on the basis of their record over the past four years. It is hard to assess who was right given that the election was almost unwinnable for the Labour Party. Bell argues that, had the parties been closer in the polls, the positive approach might have cost the Conservatives dearly on polling day. 'There were numerous negative ads that I refused to even present to the PM in 1983 because I felt it might jeopardise our relationship with the party,' he says. 'There were always other agencies trying to move in on the account and so we had to make sure we kept them happy.' The men from Saatchis did at least get some of their favoured work past the approval process. They created a poster that compared eleven policies from the Labour Party's manifesto with eleven from the Soviet Union's Communist Party. The headline ran: 'Like your manifesto, comrade.' It tapped into the cold war paranoia that was at its height in British society in 1983. It was funny and aggressive and became the most memorable poster of the campaign.

Despite the frostiness from Parkinson and his staff at central office, Bell was almost always able to convince the prime minister to consider the agency's work. Even when, at the start of the campaign, he presented agency research that was highly critical of Thatcher's prime ministerial style, she accepted his views. 'Tim had a more sensitive set of antennae than most politicians,' Thatcher later remarked. 'He could pick up quicker than anyone else a change in the national mood. And, unlike most advertising men, he understood that selling ideas was different from selling soap.'

Bell is candid about how he sold his ideas. 'There is an old adage about the adman on his wedding night,' he tells me. 'He sits at the end of the bed explaining to his wife at great length just how great the sex is going to be and, by the time he's finished, she's too tired to actually do it. I did things differently: I went into those meetings with confidence and conviction. I didn't try to explain everything – I just assured them this was the right approach to take. They seemed to like that.'

Parkinson recalls the tricks Bell would use to convince the prime minister. 'We never met Charles or Maurice Saatchi throughout the 1983 campaign,' he says. 'But once in a while Tim would unveil a poster with great ceremony and say in this hushed way, "This particular poster is by Charles himself." Who knows whether Charles had anything to do with any of the work? But Tim created this sort of mystery around him that even impressed Margaret.' For the most part, though, Thatcher thought Bell *was* Saatchi & Saatchi. 'I think she thought he wrote, designed and directed all of the ads himself,' says Parkinson.

Bell was able to push through one more combative

proposal: to produce an election broadcast focusing on the winter of discontent. Central office saw it as off-message, a throwback to the 1979 election rather than a celebration of what had been achieved since. But Bell was adamant that the public needed reminding of how bad things had been under Labour. A dramatic montage depicting strikes, snow and heavily littered streets was accompanied by a chilling voiceover from the actor Anthony Quayle, who asked viewers repeatedly, 'Remember when . . .?' Every time Bell managed to squeeze a piece of negative advertising past Parkinson and Thatcher, it appeared to have a big impact. 'They were very good at bringing a real style to films like that,' says Parkinson. 'But however good the ads were, they were not central to the campaign. I like Tim and consider him to be a friend but I feel that the media have been extremely generous to him and the Saatchis over the years. The ad campaign was not really relevant to the election results, and there is proof of that.'

In the final week of the campaign a rogue opinion poll was published suggesting that Labour was eating into the Tory lead. Saatchis was characteristically aggressive in its response. Bell suggested that the Tories take out three consecutive pages in every national newspaper. The first page would outline eleven reasons to vote Conservative; the second would bullet-point eight reasons not to vote Labour; and the third would feature a single line explaining why it was pointless to vote for the SDP–Liberal Alliance. To purchase such a huge amount of advertising space would cost the party in the region of £1.5 million. With most polls still showing a Conservative lead of close to twenty points, Parkinson decided that the ads would be a needless extravagance.

'I rang the prime minister and told her that I wanted to cancel the final week of media spend and save the money,' says Parkinson. 'It would be wasted funds to beat an opposition who were already on their knees. She agreed.'

Bell was astonished when Parkinson broke the news to him. He knew the funds were available and couldn't understand why the party wouldn't want to make absolutely sure of victory. 'I told him that it would look like we were trying to buy victory,' Parkinson tells me. Bell had felt sidelined throughout the campaign, unable to wield the same influence he had in 1979. Parkinson claims that Bell met directly with the prime minister on only five occasions during the whole period. Eventually the adman took matters into his own hands. 'He turned up at a press conference and tried to grab the prime minister on her way out,' says Parkinson. 'She said she didn't have time to see him, but he was adamant that if he could just talk to her directly she would agree to the ads. I took him aside and said, "Look, Tim, you are not Michelangelo and this is not the Sistine Chapel!"'

It was a bold move by the young party chairman. Conservative treasurer Lord McAlpine told him, 'If we win on Thursday, you'll be a hero. But if we lose by one, you should emigrate without delay.'

The resounding victory at the polls justified Parkinson's veto. He was guided by more than gut instinct. A week previously, Chris Lawson had called his old colleague Bob Worcester, who was working on Labour's private polling. 'He told me they were thinking of saving themselves a few million by pulling the last week's ads,' Worcester told me. 'He wanted to know if my private polls would back up the decision. Obviously I couldn't tell him anything because I was employed by the Labour Party. I told him it was his call. But I think we both knew they had it in the bag.'

Parkinson speaks fondly of Tim Bell as a person, but he was deeply suspicious about the industry he represented and, specifically, Saatchi & Saatchi's motives in 1983. 'They built themselves up into great central figures, and there's no doubt at all that, had I allowed it, all of those newspaper spreads would have won them all sorts of plaudits – you know, the advertising scoop of the year. But it would have cost us millions and, as the events proved, we got a majority of 146 without it. So it would have been a total waste of money.'

Saatchis had stood to gain more than awards from its proposed ad splurge in the final week. At that time, the industry convention was to charge a client about 17 per cent of a campaign's media spend in fees. By cancelling £1.5 million worth of advertising in the final week, Parkinson had cost the agency close to £250,000.

Parkinson thought that his decision might have finished off the influence of admen over election campaigns for ever. 'People say, "Advertising is absolutely essential,"' he says. 'But that campaign cost something in the region of £28 million and we got 397 seats. I was bombarded in that final week by telegrams and messages from senior figures telling me to spend the money and advertise more. But the proof of the pudding is in the eating; we didn't spend the money and we got our majority. For me, that blew out of the water once and for all the idea that it's advertising that does the trick.'

Perhaps it should have done. But it did not. Over the coming years, the Conservative Party's relationship with Saatchi & Saatchi would become deeper and more complex.

Perhaps the 1983 election was a flawed test case: the Labour Party was in such disarray that the Conservatives would have won without any campaign whatsoever. Advertising by either side was irrelevant. Over the coming years, the electoral margins would draw closer and Parkinson's successors would not dare to take the same chances as he did in 1983. But the admen themselves were growing bolder: Tim Bell and the Saatchis were now veterans of two electoral victories and they were unafraid of publicising the fact. Despite the fractious nature of the 1983 election, they would dig in with the Tories, convinced that their own fate was inextricably linked to their key client. Now they had experience and credibility on their side and would bill themselves for years to come as the admen with the political Midas touch. Everything Parkinson thought he had exposed about the business in 1983 would soon be forgotten.

6

CRYING OUT FOR CHANGE

“IF UNEMPLOYMENT IS NOT BELOW THREE MILLION IN FIVE YEARS, THEN I’M NOT WORTH RE-ELECTING.”

Norman Tebbit 1983

NO WONDER THEY’VE CALLED THE ELECTION A YEAR EARLY.

THE COUNTRY’S CRYING OUT FOR CHANGE. VOTE LABOUR

I first met Neil Kinnock in 1992, when I was seventeen years old. He had just stepped down as leader of the Labour Party after the election defeat of that year. My father had been complicit in the unsuccessful campaign and was invited to Kinnock's farewell party, and he took me as his guest. I got talking to Kinnock but he seemed even less keen on discussing politics than I was. Instead, we talked about football. We'd both had a couple of beers. I remember him describing in detail the correct way to execute a headbutt on someone without hurting yourself. He also told me a brilliant story about an altercation he'd had with a dwarf outside a South Wales pub in his youth. He was a wonderfully colourful and entertaining man who – despite never actually mentioning politics once – helped spark my interest in the subject. He seemed like a normal human, not the weird, dysfunctional spod I'd assumed all politicians to be. Rightly or wrongly, I think his dwarf-fight story (to summarise, the dwarf ambushed him outside the pub, knocking him down with a sack of coal and kicking him while he was on the floor) convinced me that politicians weren't all bad and that politics could, therefore, be a force for positive change. I suppose we all discover our passions in different ways.

I know the conversation wasn't a weird drunken dream because, twenty-one years later, when I met Kinnock for tea in Westminster, I asked him about the dwarf tale again. He seemed surprised that I recalled it but confirmed my memories were accurate. But on this occasion we were here to talk about more than that. I wanted to ask him about the aftermath of Labour's 1983 election disaster; about how he had taken over the leadership of an unelectable party; and about how he managed to drag Labour kicking and screaming into the age of modern political communications.

He went back immediately to 1979, when he had been driving through his own constituency in Bedwellty, South Wales, and seen the Conservatives' 'Labour isn't working' poster displayed by the roadside. He had wondered why the Tories would waste their money on advertising in such a Labour stronghold, but realised it was an act of bravado, a reminder that the Tories could waste money on futile advertising while Labour scrabbled to pay for a half-respectable campaign. But he was not despondent. 'It was a great poster because it was so creative,' he says. 'Its claims might not stand up to analysis, but that didn't matter because it tapped into the public's state of mind in a clever way. I thought to myself, "Imagine what we could achieve if we had creativity like that in our ranks." From that moment there were people like me in the party, sensible people, who realised that Labour had to embrace that kind of communication if it was to get re-elected.'

He recognised that with the right ideas, money wasn't important. And he sensed that the talent was out there to help him keep pace with Tory advertising. 'The best creative talent usually tends to be left-wing,' he says. 'Writers, artists and actors have very often experienced periods of not working and having no money. They understand that plight and it informs their politics. I knew that there must be creative minds out there who could help us.'

Kinnock was convinced that the party's image was not a superficiality – it spoke volumes about what they stood for. He was determined to make Labour more creative.

'[Creativity] was non-existent in the party then,' he says. 'In a sense, what typified it was the Labour Party flag. The insignia and letterheads were mid-1930s representations of the words "Labour Party". They had even dispensed with the flame and the crossed spade and the word "liberty", which used to sit underneath the logo. That's what we're after – liberty. We represent workers by hand or by brain, the spade or the plume. That was dispensed with and exchanged for what I always thought was a pretty ugly and dated logo that said very little. It denoted a mentality which was out of touch with the whole idea of design and dynamism and representational art, which can mean a lot to political parties, as it can to trade unions and companies.'

But Kinnock struggled to convince other key figures in the party. 'The establishment in the party, represented by Tony Benn and Dennis Skinner on the NEC, thought logos and image were at best superficial and at worst corrosive, not just to our identity but to our purpose. It represented such a compromise with the commercialised world as to be repellent as far as they were concerned.'

Labour's internal difficulties had not gone away. Kinnock battled with the far-left Militant Tendency, who had taken control of numerous Labour councils in the north, and became caught up in the miners' strike of 1984–5. While his battle with Militant won the party some favourable coverage, demonstrating its desire to oust radical elements, the violent picketing of the miners' strike, led by NUM leader Arthur Scargill without a democratic mandate from his members, sparked damaging memories of the winter of discontent. Kinnock found himself in an impossible position: sympathetic to the brave rank and file of striking miners but vehemently opposed to the cavalier nature with which Scargill led them. In short, Kinnock's early years as leader were so consumed by such issues that he had little time to focus on the modernisation of his party. But soon he would discover an ally who would help deliver his vision with a gusto and radicalism that he might never have dreamt of.

In the summer of 1985 the Conservative MP for Brecon and Radnor in South Wales died, leaving a 9,000 Tory majority. With Thatcher's poll ratings suffering a mid-term lull, Labour's hierarchy saw Brecon as a very winnable seat and sent several campaign officers to get behind their candidate, Richard Willey. But the campaign was characteristically disjointed and confused, with the various party workers failing to deliver a coherent message or organised strategy. Then one day Peter Mandelson, a young producer from London Weekend Television, arrived in Brecon and offered his services to Willey for free. He had known the candidate's father, Fred Willey, a former chairman of the parliamentary Labour Party, and was keen to help. In fact, he had taken a fortnight's sabbatical from his television job to do so. For the next fortnight he became Willey's 'minder' – liaising with the press, accompanying him on the campaign trail and organising his schedule. Neil Kinnock's chief of staff, Charles Clarke, kept a close eye on the campaign and quickly noticed that Mandelson had successfully lent it some much-needed vigour and professionalism. He reported as much back to the party leader. Labour lost the election but slashed the Tory majority by almost half. Peter Mandelson had successfully put himself on Kinnock's radar. 'He sort of came to people's notice at that stage,' says Kinnock. 'We realised at Brecon how he was able to make a big impact without any formal position. That was when we began to think he might do something good for the party as a whole.'

The party leader, in conjunction with the new general secretary, Larry Whitty, had begun to chip away at Labour's complex and convoluted organisation. The number of departments at Walworth Road had been cut from twelve to four. Nick Grant, the head of press relations during the 1983 debacle, had left and a new role had been created: the director of campaigns and communications. This, Whitty and Kinnock hoped, would be filled by an overarching media supremo who would be able to co-ordinate every element of the party's image, from press to broadcasting and advertising. Mandelson applied for the job but was a rank outsider. The influential members of the national executive committee were largely from union backgrounds and were sceptical about the credentials of a slick young media professional from London. But Mandelson was the preferred candidate of both Kinnock and Whitty. He had worked hard to build a coalition of support among senior MPs, including deputy leader Roy Hattersley and left-winger John Prescott, and had lobbied contacts at his former employers, the TUC. He had even rallied Bob Worcester, whom he knew vaguely from booking him as a guest for LWT. Mandelson was on track for a successful and lucrative career in the media, but he was intent on a seemingly less glamorous life in politics. Soon, he had one.

Mandelson was elected by the NEC under Kinnock's recommendation by a slim margin. 'People were sceptical because he was the only candidate from a TV background,' says Kinnock. 'Most people thought contacts in the press were more important. But I thought we needed someone with a fresh perspective. Mind you, I don't think we would have ever got him through the vote had a couple of union members not nipped out for a fag when the votes were cast.'

From the moment he was appointed, Mandelson knew that he would have a mandate for change and renewal. But with a limited budget, little traction among the party hierarchy and scant working knowledge of how to manage the sprawling communications operation of a national party, he was overwhelmed by the magnitude of the job.

'To begin with it was incredibly hard,' Mandelson tells me when I meet him at his office in central London. 'People say I revolutionised communications in the Labour Party, which is very kind but not true. It was Harold Wilson who started to modernise things with David Kingsley and the Three Wise Men. But since then things had slipped under Callaghan and Foot. I simply revived what had already been done twenty years beforehand.'

Mandelson was steeped in Labour Party history: his grandfather on his mother's side was Herbert Morrison, a former Labour cabinet minister. But he was far from the cloth-cap Labour archetype: he had grown up in leafy Hampstead Garden Suburb, the son of an advertising manager at the *Jewish Chronicle*, and had been active in Labour politics while a student at Oxford. Like many young activists of his generation, he was disillusioned with the direction Labour's politics had taken, but unlike the many who gave up completely, he believed there was a new way of interpreting Labour values for a changing society with a broader middle class. 'From the start I thought there was an activist base whose votes were already in the bag,' he says. 'We didn't need to convert them to anything. It was the new breed of middle-class aspirational voters that we needed to convince that Labour could be their party.'

Introducing the modern techniques that might help them do so wasn't going to be easy, with much of the Labour Party hierarchy implicitly opposed to Mandelson and his ideas for modernisation. 'They didn't know a lot about me when I arrived at Walworth Road but they knew enough to know they didn't want me,' says Mandelson. 'Pushing through the changes I wanted to make was like pushing a very large boulder up a hill. Every time I released any of the pressure it threatened to roll back and take me with it. There was jealousy from my colleagues. There was mistrust too. They thought I was the man to dress their party up like a box of cornflakes and sell it to the masses. They were all asking, "Why doesn't he consult more?" and "Who the hell does he think is?"'

I ask him if he came close to quitting the job in the early days. 'I didn't come close to quitting, I came close to a breakdown,' he tells me. Mandelson was splitting his time between his official base at Walworth Road and Kinnock's offices in Westminster. He would arrive at work every morning at seven and get home late most nights. Weekends were spent at his cottage in Wales, where he would scour the papers for the latest brutal attack on Kinnock and the party. The influential journalists he spent his time trying to lobby were just as hostile as his Walworth Road colleagues. There was no respite for the young spin doctor. One Sunday in 1986 he was driving back to London in pouring rain when the pressures of his role became too much and he burst out in tears and had to pull over to the side of the road. The next day he saw a GP, who prescribed sleeping pills and rest. He was burning out before he'd even begun, but he refused to give up on the mission he had been set. 'I had no choice,' he says. 'I could have just left things the way they were, but that is not what Neil had asked for and not what the party needed. So I ploughed on for two reasons: arrogance and desperation. Arrogance in the sense that I didn't realise the limitations of my own role and power. I was too big for my boots from the word go. And desperation because I'd been given a job about which I knew nothing, for which I had no training or preparation at all. And so I was ready to embrace anything or anyone who came to me with an idea.'

Marcia Williams was one of the first to call. The former private and political secretary to Harold Wilson, she was Labour Party royalty. Mandelson had known her vaguely since he was a child and she recognised that he could be the man to revive Wilson's ideas on communications and advertising. 'She introduced me to Peter Lovell-Davis, who was one of Wilson's Three Wise Men,' says Mandelson. 'I was invited to his house in Highgate, where he had this huge archive of marketing memorabilia from the sixties and seventies. One poster in particular stood out. It said: "Labour's got heart and soul". I loved that. I scooped up a pile of this stuff in my arms and took it home. And it became the basis of the changes I eventually made to the party image.'

The next figure to come to Mandelson's aid was former adman turned political consultant Philip Gould. Gould shared a background and a set of values similar to Mandelson's: he was from Woking, in Surrey, an aspirational Labour man who was frustrated by the old-fashioned dogma that he felt hindered the party. A politics graduate, he had worked as a planner in ad agencies, a role that encompassed researching and analysing consumer attitudes. His analysis of voters in Britain showed shifting social patterns that Labour had failed to keep pace with. Like Mandelson, he knew that the large industrial working class was shrinking and that the party had to find a way to appeal to a wider group. When Gould heard that Mandelson had been appointed as Labour's new communications boss, he initiated a meeting. The pair shared a friend in Robin Paxton, an LWT producer and former colleague of Mandelson's. Paxton invited them both to a party at his house. Mandelson first realised that it wasn't going to be an informal chat over a glass of wine when, a few days in advance of the party, he received an eleven-page letter from Gould outlining how he might help overhaul Labour's presentational policies. 'I decided to pay him £600 to do an initial stocktake of all Labour's communications,' Mandelson says. 'It was a large chunk of my budget but it turned out to be worth it.'

Gould's subsequent report was damning: he found a multitude of different outlets producing communication materials for the party, with no central co-ordination whatsoever. Kinnock's office would commission one set of admen to produce a campaign, while officials at Walworth Road commissioned a conflicting set of ads from a separate company. 'The interviews I did in the autumn of 1985 revealed an astonishing morass of communications networks within the party,' Gould wrote in his memoir *The Unfinished Revolution*. 'Committee upon group upon committee, leading to a chaos of indecisiveness, one-upmanship, hedging and ultimate stagnation.'

He did not leave it at communications. Gould conducted qualitative research using the same focus-group techniques he had employed for brands in his advertising days. His conversations with young voters revealed a growing sympathy with Thatcherite values: the Falklands War was a source of great pride and reflected national strength; enterprise, achievement and individualism were the prevailing themes, and most groups perceived unemployment as the fault of individuals, not the government. Gould's research revealed that many of those who held these beliefs were traditional working class. The document noted that 'Everyone wants to be middle class these days.' The Conservatives were perceived as the party who could help people achieve that dream.

As Gould put it in his memoir: 'This was the situation I found in 1985 – far worse than I could possibly have anticipated, far worse than many even now appreciate: a political party separated from its natural supporters by a chasm of fear, mistrust, even anger; a campaigns and communications operation too pitiful even to begin the task of building a bridge across it; and a party not really understanding that it had to try.'

But Mandelson did understand the need for change – and with Kinnock's support he set about trying to make it happen. 'Philip's report was extremely damning, so I had to smooth out the edges,' he tells me. 'Senior figures on the NEC were very hostile to anything I had to say. They saw me as a fake socialist who was trying to sell their party like breakfast cereal. Trade union leaders were throwing insults my way, and even [deputy leader] Roy Hattersley started to criticise me. Which was ironic because I had supported him rather than Neil in the leadership election in 1983.'

Mandelson soon found that Gould was an asset in appeasing the sceptics on the NEC. 'He presented himself as an outside expert, so they found it easier to accept him,' says Mandelson. 'He had a way of making his research sound very academic and convincing, and people would go along with what he said. He generally had more patience than me when it came to talking ideas through. But he wasn't an employee of the party and so he wasn't under the same pressure as me.'

Armed with Gould's dossier, Mandelson met with Kinnock and outlined a plan to put himself at the centre of all the party's communication decisions. This, he argued, would secure a consistent message. He would also establish a tightly knit group of outside experts and well-regarded professionals who would offer their creative services for free. The group, which would be anonymous, became known as the Shadow Communications Agency and was run from the offices of Boase Massimi Pollitt. The idea for the SCA was conceived by BMP's Chris Powell, who based the model upon the Tuesday Team, a group of American ad professionals from various agencies who met weekly to strategise campaign communications for the Republican Party. In 1983 he wasn't ready to have his name associated with a deeply unpopular Labour Party. Now he was ready to help slightly more publicly. 'The big difference from my point of view was that Peter actually believed in advertising and was interested in it,' says Powell. 'Back in those days he listened and absorbed everything we had to say. And he had real power to sign things off. Neil had given him that power and it was revolutionary. Suddenly, we didn't have to sell our ideas to a hundred different committees filled with people who instinctively regarded ad people as the enemy. Now we only had Peter to answer to, and he backed us all the way.'

Back at Walworth Road, Mandelson sat on a wobbly chair in front of a three-legged desk propped up against a filing cabinet, beside a decaying spider plant and a World War II-era telephone. It neatly symbolised the decrepit nature of the Labour Party machine. But rather than attempt the convoluted and futile process of modernising the party from the inside, Mandelson, Kinnock and Gould decided to use outsiders to help them. 'The aim was not to bypass the party machine at Walworth Road,' Mandelson says. 'It was to re-professionalise the party by means of an infusion of people from outside.' By the summer of 1986 Gould was working as the co-ordinator of the SCA, and Mandelson had assembled a group of award-winning admen from some of London's top agencies. He was spending less time at his rickety desk in Walworth Road and more at the lavishly appointed headquarters of BMP in Paddington. Alongside Powell and his colleagues sat executives from Abbott Mead Vickers and TBWA. Bob Worcester was another founding member, as was Colin Fisher from leading market-research firm SRU.

Kinnock could see that his new young communications chief was making rapid progress. 'In 1983 nobody would touch us in the ad world,' he tells me. 'But now the big talents were offering their services as long as we kept it secret. I understood their point of view, I suppose: we were unpopular with their corporate clients, and their links with Labour might cost them their jobs – or at least their second BMW.'

Powell disagrees, insisting that it was an open secret that he was advising the Labour Party by 1985. 'I only ever heard of it compromising the agency once, when someone claimed that Tesco crossed us off a list of potential agencies because we were a bunch of lefties,' he says. 'But mostly clients found it a strange curiosity that we worked with politicians. It was as if we were working with rare wild animals – they always wanted us to tell them stories about them. In that sense it was an advantage rather than a hindrance.'

With the team in place, Mandelson prepared for his first major statement as communications chief: the 1986 party conference. 'I'd resolved to make it substantially different from anything that had gone before,' he says. Kinnock was conscious of the need to accelerate the process of modernisation. 'We had wasted two years on fighting the militants and dealing with the miners' strike,' the former leader tells me. 'Now we had a year to convince people that we had changed and were a modern, forward-looking party.'

Kinnock suggested using a red rose to replace the 'ugly and offensive' logo that depicted the party name in a dated typeface. He showed Mandelson the rose he had used in his personal campaign materials in 1983 and asked him to commission something similar. The pair contemplated numerous roses over a period of months before they came to a final decision. 'Eventually, I took a picture from my father-in-law's gardening catalogue,' says Kinnock. 'Peter used it as a reference for the designers. To this day, I still insist that the stem was too long, but he thought otherwise.'

Kinnock was aware that a change to the party logo would send tremors through the various committees at Walworth Road and he encouraged Mandelson to slip it through a subcommittee meeting prior to the conference, presenting it as a piece of campaigning material as opposed to a new universal symbol for the party.

'We put it in front of a subcommittee at Walworth Road and tried to be casual about it,' says Mandelson. 'The chair of the committee, Gwyneth Dunwoody, must have known what we were up to but she just sort of bounced it through the meeting and we had it signed off.' Three weeks later, thousands of Labour Party delegates would arrive at the party conference in Blackpool to find the new rose emblazoned upon a pistachio-green backdrop behind the main stage, accompanied not by 'Labour Party' but by the single word 'Labour'. It was at this moment that the seeds of New Labour were sewn, introduced via the back door by Kinnock and Mandelson. 'The truth is that Neil knew the NEC would have rejected the plans, but we simply had to find a way to get them through,' says Mandelson.

Delegates at the conference were handed salmon-pink folders containing policy and publicity documents, under the title 'Putting People First'. This too represented a radical departure from traditional party presentations, and even Kinnock found this one difficult to swallow. 'A week before the conference he called me into his office, and he looked ashen-faced,' Mandelson recalls. 'He asked me why his preferred title – "Freedom and Fairness" – had been replaced with "Putting People First". I told him it had tested badly in focus groups. Then he told me that we'd never convince the delegates from the National Union of Mineworkers to walk around conference holding pink folders. So I lied and told him they had gone to the printers and it was too late to change.'

At every turn Mandelson was finding ways to circumvent stifling party procedures and force through his new vision for Labour's image. He was unable to change the behaviour of all the party activists but he could attempt to manipulate the way in which they were presented. A tradition remained for singing the socialist anthem 'The Red Flag' at the conclusion of each conference. This, thought Mandelson, was a throwback to a bygone era that gave the average voter an unhelpful impression of radicalism. He was unable to stop the singing, so he choreographed the speeches to make sure that the concluding hymn would be sung after the TV cameras had stopped rolling. Within less than a year the man who would later be labelled as the Dark Lord of spin was mastering his art.

It seemed to be paying off. Delegates of all creeds took enthusiastically to the new campaign materials, embracing the pink folder and new logo. Some were even asking party workers for spare folders to take home to their families. Mandelson was vindicated. 'People responded to it because it was attractive, it was new, it was professional and smart. And for the first time in a long time people thought, "God, this is our party!"' he says.

When Margaret Thatcher called a general election on 11 May 1987, Labour remained roughly where they had been in 1983. The economy had stabilised under the Conservatives, while Labour remained besieged by infighting, with the tabloid press falling over themselves to report Militant's extravagances in councils around the country. The Greater London Council's 137 Rule decreed that council funding be made available to every special interest group, from Brent Friends of the Earth to the Rastafarian Society. Such stories were open goals for a largely right-wing press gunning for Labour.

The previous January Labour had lost a by-election in Greenwich to the SDP–Liberal Alliance. 'There was a very real sense that we were fighting to remain the official party of opposition in 1987,' says Charles Clarke, Neil Kinnock's chief of staff at the time. 'Nobody really saw it as a battle to win outright – we just had to stay in second place.' But Mandelson was on the front foot from the moment the campaign began. 'It was life or death for the party,' he says. 'If we messed up again like we'd done in 1983, we knew we could be facing extinction.'

While the public had watched Labour sinking ever deeper into internal strife in the early months of 1987, a secret team led by Mandelson had been working tirelessly behind the scenes to ensure that a polished and united campaign was ready for spring. When the election was finally called, voters, the press and the Tories would be astonished by the slickness of Labour's presentation.

In 1986 Neil Kinnock had appointed the MP for Dagenham, Bryan Gould, as campaign co-ordinator, and he had launched himself into the role with zeal and determination. 'I was driven by the debacle of 1983,' Gould tells me over Skype from New Zealand, to which he returned after retiring from politics in the mid-nineties. 'It was disorganised and pathetic and I knew we could do better. So months beforehand I had drawn up Labour's first-ever campaign grid. It mapped in detail the whereabouts of fifty key figures every day throughout the campaign. We knew what they'd be saying and when they were saying it. We made sure that our key people would be appearing in the right settings on the right days and sticking to our preferred agenda.'

Crucially, his attitude towards image and advertising was thoroughly pragmatic. 'It had become clear since 1979 that advertising was very important and that for some reason we had let the Conservatives take the lead,' he says. 'I'm not one to say that great ads can win an election, but I was interested and open to anything that could make even the smallest difference. Mandelson struck me as extremely clever, and so did Chris Powell. I embraced everything they brought to me. We simply had to try everything we could.'

Powell and his SCA colleagues had devised the line 'The Country Is Crying Out for a Change. Vote Labour'. Philip Gould's latest research had shown that huge swathes of the population were hostile to Mrs Thatcher's government – but too scared of Labour's radical tendencies to vote for them. He wrote in a memo to Mandelson just prior to the campaign: 'If we lose this election it will not be because [the Conservatives] have done well but because of the failure of the opposition parties to provide a convincing alternative. The election, in effect, will be lost by default.' With unpopular policies such as nuclear disarmament and the renationalisation of industries still plaguing the party's manifesto, it was decided that they would campaign on an emotional basis: stressing their humanity, their love of the NHS and their passion for social issues.

To execute the message Chris Powell had assembled some of the top creatives in London. Boase Massimi Pollitt was arguably the most highly regarded agency of them all: it had been winning awards and admirers since it launched in the seventies, thanks to a knack for applying modern creativity to mass-market brands. At the time, there were so-called 'cool' agencies such as Collett Dickenson Pearce and Bartle Bogle Hegarty who made stylish, funny and ambitious adverts for niche brands in fashion, tobacco or alcohol. Then there were behemoths such as J. Walter Thompson and Ogilvy and Mather who used rather more broad hard-sell techniques to advertise major consumer products for clients such as Unilever and Kellogg's. BMP had established itself as the agency that could do both: mesmerising ordinary consumers, from housewives to schoolkids, with charming, witty ads that not only helped sell products but also won the applause of its industry peers. John Webster was the agency's legendary creative guru, a man responsible for creating the celebrated Smash Martians, the Honey Monster and George the Hofmeister bear. He had creative flair and a common touch – a combination that seemed perfectly suited to political advertising.

After the confused and clunky party branding of 1983, the 1987 ads were a revelation. The design was neat and sophisticated. The words delivered the emotional punch Labour needed but with none of the fiery radicalism of the past. One stand-out press ad read: 'The Conservative manifesto doesn't say anything about reducing unemployment. It doesn't say anything about improving the health service. It doesn't say anything about investing in education. It doesn't say anything about building more houses. It says a lot about the Conservatives.' The slogan was: 'The country is crying out for change. Vote Labour.' It was sober, it was charming and it was convincing. Eyebrows were raised in the press. *The Economist* noted of the Mandelson era that Labour was 'determined never again to seem dowdy or old-fashioned'.

Powell was amazed by the freedom his team were allowed by Mandelson and Kinnock. 'They were committed to letting us be the experts,' he says. 'Almost anything we put forward they agreed with.' But for all the intelligence and sophistication the SCA brought to the campaign, they trailed the Tories in one crucial respect. 'People used to say that if you wanted to sell food or drink to housewives, you came to BMP,' says Powell. 'But if you wanted to destroy your competitor, you went to Saatchis.' There was a grace to Labour's advertising that, while pleasing on the eye, lacked the same streak of brutality that ran through the Tory ads. 'It was maybe easier for them to be a bit more extreme with their tone because they weren't fighting against this dangerous, radical reputation,' says Powell. 'We had to show we were dependable and professional. If we were too aggressive, it would confirm people's suspicions about us.'

Not that they were completely devoid of Saatchiesque trickery. A controversial poster drew upon a remark made by Norman Tebbit in 1983. It read: 'If unemployment is not below three million in five years, then I'm not worth re-electing.' Beneath it was a cheeky pay-off: 'No wonder they've called the election a year early.' It was straight from the Saatchi school of mischief: bending facts, courting controversy, attempting to antagonise the opposition into a response. It worked. Mandelson eventually assembled a press conference where he played a distorted recording of Tebbit's original speech through a cranky tape recorder. Philip Gould later wrote: 'Tebbit's words bore little relationship to the words on the advertisement but it didn't matter. We had the tape, Tebbit was speaking, Peter was icily confident, the journalists were seduced.'

The campaign team thought they had one other trump card up their sleeves. Gould had noted in his pre-election memo to Mandelson that 'Presenting Labour in a positive light will be difficult. Presenting Neil Kinnock in a positive light, much less so.'

For that reason Kinnock was front and centre of the campaign, delivering a performance which Mandelson describes as 'barnstorming'. 'He was simply on fire,' he says. 'Everywhere he went he spoke with passion and fire. He would always stray off script and whip the crowds up into a frenzy. Thatcher was perceived as cold and heartless. Neil was demonstrating that he was the opposite.' At a Welsh Labour conference in Llandudno in May, Kinnock delivered his breakthrough moment: an off-the-cuff broadside against social injustice. 'Why am I the first Kinnock in a thousand generations to be able to get to university?' he asked. 'Why is Glenys [his wife] the first woman in her family to be able to get to university in a thousand generations? Was it because our predecessors were thick? Did they lack talent, those people who could sing and play and recite and write poetry? Those people who could make wonderful, beautiful things with their hands? Those people who could dream dreams and see visions? Was it because they were weak – those people who could work eight hours underground and then come up and play football? Does anybody really think that they didn't get what we had because they didn't have the talent or the strength or the endurance or the commitment? Of course not! It was because there was no platform on which they could stand! There were not the conditions that allowed people that were free under British law truly to live that freedom!' It was a rousing and spectacular articulation of socialism's most appealing principles and his own personal passions. Kinnock knew he had hit his stride in readiness for a bloody election battle. 'As I finished that speech I remember seeing officers of special branch with tears running down their cheeks,' he says. 'That's an undying image of mine.'

The policies and party might still have had a bad name but, it seemed, Kinnock was something the admen could sell.

Hugh Hudson had been filming Kinnock on that night in Llandudno. He was part of a generation of successful British ad directors who had graduated to making Hollywood movies in the eighties. His work in advertising was regarded as groundbreaking: he had a sophisticated visual style which elevated even the most banal ideas to artful mini-epics. His mentor had been the legendary American graphic designer Robert Brownjohn, from whom he inherited an ambitious visual approach. He was able to paint stirring pictures for brands such as Benson and Hedges and Fiat. Later, in Hollywood, he had won plaudits for films such as *Revolution*, starring Al Pacino, and had picked up an Oscar for directing *Chariots of Fire*. No one of such pedigree had ever been used to make an election broadcast before. By collaborating with Hudson, Mandelson showed just how elevated his ambitions for Labour had become. 'He wrote to the party offering his services to us,' says Mandelson. 'In another era I'm sure the letter would have been lost. But Philip [Gould] and myself, plus Patricia Hewitt [Kinnock's press secretary], went to meet him and told him the brief: to make Neil look like a leader. We wanted to tell the whole story, to show the dimensions of Neil's character that the press were not giving to the public.'

Hudson's ten-minute film centred upon a heartfelt interview with Kinnock in his home (with the questions fired from off-camera by a young Alastair Campbell). This was cut together with passionate excerpts from his speech in Llandudno and testimonies from relatives and party grandees such as Barbara Castle, Denis Healey and James Callaghan. The execution was sublime. Kinnock delivered a naturalistic and sincere interview unthinkable of today's politicians – reflections on his marriage to Glenys; the description of his childhood in Wales – all strung together by Hudson's artful cinematography, sweeping images of Neil and Glenys walking arm in arm along windswept clifftops and a rousing soundtrack. It painted a rounded and impressive picture of a serious man of warmth and values. It was the perfect reply to his characterisation in the press as an indecisive and inexperienced windbag.

'It was a blockbuster,' says Mandelson. 'I mean, I remember when we first saw the rough edit, I'm pretty sure there were tears running out of my eyes. For a good time we were speechless, and Hugh turned and said, "Do you not like it?" He took our silence for disapproval. And I said, "Hugh, on the contrary. It is absolutely brilliant. And it's going to take the country by storm."'

And it did: Kinnock's personal poll rating jumped overnight by 16 per cent. According to Philip Gould in his memoir: 'Some people say that the broadcast was irrelevant, that Labour still lost. They are wrong. Almost overnight Labour had shunted the Alliance to the sidelines. By the end of the second week the polls had begun to shift. Labour was on the move.'

But the broadcast didn't pass without controversy. Mandelson and Hudson's boldest decision had been to conclude the film with the end title 'Kinnock', as opposed to 'Labour'. Inside and outside the party critics saw it as overpersonalised and presidential in style. Mandelson remains unrepentant. 'If you had a Labour Party in 1987 which was as unpopular and unattractive as it was, you would go for your strongest selling point, and that was Kinnock at the time,' he says. 'We were relying on our loyal supporters. But to pick up floating voters the best option was to present a very young and dynamic leader who had taken on the Militant Tendency and wrestled them to the ground.'

Mandelson says that this was part of a continued theme in political campaigning. 'One of the trends of post-war politics is that in the hierarchy of party, politics and leader, leader emerged as the number-one determinant of people's voting intentions. As people's affiliation to parties has faded, what's become more important to them is, "Of all the leadership candidates, who will be best at leading the country?" So people in charge of campaigns need to be thinking in terms of presentation of the leader.'

The film received such a positive response from the public that BMP's Chris Powell came up with the idea of running it a second time. 'We ran ads over and over again, so I thought, "Why not do the same with election broadcasts?"' he says. 'But what I didn't account for was that the PR potential was non-existent the second time round. All the papers had already written about it by then. People often don't realise that the main point of these broadcasts is the PR they generate around them. We all played the game for years. We'd produce a big poster on one single site, invite the press to come and snap it, then take it down again hours later once they'd gone off to write about it. Until one day when we cheekily took down another client's poster for a short while in order to stick up a Labour one. But some of the press turned up late, by which point the original poster was back up again and the whole ruse was exposed.'

The media were becoming increasingly aware of these shadowy admen and their influence over Labour's campaign. The Kinnock movie was seen as the ultimate evidence of the party's new love affair with such men. In their election special, satirical puppet show *Spitting Image* delivered a cutting spoof of the by now infamous broadcast. It opened with: 'And now, by popular demand, yet another chance to see an election broadcast by the ahem . . . ahem . . . party.' Later, it showed latex incarnations of the Kinnocks standing outside Number 10, while a Hollywood-style voice-over said: 'A man with an impossible dream; a man with a rather fruity wife; a man with a new advertising agency.' On cue, two stereotypical adman caricatures in sharp suits and trendy haircuts appeared, gathering bouquets of flowers and awards. It was a savage parody of the adman as a self-serving snake-oil salesman, exploiting a desperate party to further his own reputation. The spoof ended with the line: 'That was an election broadcast on behalf of a new Porsche for the account director.'

But however hard the admen spun, they couldn't legislate for Kinnock's own flaws. At the start of the third week, during a television interview he accidentally implied to David Frost that Labour's response to a Soviet invasion would be civilian resistance. 'He wants *Dad's Army* back,' quipped the SDP leader David Owen. The Tories had a field day. Labour's unilateral disarmament policy was back at the top of the agenda and Kinnock was very much on the back foot.

A week before the election, Mandelson decided to bring Kinnock into BMP's Paddington offices to meet with Powell and the rest of the SCA. 'I think he thought it would be a morale booster for us as the polls were flagging and we were exhausted,' says Powell. 'We prepared a meal in the office. But Neil arrived with Glenys and she took one look at the food and insisted that they already had arrangements to eat elsewhere.' It was about to get worse. As Powell and his team started to present strategies for a final push in the last seven days, Kinnock put his head in his hands. 'He was saying, "None of this is of any use! It's me! They're never going to elect someone like me!"' recalls Mandelson. 'I looked at Chris and sort of blanched. There was an awkward silence, and Neil just kept saying, "It's me! I'm unsellable!" Myself and Patricia Hewitt just raced in to try and change the subject. Even at his barnstorming best in '87, Neil was always very fragile.'

I asked Kinnock if he had enjoyed the 1987 campaign. 'I wouldn't say I enjoyed it, no,' he said. But you had been on great form, I reasoned. 'Only in the same way that the British expeditionary forces were on form at Dunkirk,' he insisted.

The British public went to the polls on 11 June and confirmed that, however hard they spun, however professionally they campaigned and however slick their communications, the Labour Party remained unelectable. The Conservatives retained a three-figure advantage in terms of parliamentary seats and remained ten points ahead of Labour in the popular vote. The only positive to emerge was that the threat of the SDP–Liberal Alliance had been seen off: Labour secured 31 per cent of the vote to the Alliance's 22 per cent.

'I don't think victory was ever realistic,' says Chris Powell. 'When you have a leader who was perceived in the way Neil was, and a set of policies as outdated as we had, it doesn't matter how good your communications are. We won every sort of professional poll on who had run the best campaign. And yet we ended up with only a few more seats than in 1983. It was a revelation in a way. It demonstrated that policies and leadership trump advertising and communications every time.'

As *Private Eye* put it, Labour had achieved 'a brilliantly successful election defeat'. It had been run with efficiency, gloss and professionalism. Kinnock's vision and bravery had allowed Mandelson to act with a boldness that had transformed the party's image beyond all recognition in a short space of time. The day after the election, Larry Whitty, Labour's general secretary, left a note on Mandelson's desk that read: 'Can I record that I believe your efforts, political judgment and imagination have made this the most effective campaign the Labour Party has ever waged. Well done – and thanks.' Around the same time, the *Observer* journalist Robert Harris wrote a piece in glowing praise of Mandelson's communications revolution and, for the first time, dubbed him 'the Machiavelli of Walworth Road'.

A tone had been set for the future. Mandelson was the coming man: together with Philip Gould, he had established a new vision for Labour that he had shown himself capable of delivering. With the party at a low ebb after a third successive defeat, it was more open than ever to fresh ideas that just might offer a brighter future. Mandelson and Gould had been the only winners in 1987, and their influence was about to grow over subsequent years. In the view of many, it would soon spiral out of control.

'I think that without the brilliant campaign and advertising we ran in 1987, things would have been a great deal worse,' says Bryan Gould. 'We had seen off the threat of the Alliance and cemented Neil's position as leader to continue fighting for policy change. But something changed within the shadow cabinet. They were more enamoured than ever by Philip Gould's polling and more willing to give in to public opinion. Previously, I had thought the role of the politician was to devise a policy that you thought was right and then consider it an obligation to try and explain it and win support for it from the public. But after '87, the spin doctors were the stars, and if they said the public didn't like a policy, we dropped it.'

Labour's transformation in a few short years had been startling, but it came at a price. Bryan Gould could see that the pursuit of victory by any means was in danger of usurping the values that once underpinned the party. I asked him if he thought that being driven entirely by polls reduced an MP's role to regurgitating public opinion back to the public. He paused. 'Well, Sam, you might well ask me why I'm sat here at my desk in the eastern Bay of Plenty in New Zealand and not back in Westminster.'

7

THAT BLOODY WOMAN

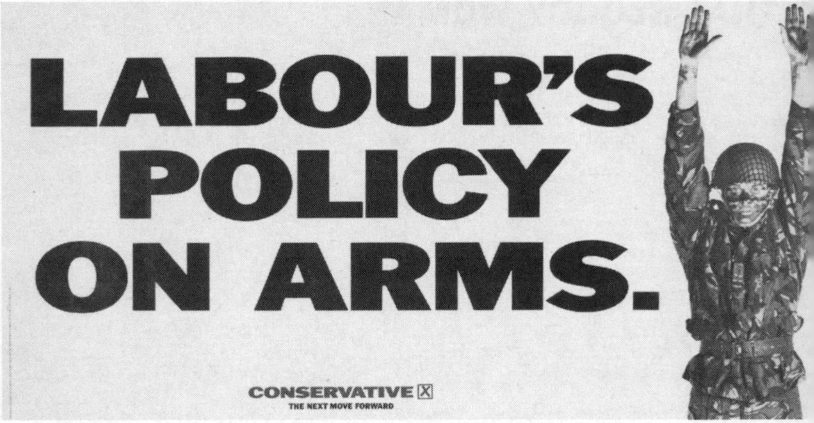
LABOUR'S
POLICY
ON ARMS.
CONSERVATIVE
THE NEXT MOVE FORWARD

On 4 June 1987 Margaret Thatcher visited the Alton Towers theme park in Staffordshire, suffering from intense toothache. Refusing the offer of painkillers, which she thought might slow her down, she cut a grim figure amidst the frolicking children and white-knuckle rides. It was one week before polling day; if she won, she would make history as the first prime minister of the twentieth century to win three successive general elections. But the signs were not good. 'By that stage, she was worried, worked up and worn out,' says David Young, her closest cabinet advisor during the campaign. The tooth wasn't helping, nor was the incongruous fairground setting, but her chief concern as she stood in front of the press that day was an opinion poll that had just been leaked. Over the past three weeks her lead had been chipped away by Labour's vibrant campaign. Now the latest figures had them at neck and neck, with Neil Kinnock's party clearly in the ascendancy.

Thatcher was unimpressed by the Conservative campaign, sceptical about the abilities of those who had shaped it and paranoid about the motivations of the political colleagues who surrounded her. 'She was an ageing prime minister in a hurry,' says Michael Dobbs, her advisor, who was now Saatchi & Saatchi's man at Tory central office. 'She had stopped listening and started to mistrust those around her. She had become very isolated.'

As she attempted a smile for the assembled media, trying to disguise the pain that throbbed inside her mouth, she overheard a cameraman remark: 'That's it: she's downhill all the way now.' He was very nearly right.

'It was not a happy campaign but it was a successful one and that is all that counts,' Thatcher wrote in her memoirs of the weeks leading up to the 1987 general election. She would go on to win, but the consensus among those involved is that victory was achieved in spite of the campaign, not because of it. 'Labour could definitely have won it but they would have needed a much better proposition than Neil Kinnock,' reflects Norman Tebbit. As party chairman, he was responsible for co-ordinating a campaign which even he describes in retrospect as 'a mess'.

Tebbit had already told me about the battles that had surrounded the 1987 election campaign. The most infamous flashpoint had taken place in Downing Street on so-called 'Wobbly Thursday', seven days before the country went to the polls. It was then that Tebbit had very nearly come to blows with David Young. 'David has spoken about how he grabbed me by the lapels and shouted in my face about how we were going to lose that election,' Tebbit told me. 'But he was insufficiently honest to tell the truth about how I had been right all along about the polls.'

A week after visiting Tebbit, I went to see Lord Young at his offices in central London. Young was never a Member of Parliament but he was an active Conservative, valued highly as an advisor on business and employment. Thatcher had made him an honorary peer in 1984 in order to appoint him to the cabinet, but it was in fact Tebbit who had given Young his first position of significance in the government, by appointing him as the chairman of the

Manpower Services Commission in 1981. 'Norman had given me a first chance and we had got on very well, but the events of 1987 put us in two very separate camps,' he says. Whereas Tebbit is abrasive and a bit intimidating, Young is smooth and understated. He told me almost immediately that 1987 had been the darkest time of his political career and was quick to open up about his own mistakes during the campaign. As a chief political lieutenant, it was easy to see why Thatcher came to favour Young over Tebbit.

Since she appointed him party chairman in 1985, Norman Tebbit had reorganised Conservative central office, putting several noses out of joint in the process. He had forced out long-serving party administrators and had started to impose his own methods of campaigning. But in 1986 heavy defeats in by-elections and council elections had reflected badly on him, and Thatcher was growing concerned that she had appointed the wrong man to this crucial role. 'Norman was a great communicator but a terrible organiser,' says Young, then Minister Without Portfolio. A successful businessman, he had pleased Thatcher with the work he had done at the Departments of Employment and Trade and Industry, and she had come to see him as her most competent and trustworthy minister – a position previously occupied by Tebbit. 'She asked me to go into central office and help get things organised properly,' he says. 'This obviously didn't go down very well with Norman.' Rumours around Westminster suggested that Tebbit was ready to turn against Thatcher publicly – and perhaps even challenge her leadership of the party. 'I don't think Norman was manoeuvring for her job but when leaders have been in power that long they tend to get paranoid,' says Young. 'At that stage, she saw everyone as a potential threat. But I was an honorary peer and therefore couldn't be party leader. In that sense I was a political eunuch and no threat to her whatsoever. That's why she knew she could trust me.'

But Thatcher remained unhappy. For her Saatchis just wasn't Saatchis without Tim Bell's involvement. Michael Dobbs was now the key conduit between central office and the agency. Dobbs was not particularly popular with the prime minister at the time: they had shared a frosty relationship even when he had worked for her in the late seventies. 'When she was first elected prime minister she couldn't find a suitable job for Michael, so she asked me to offer him something at Saatchis,' recounts Bell. 'I did it as a favour to her, but he soon rose through the ranks.'

Bell had been retained by Saatchis as a consultant on the Conservative account in return for a £24,000 fee. But when plans for the general election began in earnest, the agency refused to involve him. The relationship between Bell and the brothers was so bad that they weren't speaking. The Saatchis were paranoid that their former chairman might attempt to poach the account for the new agency he had formed with former Collett Dickenson Pearce boss Frank Lowe. But to exclude him from their campaign was a gamble: his absence was bound to disappoint the prime minister. 'We knew from the very outset that we didn't have a ready-made replacement for Tim Bell,' says one senior Saatchis executive of the time. 'Maurice [Saatchi] wasn't it. I'm not sure if he knew Margaret Thatcher very well or in fact if they even liked each other that much either. Charles [Saatchi] had no interest in politics, only the agency. I myself had political instincts that were considerably to the left of the Conservative Party at the time. I actually told

Norman Tebbit this and he didn't care – he just wanted me to do my job, and that's the way I saw it too.'

But from the moment he learnt that the Saatchis were excluding him, Bell knew that two teams would end up fighting the election campaign for the Conservatives. The official team would be Saatchi & Saatchi, in conjunction with Norman Tebbit and central office. The rogue outfit would consist of Bell and his fellow 'exiles' such as Gordon Reece – in secret liaison with Margaret Thatcher and David Young at Downing Street. 'We knew that Tim would find a way of communicating with the prime minister right from the start,' says the senior Saatchi executive. Charlie was very angry about it. Really, it was a sideshow; the public didn't know or care about it. But there were little conflicts that surrounded everything as a result, which, although small in retrospect, didn't make anyone's jobs any easier.'

The Saatchis might have given in to the prime minister and invited Bell back into the fold for the duration of the campaign. Alternatively, Bell could have stepped aside entirely and left the country for the duration so as to avoid damaging feuds. But that wasn't how the big beasts of eighties adland went about their business. Ego, hubris and paranoia defined the atmosphere – no one was willing to give ground. 'At that time, we weren't very friendly to people who left,' admits Jeremy Sinclair, then creative director at Saatchi & Saatchi. 'We were like family. When someone left, our response tended to be: "What the bloody hell do you think you're doing?"'

But Sinclair denies that they were ever concerned about losing the account to Bell. 'In a business sense, we had probably got about as much as we were ever going to get out of the Conservative Party by then,' he says. 'They had made us as famous as they were ever going to. But we had an emotional attachment to it. We thought that Kinnock – and Foot before him – were dangerous people capable of taking the country backwards. When Tim left we didn't think, "Oh my God, we're going to lose the Tory account." It was more like, "Buddy, you're not supposed to do this."'

When the general election was finally announced in May, there was at least a loose consensus among everyone involved in the campaign: to attack a still-fragile Labour Party and remind the British public of the opposition's myriad shortcomings. While an attack on Labour would define the national message, Tebbit was convinced that the real battle would be fought in a handful of local campaigns. 'I had conducted detailed research and calculated that we had to focus most of our energies on a few key seats where we only had a narrow lead,' he says.

But Thatcher obsessed over the tone of the national advertising campaign. She was supported in this by David Young, but some of Young's cabinet colleagues were unsure about his ability to guide the party to election victory. '[Young] was a businessman . . . without ever having stood for office or even being a local party worker,' the chancellor Nigel Lawson later recorded in his memoirs. 'As a result he knew less about election campaigning and had his finger further from the public pulse than any other cabinet colleague. He was, however, a great believer in the power of advertising . . . He seemed to believe that it was the choice of advertising agency which would determine the outcome of the election. Margaret, who was always inclined to believe that if a policy was unpopular it could only be because of poor presentation, had a weakness for this line of thinking.'

She agreed with the areas of focus but was disappointed that Saatchis was preoccupied with attacking Labour rather than celebrating Conservative achievements. Even Bell tried to reason with her on this point: 'I tried to explain the basic rule of political advertising: to encourage thanks for *favours not yet received*,' he says. 'Voters aren't half as likely to vote on the basis of what you've done as what you might do.'

The most iconic poster produced by Saatchis during the campaign attacked Labour's commitment to nuclear disarmament. Labour leader Neil Kinnock had slipped up in a television interview by suggesting that, in the event of a Soviet invasion, he would encourage Brits to retreat to the countryside and wage resistance through guerrilla warfare. It was an open goal for the creatives at Saatchis: their poster featured a British soldier with his arms aloft in surrender, accompanied by the headline 'Labour's policy on arms'. Tebbit, a naturally confrontational politician, found the comedic attacks on Labour very appealing. 'The best one they came up with had a Soviet bomber with a huge hammer and sickle, under the headline "If a Labour government drops Britain's nuclear programme, will they drop theirs?" I thought that was great but we never had to run it because the surrendering-soldier poster was so successful.'

Kinnock: The Movie and Labour's slick campaigning had made inroads into public opinion. The Conservatives had begun the campaign with a healthy ten-point lead in the opinion polls. By week three it was cut down to six. Then came Wobbly Thursday.

'The trouble with an election campaign is that you go

febrile,' says David Young. 'You start to believe everything the opposition says and nothing that your own side says. When the *Daily Mail* poll said that Labour had cut the lead to two points, we thought we were done for.'

Thatcher had called Young immediately after her press engagement at Alton Towers to discuss the damning poll. The pair had arranged to meet at Downing Street that evening for an emergency summit, and she asked Young to make sure Tim Bell was there too.

'David [Young] had to smuggle me in past the bins,' says Bell. 'It was important that none of the press saw me. But Margaret was past caring about upsetting Tebbit or the Saatchis. As far as she was concerned, this was a crisis – they had mucked up the campaign and we were heading for defeat.'

Before she met with Bell and Young, she had called Young at central office, complaining about what she described as 'an unfocused and confused campaign that concentrated too much on Labour and not enough on our own economic record'. The pair, according to Thatcher's memoirs, had 'a ding dong row that cleared the air'. Tebbit recalls it differently: 'She was convinced by this *Daily Mail* poll, that was all she wanted to talk about,' he says. 'But I knew it was a rogue poll. It ran contrary to every other poll that I had commissioned. It was an old trick the Tory press always used a week before election day. It was designed to remind Tory supporters that the result wasn't in the bag and to go out and vote. I assured her that we were heading for a majority of over eighty seats. The truth was I calculated it at more like a hundred but I didn't think she'd believe that, so I told her something more modest. She took my calmness for complacency.'

Thatcher decided that she had been too passive in the campaign. She was frustrated with the tone of the Saatchi advertising and wanted to see ads that were confident and celebratory. She'd had enough of the attacks on Labour. Both Young and Bell agreed to do whatever she asked, although in truth they weren't convinced by her thinking. 'I didn't think the posters would make much difference to people's voting intentions at that stage either way,' says Young. 'But they still played an important role in the campaign because they boosted the morale of party workers and, crucially, Margaret herself. She was exhausted and demoralised. I wanted to do whatever it took to make her more confident and energetic for the final push.' Bell was excited by the prospect of getting his hands dirty. 'David said to me, "She hates this advertising, you've got to do something about it,"' he says. 'So I rushed back to the office and tried to come up with my own campaign.'

Bell's mission was to come up with a campaign-saving idea in less than twenty-four hours, without anyone finding out that he'd been asked to do so. He went back to his offices at Lowe Howard-Spink and Bell in South Kensington and sat down with his partner Frank Lowe behind the closed doors of a conference room. The pair agreed that no one else in the agency could know about the brief and that they would write the ads together that night. The only trouble was that neither of them had ever written an ad before in their lives. Like Bell, Lowe was an account man whose expertise was in schmoozing clients, developing strategy and cajoling creatives into delivering the best work possible. But if either of them had even the slimmest of credentials, it was Lowe: for ten years he had run Collett Dickenson Pearce, an agency renowned the world over for its creativity. While there he had nurtured the careers of Alan Parker, Ridley Scott, Charles Saatchi and a generation of legendary admen. He had overseen some of the most iconic campaigns in advertising history, such as 'Heineken Refreshes the Parts Other Beers Cannot Reach', 'Happiness Is a Cigar Called Hamlet' and Ridley Scott's career-making commercials for Hovis bread. He was a so-called 'suit' who was unusually respected and admired by the creative fraternity. Bell told him that it was down to him to write the ads. 'Frank was a big Labour supporter so he wasn't really sure about the idea,' says Bell. 'But he had a winning mentality like I did and saw it as another battle. We wrote these ads which were all about loads of new doctors, nine million new whatever it was, a whole series of positive achievements. I supplied him with the info and he wrote the ad. Then his art director Alan Waldie turned them into brilliant layouts.'

For the all-important slogan, Bell looked to successful campaigns from the past. 'I found this great line from the 1959 campaign that said, "Britain's a success. Don't let Labour ruin it." Then Frank just cobbled together some nice facts about the number of new hospitals and schools that had been built over the past four years, which we ran as bullet points underneath. And that was that.'

The posters were sent over to David Young the next morning, who immediately took them to Number 10, strategically placing them propped up on a shelf in Thatcher's office. 'She walked in, glanced at the posters and said, "That's it! That's what I want! Who did these?"' says Young. 'I told her Tim had done them, and she said, "Well, of course he did! They're perfect!"' But she was mindful of the furore the new campaign might spark. 'She knew that

Tebbit wouldn't be happy but was determined to use the new ads. But she simply didn't have time to deal with the fallout. I promised her that I would handle the situation,' says Young.

Young immediately called a meeting at Downing Street with Tebbit and Michael Dobbs. He knew that what they had done was an affront to Tebbit's authority as party chairman. But his loyalty was to Thatcher: Stephen Sherbourne, Thatcher's parliamentary private secretary, had told Young bluntly, 'David, you would do a marvellous thing if you could get this whole thing done without even going to her, and just tell her it was all off her hands.' The pressure was on.

Tebbit arrived within the hour and entered the meeting room where Bell's posters were still propped up. 'What's this?' the party chairman demanded. 'The prime minister hates the Saatchi ads. She wants to go with these,' Young replied. Tebbit paused. Young held his breath. 'Norman's face actually went red and he asked, "Who the fuck did these?" And I said, "Tim Bell." He hit the roof. "How dare you do this? This is outrageous! I won't allow it!"' Young had been on the campaign trail for nearly a month, was exhausted, stressed and under immense pressure from Thatcher to fix a campaign that she thought had spiralled out of control. 'I grabbed Norman by the lapels and shouted in his face, "Norman, listen to me, we're about to lose this fucking election! You're going to go, I'm going to go, we're all going to go! It's about the future of this flaming country!"' According to Young, Tebbit shoved him backwards across the room. Tebbit recalls: 'It wasn't David's style. I think he was even more surprised by his actions than I was!' Young concurs: 'I'd never done anything like that before, but I was at breaking point. Everything seemed to be going wrong and I felt that all the pressure was on me to fix it. I just snapped.'

Young implored Tebbit to make an objective assessment of the posters. Eventually Tebbit conceded: 'Okay, they're better than the ones we have, I suppose. But what will we tell Saatchis?' Young asked Tebbit to summon Maurice Saatchi and Michael Dobbs to Downing Street immediately. He reached an agreement with Tebbit that they would allow Saatchis to take credit for Bell's posters in order for them to save face.

As the pair waited anxiously for the team from Saatchis to arrive, the results of a new poll were handed to them by an aide. They confirmed Tebbit's suspicions that the previous day's *Daily Mail* poll had been a red herring. They showed the Conservatives on 44 points, Labour on 34 and the Alliance on 20. The chairman was vindicated: 'The problem was that Tim Bell had whipped up anxiety in Number 10. He had encouraged the prime minister and David Young to think the campaign was boring. He was right, it was boring. That was intentional. If you start a campaign ahead in the polls, your motto is simply "Don't fuck this up." Let the opposition make all the running and don't do anything too rash.'

When Maurice Saatchi arrived, the two ministers presented him with the posters and explained what had happened. The ad exec was ruffled. 'No, I can't possibly do this, I won't take it, this won't do!' he said. Young approached him and grabbed him by the lapels, just like he had with Tebbit. 'I said, "Now look, Maurice, you've got to do it!" He said, "No we can't possibly . . ." And I said, "Maurice, how much are you worth? How much are your companies worth? Do you know how much you'll be worth this time next week if we lose this election? You'll be broke, I'll be broke, the whole country will be broke! Now forget your bloody pride. This is the programme she wants and this is the programme you're going to do!"'

Saatchi regarded Bell's posters. 'They're a bit amateurish,' he observed. Young told him that it was a rough outline of what Thatcher wanted. He was happy to let Saatchi's own creative teams play around with the idea as long as they stayed true to the positive tone. Saatchi reluctantly agreed and returned to Charlotte Street, where his team worked through the night on the new concept. Bell and Young met later at a friend's Westminster flat for a debrief. 'Tim was taken aback that I had told Saatchi that he had been behind the new ideas but, either way, we shared a bottle of champagne to celebrate the new poll results,' says Young.

The next morning, Saatchis delivered a reworked slogan that now read: 'Britain's great, don't let Labour wreck it'. It was the tiniest of tweaks – but at least it gave the world's biggest agency some small claim over the final campaign. 'Changing the slogan from "ruin" to "wreck" sums up the fundamental difference between the Saatchis and me,' says Bell. 'They like shouting at people and I don't. I prefer to convince through charm and niceness. They prefer using aggression and bullying.'

On Thursday 11 June 1987 the British people re-elected Margaret Thatcher for a third time, with a majority of over a hundred parliamentary seats. 'I watched the results come in at a BBC studio and right up to the final hours a great many journalists still had it down as a Labour win,' recalls Tebbit. 'The only thing that surprised me was that we won by more parliamentary seats than even I had imagined.'

Shortly afterwards, Thatcher met with Tebbit to try to heal the rift between the pair. She asked him to remain in government, conscious that – despite their arguments – he was the cabinet's strongest advocate of her principles and policies. He informed her that he would be retiring to the back benches in order to spend more time caring for his wife. Belatedly, it occurred to Thatcher that her anxiety about him attempting to replace her as leader had been misplaced. 'I was very proud of the way I planned the campaign in '87,' he says. 'But I should have managed the prime minister better. I didn't, the rift between the admen somehow came between us and towards the end the whole thing became a bit of a mess.'

Many credited the Tory ad blitz in the final week of the campaign as crucial to the election's eventual outcome, and in the aftermath of Thatcher's historic victory the media began to focus as much on the adland battle for recognition as on the political implications. The *Daily Mail* ran a story, written by Nigel Dempster, under the headline 'Not Saatchi triumph after all', alongside a picture of Bell and Lowe. Tebbit was said to be furious at the ugly fallout. Meanwhile, the Saatchis were disgruntled and launched a so-called bear raid on Lowe Howard-Spink and Bell, wiping £12 million off the company's value in a single day, and stories about Bell's private life began to emerge in the newspapers. The whole affair quickly came to the attention of Margaret Thatcher, who told Gordon Reece: 'It really is unseemly. I've just won an election by over 100 seats and all they do is bicker over who wrote which ads.'

She eventually telephoned Bell. 'I understand that those brothers are trying to damage your company,' she said. 'Tell me what I can do to help.' Bell was resistant, telling her: 'Margaret, please don't. You've got a fucking country to run, I'm perfectly capable of looking after myself.' But Thatcher insisted. She called the industrialist James Hanson, who was a major client of both the Saatchis and Bell. He summoned all of the warring parties to his office. But while Bell turned up, Maurice was the only Saatchi brother in attendance. 'Where is [Charles]?' asked Hanson. 'He's not going to ever speak to Tim Bell again,' replied Maurice. 'Well,' said Hanson, 'all I can say is that you'd better get him on the phone now or something very unpleasant is going to happen to you both.' Charles was dialled into the meeting, which descended quickly into a slanging match between the opposing admen. Eventually, Hanson put his foot down, telling the Saatchis that he was prepared to launch his own bear raid unless their activity against Bell ceased. 'In the meantime, I'm going to invest a quarter of a million pounds in Lowes in order to return their share price to the correct levels and you will stop this nonsense and not do it any more. Do you understand?' A joint statement was issued by both sides, with Lowe congratulating the Saatchis on their winning campaign and the Saatchis expressing gratitude for Lowe's assistance. Bell wasn't mentioned.

'I don't think Tim's a malicious person,' reflects Jeremy Sinclair. 'He's got all sorts of interesting characteristics but he's not malicious. He wouldn't have done what he did during the campaign to kick us. He would have done it just because someone had asked him his opinion and he gave it.'

A BBC *Panorama* documentary broadcast a week after the election claimed that Thatcher had dispensed with Saatchi & Saatchi in the final week of the campaign, in favour of an unnamed rival agency. The Saatchis were so angry that they issued a legal writ against the BBC. Bell says that 'there were two sides in the campaign, but we both had the same aim: to win the election for Margaret Thatcher'.

But if their motivation was as selfless as Bell implies, why did they battle so fiercely for credit once the election was won? If, as Jeremy Sinclair suggests, their work was motivated by an emotional attachment to the cause and a desire to stop the 'dangerous' forces of the Labour Party, what did it matter who wrote which poster? The truth is that the controversy raging in the press after the election not only impacted upon the share prices of both Saatchi & Saatchi and Lowe Howard-Spink and Bell, but it also had a very public effect on their reputations among existing and potential clients. More than anything else, ad agencies are in the business of selling themselves. Securing victory for the Conservatives was important, but securing the credit for that victory was paramount.

Shortly after the election, Saatchi & Saatchi resigned the Conservative Party account. Publicly. They claimed that their widespread business interests meant that they could no longer serve as unbiased political advisors. But one senior Saatchi executive of the time says: 'We resigned because Maurice and Charles could see that Mrs Thatcher no longer liked us very much. And that continuing in a relationship that problematic would probably mean that we wouldn't be able to do our best work, we would suffer reputational damage in the long term and there would be more potential for bad rumours and press. So quitting was absolutely the right thing to do at the time.'

Nevertheless, the Saatchis would be back at the next

election. Thatcher would not. 'There was a sense after 1987 that [Thatcher] had allowed things to get a bit chaotic,' says Dobbs. 'It might not have been entirely her fault but some people in the party blamed her for the campaign that year. After her victory speech at central office on election night, a senior cabinet minister turned to me and said, "That's her finished now. She'll never fight another election again."' He was right. Even David Young, her most trusted colleague, saw what was coming once the 1987 election was over. 'People resolved they would never fight an election like that again,' he says. 'The poll tax was already on the agenda and there was a growing sense that [Thatcher] had lost her political antennae. The knives were already being sharpened.'

Certainly, the admen with whom she had become so enamoured had played their part in her downfall. It was her fixation with their work that had distracted her from more pertinent aspects of the campaign. It was their personal squabbles that had spilled over into her government. It was their disagreements over relatively trivial posters and headlines that had driven a schism between her key ministers and caused embarrassing controversy in the press. But, despite all of the impact they had on the narrative of the election campaign, they seemed to make little difference to the election result.

'The clashes of 1987 were just about admen's egos and politicians' paranoia,' says Tim Bell. 'The reality was that the result was in the bag months before polling day. We could have stuck a huge poster up in Piccadilly Circus saying "Fuck off" and people would have still voted for us.'

8

DON'T LET IT END IN TEARS

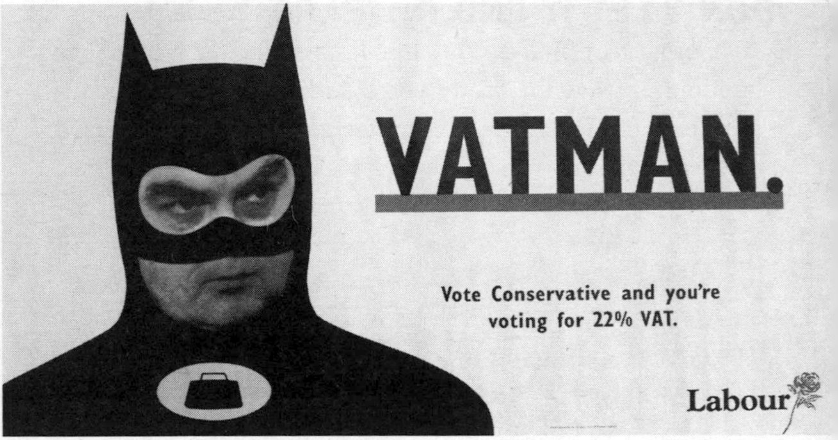
VATMAN.
Vote Conservative and you're voting for 22% VAT.
Labour

Peter Mandelson used to enjoy his visits to the fashionable offices of Boase Massimi Pollitt, the ad agency in Paddington that for many years had served as the headquarters of the Shadow Communications Agency. 'He used to spend a lot of time here,' says Chris Powell. 'It was a decent environment, nicer than his own office. And there was always a bit of hostility towards him at Walworth Road among the old guard. Here we were pleased to see him.'

The SCA continued to thrive after their acclaimed work during the 1987 election. Mandelson was now as much an adman as a politician, devising Labour's marketing strategy with Philip Gould and briefing Powell's creative team in Paddington. But those at Walworth Road who thought that he had been seduced by the superficial glamour of what John Prescott would later call 'the beautiful people' were wrong. In 1988 he walked away from his high-profile job as the party's communications director in favour of running for selection as Labour's parliamentary candidate in the north-eastern constituency of Hartlepool. It was a blow from which the party would take years to recover.

Mandelson had thought the party leadership would be happy for him to keep his job as director of communications. He was wrong. 'Neil [Kinnock] felt I'd let him down badly,' says Mandelson. 'And I don't think he ever forgave me for it.'

'He deserves it but he's left us in the shit,' is what Kinnock told his chief of staff, Charles Clarke, when Mandelson successfully won his candidacy in December 1989. Labour had been building upon the modest successes of 1987, and the party had established a double-digit lead in the opinion polls over an increasingly unpopular Maragret Thatcher.

But the next campaign would have to be every bit as carefully stage-managed as in 1987. Losing Mandelson, the man who had revolutionised Labour communications in four short years, was a colossal blow. 'Peter was the first person to take control and give us the freedom we needed to deliver a powerful campaign,' says Chris Powell. 'We knew right away that things could fall apart without him at the centre of things.'

But however much he enjoyed straddling politics and adland, Mandelson understood that no amount of spin would work without real political change. 'I believed I could make more of a difference as an MP,' he says. 'But I felt sure that that didn't have to stop me managing the way we ran communications.'

The formidable Charles Clarke summoned Mandelson to the shadow cabinet room in the House of Commons. The two were old colleagues; it was Clarke who had spotted Mandelson's potential during the Brecon by-election in 1985. He had backed him for the job as director of campaigns and communications, and the pair had formed a tight team around Neil Kinnock. But their meeting at the tail end of 1989 was less than friendly. 'I've never known Neil so angry over anything,' Clarke told the spin doctor. 'You cannot stay, you'll have to leave and we'll find someone to replace you.' Clarke added that, if it had been up to him, he'd have Mandelson empty his desk that very afternoon.

'I felt very strongly that you couldn't both be fully engaged in running an election campaign and be running your own campaign as a Member of Parliament. [Peter] didn't agree,' says Clarke when I meet him for coffee in the lobby of a hotel in Holborn. Clarke is a physically imposing individual with a manner that exaggerates that impression. He is brusque; he speaks quickly, seriously, with an overwhelming amount of conviction. (As an aside, I asked the man who served as home secretary under Tony Blair what he made of Labour's chances in the 2015 general election, which at the time was well over a year away. 'I think we're in very bad shape,' he shot back immediately. 'I expect the Conservatives to win a majority.' He looked so cross about it I changed the subject.)

In the eighties Charles Clarke was a behind-the-scenes figure able to wield immense influence over the Labour leadership. As Kinnock's chief of staff he was given a wide-ranging day-to-day decision-making mandate by a leader who was intolerant of process and detail. No policy or strategic decision came out of Kinnock's office without first going through Clarke. He was in his thirties at the time, fiercely loyal to Kinnock and often combative with anyone he perceived to be a threat to his boss.

In 1989 he saw to it that Mandelson was immediately punished for what he and Kinnock perceived as a betrayal to the party. 'Peter thought that he could do both jobs,' explains Clarke. 'I simply thought it wasn't feasible. And so we had an argument about that. Neil agreed with me and so Peter went.'

Suddenly, the forthcoming campaign for an election that

had looked eminently winnable was completely derailed. 'Charles was extremely upset and annoyed that I, as he put it, "Put my personal career before the interests of the party,"' says Mandelson. 'And he didn't forgive me.'

The organisational processes Mandelson had put in place; the experts he had brought into the SCA; the creativity and professionalism he had applied to the 1987 campaign: all of it would be allowed to wither away in the run-up to 1992. Labour was about to take several giant steps backwards. To this day, Mandelson is convinced that Clarke and Kinnock made a terrible error and that he could have easily combined his battle for a parliamentary seat with a continued role on the campaign team. 'Oh, I could have. I could've made sure that there was a continuity and that the machine was kept together, without any shadow of doubt. And during the actual campaign itself, you know, I would have been in Hartlepool but still on the other end of the phone. But the truth is, the campaign machine, after I stepped out of it, ran down. It was never the same again. Neil blamed me for that.'

Kinnock was a fragile leader, a dazzling orator on his day but riddled with insecurities about his standing with the public. Mandelson says that, by 1992, Kinnock was running out of steam. 'He kept telling me, "I just can't find the words,"' he says. With his most trusted image advisor gone, the leader's confidence received a damaging blow.

Mandelson's close friend, Colin Byrne, applied to replace him as the head of campaigns and communications. Kinnock voted for Byrne at the NEC but the PR man was defeated by John Underwood, a former TV reporter. 'They didn't even let me play a role in selecting my successor,' says Mandelson. While Kinnock preferred Byrne,

Clarke was said to have objected to his appointment on the basis of his close friendship with Mandelson. The NEC duly appointed Underwood. Rather more traditional than his predecessor, Underwood was thought by many to pander too much to central office and the shadow cabinet, dropping most of the creative talents that Mandelson had recruited to the SCA.

Philip Gould found himself trying to hold together what remained of the 1987 campaign team. But even in 1990, two years before the campaign, his outlook was bleak. 'In short, Labour has stalled,' he wrote in a memo that June. 'Labour has not changed enough . . . At the death, in the polling booth, people may be more likely to vote for the devil they know and dislike rather than the devil they do not fully trust. As things stand, the Conservatives are on course for an election victory. Without a campaign manager – one person in charge – Labour will find it hard to win.'

Kinnock appointed shadow minister Jack Cunningham as his campaign chief. But it was clear that the rapier efficiency of the 1987 campaign had faded away. 'There was not enough focus or action,' says Chris Powell. 'While Peter was in charge, we felt we had a direct conduit to the leadership and had our ideas signed off quickly. In the run-up to 1992 all we had were weekly talking shops presided over by Jack Cunningham, but nothing ever got done. We made hardly any ads. It was weird, because Neil was so conscious of communications and Jack [Cunningham] was an intelligent guy. But we never really got the opportunity to do anything.'

Meanwhile, an unofficial campaign team had formed in a flat in north London that would help worsen the sense of mutual suspicion that was spreading within the party. Mandelson had moved in with Colin Byrne and Kinnock's former press secretary Patricia Hewitt, who remained a highly influential figure. Charles Clarke was furious, seeing it as an open act of insubordination. 'It led to a whole set of circumstances where I felt Peter was trying to influence the campaign from the outside,' says Clarke. Philip Gould recorded in his memoir that Clarke refused to cover the flat's fax-machine bill once he knew Mandelson was living there. 'I have no recollection of that,' says Clarke. 'It may well be true. It certainly doesn't ring false. But I did feel it was a very bad state of affairs. It wasn't a comfortable state of affairs that took place.'

Hewitt had been another big loss to Kinnock: his former press secretary had left to take up a role at a political think tank and now, alongside Mandelson and Byrne, was attempting to guide Labour's campaign from the outside. As with Mandelson, Clarke had made his former colleague Hewitt unwelcome in the inner circle. 'We had an interesting relationship, sometimes good, sometimes bad,' says Clarke. 'Occasionally it was competitive, for which I am probably responsible. It became less easy and so she went. We never had an explicit discussion about it. But I've always worried about it.'

Despite the various upheavals, Labour retained a ten-point opinion-poll lead throughout much of 1990. Then, in November of that year, Margaret Thatcher was deposed as prime minister by her cabinet colleagues and eventually replaced by the chancellor of the exchequer, John Major.

Thatcher's unpopularity had become Labour's biggest electoral asset. With her gone, Kinnock saw the writing on the wall. 'When the news about Major came in, I told my team: "Let's eat, drink and be merry tonight, chums, 'cause our problems start tomorrow,"' he says.

Internally, there remained a deep schism between the official campaign team at Walworth Road and the SCA in Paddington. Meanwhile, Mandelson, Byrne and Hewitt endeavoured to shape campaign policy from their own north London base. John Underwood had left his post as director of communications after just one year and the newly appointed David Hill, while more popular, was still acclimatising to the job. Philip Gould and his business partner Deborah Mattinson had carried out research gauging Labour's policy weaknesses and had discovered unequivocally that the party was deeply mistrusted on tax. Mattinson had delivered a presentation to the shadow cabinet in 1990 showing that 70 per cent of voters believed they would pay more tax under Labour. She and Gould urged the shadow chancellor John Smith to address the matter; Smith told them angrily that he wouldn't be lectured by admen and pollsters.

Smith had publicly committed a future Labour government to a rise in pensions and child benefit, policies which the Conservatives claimed would require tax rises in order to be paid for. At the start of the year, with Labour continuing to lead in almost every opinion poll and the recession deepening, the party resolved to fight a safety-first campaign. 'It was almost as if they had decided to avoid ads altogether,' says Chris Powell. 'There was a feeling that the less we said as a party, the less chance we had of slipping up before the election.'

But their silence on taxation was to prove fatal. The Conservatives began 1992 by launching an attack on

Labour's proposed spending, suggesting that it would cost the average voter £1,000 extra in tax per year. Their 'Labour's double whammy' and 'Tax bombshell' posters would set the agenda for the campaign ahead. 'It took us two months to hit back with a poster of our own,' says Powell, who was increasingly frustrated by the inaction of campaign boss Jack Cunningham and the lack of decisiveness in the party since Mandelson's departure. 'In March we put out a poster depicting Norman Lamont as Vatman, which was the one thing we were really proud of.' The poster showed Lamont behind a Batman mask, complete with pointed ears, and suggested that the Conservatives intended to increase VAT to 22 per cent after the election. Briefly, Labour pulled level in the economic debate.

But Kinnock was aware that the tax question would not go away until they outlined their spending plans in detail. 'The first time they used the "Labour's tax bombshell" poster was in late 1991, and we managed to beat it off,' he says. 'Once we addressed the accusation in detail we were able to show people that only 5 per cent of tax payers would have to pay more under our plans and, in fact, 20 per cent would pay less. But that didn't discourage the Tories. They kept banging on about it.'

Kinnock urged John Smith to publish a detailed budget at the start of the year, so that they could explain their tax and spending plans to the public well in advance of the election. 'John thought that we should wait until the Tories announced their actual budget, then surprise them with our own plans. I was so preoccupied with other things that I gave in to him. The result of that was that we never had enough time to explain and reassure the public.'

It was the sort of hesitancy and overanalysis that had

always hindered Labour in its battle against a more ruthless and cavalier Conservative campaign team. The 'Tax bombshell' poster was plastered on billboards up and down the land, despite muted Labour rebuttals. 'The problem about "Labour's tax bombshell" was it might not have been true, but it went with the grain of what people already wanted to believe,' says Kinnock. 'With political ads you need to start with what the polls are telling you about the public's preconceptions. Then you've got to communicate their thoughts back to them with a simple line and a beautiful image. That's what they did with the bombshell. People already suspected Labour were the party of high taxes, so they simply delivered that message in a punchy way.'

Norman Lamont delivered his budget in early March, in which he reduced the basic rate of tax from 25p to 20p. A few days later, John Major announced that the election would take place on 9 April. Suddenly, an election that Labour had seemed certain to win six months beforehand was up for grabs. Philip Gould recorded in his memoir: 'Maurice Saatchi told a friend after that election that the only issue the Tories had was tax, and that Labour gave it to them. "If they dealt with it, we had nothing else."'

Labour had at least one policy area they could always depend on: health. Polls consistently showed that voters saw Labour as the trusted guardians of the NHS, and the SCA resolved that this would be the central focus of their campaign. In late 1991 powerful posters produced by Chris Powell and his SCA team had helped discourage John Major from calling an early election. One depicted four skeletons hanging against a black background. Around each of them was a sign: 'Privatise the NHS'; 'Privatise education'; 'Raise VAT to 22 per cent'; 'Increase unemployment to three million'. The headline read: 'How many more have the Tories got in their cupboard?' The next depicted a stethoscope arranged into the shape of a pound sign. The headline was: 'If you want to be well, you had better be well off.' Philip Gould was later told by Conservative pollster Robert Waller that the controversy caused by the posters convinced Major to delay an election in October 1991.

In early 1992 the SCA continued their assault on Tory plans to privatise elements of the NHS. An election broadcast was commissioned to depict the differing experiences of two young girls with similar ear conditions. One was from a family who could afford private healthcare; the other received treatment on the NHS. The broadcast, scripted by BMP's top creative John Webster, was hugely emotive. To the strains of a heart-rending soul soundtrack, the NHS patient was seen waiting months for an operation, suffering constant pain and unable to concentrate at school. Meanwhile, her counterpart received immediate surgery, which, in the film's denouement, her mother pays for with a £200 cheque. Shot by Mike Newell, who had enjoyed success with his feature film *Dance with a Stranger*, it was a beautifully executed and emotionally powerful broadcast. It ended with the two girls asleep in their beds and the headline 'It's their future. Don't let it end in tears.'

'It was a brilliant and powerful broadcast and I was extremely pleased with it,' says Chris Powell. 'At the launch, it rendered a deep silence in a room full of politicians and hacks. But then things started to go wrong.'

Questions were asked about the credibility of the story it depicted. It was suggested that the details of the case on which the ad was based – that of five-year-old Jennifer

Bennett – had been falsified for effect by Labour's admen. 'It turned out that Jennifer Bennett's grandfather was a Conservative member and had told the press that the details of the case weren't correct,' says Powell. 'It shouldn't really have mattered because John had based the script on an amalgam of cases, not just Bennett's. But we didn't respond properly, and it quickly descended into a crisis.'

At a press conference in the Midlands, a number of journalists claimed that Kinnock's press secretary, Julie Hall, had told them that the ad was based specifically on Bennett's case. Hall took to the stage herself and railed against the accusations. 'It was unbelievable,' says Charles Clarke. 'I stood there watching, wanting to drag her off the stage. I think the broadcast was legitimate and the right thing to do. It was Julie's response to the criticism that turned it into such a big problem for us.'

The day after the broadcast the *Daily Express* ran the front-page headline 'Exposed: Labour's sick NHS stunts'. The *Sun* went with: 'If Kinnock tells lies about sick little girls, will he tell the truth about anything?'

The tabloid press, almost exclusively sympathetic to the Conservatives, descended upon BMP's offices. 'They filled the reception area,' says Powell. 'We were being shoved around every time we came in or out. I felt they were trying to provoke us into throwing a punch so they could get a picture of it. It was intimidating, a complete tabloid monstering.'

It seemed that however strong their communications, a hostile press would incessantly attack Labour's campaign. When Trevor Kavanagh, the political editor of the *Sun*, invited Neil Kinnock to News International's offices in Wapping to make peace, the Labour leader refused.

Instead, Charles Clarke attended the meeting without telling Kinnock. '[*Sun* editor] Kelvin MacKenzie was there surrounded by all of his senior editors, and he kept saying, "Why do you keep sending us all these fucking writs?"' says Clarke. 'I told him that it was in response to the intrusive behaviour of his reporters, who had been harassing Neil's family in Wales to get stories. I told him we would stop the writs if he called off his reporters. It was an extraordinary meeting that didn't get us very far. When Neil found out about it, he was furious with me because he wanted no dealings with them at all. They offered him his own page in the *Sun* but he turned it down.'

In the final weeks of the campaign Peter Mandelson visited Neil and Glenys Kinnock at their home in west London. 'Neil could see that the whole shadow agency we had created just wasn't functioning properly,' says Mandelson. 'Glenys kept saying, "Why don't you bring Peter back into the fold?" But Neil said, "I can't. It would just cause too many problems in the office." He knew Charles [Clarke] wouldn't stand for me coming back into the team.'

So it was that Kinnock and Labour entered the final week of the campaign with an increasingly narrow poll lead and one more major error lying ahead of them. The Sheffield rally had been planned a year in advance and was based on a US-style political rally: held on 1 April 1992, the Sheffield Arena was awash with lights, glitz and fanfare, with the hall crammed with 10,000 excited Labour Party members. It was said to have cost £100,000 to arrange. As a spectacle, it couldn't have been more removed from the traditional image of the Labour Party. Neil Kinnock arrived at the venue by helicopter and members of the shadow cabinet dashed theatrically from the back of the hall through the adoring crowd as their names were announced with triumphalist phrases such as 'The next foreign secretary!' and 'The next chancellor!'

Bryan Gould remembers the atmosphere as he arrived on stage in front of the hysterical Labour voters, convinced that they were finally on the verge of winning an election. 'It was extremely heady. We felt like we had won the World Cup,' he says. 'We had all discussed not appearing too triumphalist, but it was easy to get carried away. And one of Neil's greatest weaknesses is that he gets excitable. He was like a jumping jack, completely swept away by it all.'

Kinnock appeared to be in a state of excited frenzy, bellowing in a strangely transatlantic accent 'We're alriiight! We're alriiight!' several times. 'I looked at him and said, "Someone shut him up!"' says Gould. 'I knew how it was going to look on the news, and it wouldn't be good.'

The news images that appeared that night did little to counter widespread concern that Kinnock was unsuitable for the post of prime minister; even Labour devotees were affronted by the hubris and extravagance on display. The following day the Conservatives drew level in several opinion polls. The Sheffield rally remains in many people's minds the moment when the tide truly turned against Kinnock's bid to become prime minister.

On election day, 9 April 1992, Labour retained a narrow lead in most opinion polls. The Tory-supporting *Sun* was still sufficiently concerned about a Labour victory that they had devoted that morning's entire front page to an image of Neil Kinnock's head inside a lightbulb, beside the headline 'If Kinnock wins today will the last person to leave Britain please turn out the lights?'

Charles Clarke was bullish to the last. 'I didn't believe we'd lost until the following morning,' he says. 'I had fully expected us to get more seats than the Tories and had already spoken secretly with Paddy Ashdown about forming a coalition with the Liberal Democrats.'

In the event, despite a 2.2 per cent swing to Labour, the Conservative Party was re-elected with a twenty-one-seat majority. 'I have always felt that one of the reasons we lost was because we had just three weeks, not three months, to explain and reassure people about our tax and spending plans,' says Kinnock. 'Maybe if we'd announced them sooner, as I had hoped, we might have scraped over the line.'

He soon found out just how narrow the margin had been. 'Bob Worcester called me three days after the election and said, "Hi, Neil, I'm calling to offer my commiserations about the result and to tell you how much you lost by." I said, "Christ, Bob, that figure is written on my heart." He said, "No, the twenty-one majority is written on your heart. 1,240 should be written on your heart because that is the total number of votes that swung it in the Tories' bottom eleven seats. So you lost, my friend, not by twenty-one seats but actually by 1,240 votes.'

Did that make the Labour leader feel any better about being beaten? 'No, it made me feel worse,' he says. 'But the good news was that I was resigning that afternoon.'

Worcester was certain about the cause of Kinnock's defeat. 'It was the Sheffield rally, without doubt,' he says. 'They lost the lower-middle-class public servants after that. I was polling every day and I could see a crucial swing of voters from Labour to the Liberals the day after the rally. I think that whole performance convinced nurses, teachers and policemen that Neil did not represent what the prime minister is supposed to represent.'

Clarke is less convinced. 'People say it was the Sheffield rally that swung it, but I always thought that was bollocks,' he says. 'They also say it's the shadow budget or Jennifer's ear. The truth is, we ran a brilliant campaign in 1987 which raised expectations for 1992. We ran a campaign that was just as good in most ways and ran the Tories so close it came down to less than two thousand votes. There is no simple explanation for it.'

The 1992 general election was the first since 1979 in which the new breed of admen had a chance to prove they could make a difference. In 1983 and 1987 the Conservatives had led by such an insurmountable margin going into the campaign that it was almost impossible to work out what difference, if any, the ads made. But 1992 was a knife-edge election, in which the effective execution of campaign messages might have made a crucial difference to undecided voters. While Labour floundered over Jennifer's ear and the Sheffield rally, their rivals in the Conservative Party managed once again to set the tone and agenda of the campaign with a characteristic onslaught of aggressive advertising. 'From the moment the first "Tax bombshell" poster went up, we just felt outgunned by the Saatchis,' admits Chris Powell. 'We were pleased with some of our election broadcasts but they always had the edge on us with their poster. We knew Jeremy Sinclair and the rest of the team at Saatchis, and if we saw them at industry events we'd have a friendly drink and a chat. But when it came to elections, they just put on their gloves and came out fighting.'

9

KILL OR GET KILLED

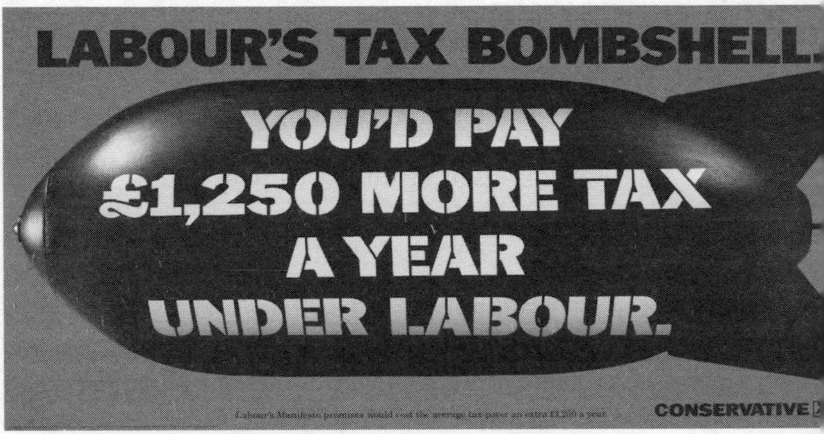

LABOUR'S TAX BOMBSHELL.
YOU'D PAY £1,250 MORE TAX A YEAR UNDER LABOUR.
Labour's Manifesto promises would cost the average tax-payer an extra £1,250 a year.
CONSERVATIVE

'The truth is that Neil Kinnock could have been prime minister. Of course he could have,' says Chris Patten. 'Certainly he had the Conservative Party worried enough that we replaced our own leader. While Margaret Thatcher was a fantastic prime minister, it's worth remembering that she won her three elections against weak leaders of a divided Labour Party. In 1992 we had a more serious opponent.'

Chris Patten was the governor and commander-in-chief of Hong Kong during the handover to China in 1997. He was later the chancellor of Oxford University. When I went to see him in 2013, he was the chairman of the BBC Trust. I remembered one of the things that Norman Tebbit had said when I'd met him a few months previously: that to serve in government you needed to be the sort of person who could run a massive department. A manager. A doer. That, said Tebbit, was what today's cabinet, filled with former policy wonks, lacked: any experience of actually getting stuff done. But Patten, a successor to Tebbit as chairman of the Conservative Party, was quite clearly a doer. He had proved that in 1992 by leading the most astonishing election coup of modern times.

That was the year John Major was written off as hopeless, the Conservatives as unelectable and the campaign as boring and unimaginative. It was also the year in which the Tories won more votes than any party in British electoral history.

The Conservative Party was almost twenty points behind Labour when John Major replaced Margaret Thatcher as prime minister in November 1990. Within a month they had turned that deficit into a 3.5 per cent lead over the opposition. Major was the antidote to Thatcher's increasingly unpopular brand of single-minded, authoritarian leadership. He was characterised in the press and on *Spitting Image* as a grey, suburban man. But it soon appeared that he was, in fact, the solution to all of his party's problems. While 71 per cent of voters were said to be dissatisfied with Thatcher's performance as prime minister towards the end of her reign, by January 1991 61 per cent of them declared themselves satisfied with Major. The election was just over a year away. The Tories were back in business.

Major knew it wouldn't be easy. Labour had proved in 1987 that they were capable of putting up a decent fight. The new prime minister was unproven and lacked the natural campaigning flair of Thatcher, and as 1991 wore on the opinion polls began to creep back in the opposition's favour. While simultaneously presiding over war in the Gulf, Major began to assemble a campaign team that was capable of pulling the Conservative Party out of one of the most difficult periods in its history. The group he ended up with might not have contained the flair, fire or largesse of Tim Bell, Gordon Reece, Cecil Parkinson or Norman Tebbit, but this relatively unsung band of admen, pollsters, spin doctors, wonks and politicians would plan and execute an almost perfectly choreographed electoral coup.

Major's first key appointment was Patten, whom he made party chairman. As secretary of state for the environment, Patten had played a prominent role in the implementation of the poll tax – one of the chief catalysts for

Thatcher's demise. But like Major he was a sober, professional and understated individual – a contrast from the firebrands who had dominated the cabinets of the eighties. As a former director of the formidable Conservative research department, he had worked closely with Saatchis during the 1979 election campaign. Patten was an experienced campaigner who was under no illusions about the task ahead. 'It was an incredibly difficult position we found ourselves in,' he says. 'It was the election nobody thought we could win. We had been badly shaken by the poll tax, rows over Europe and Margaret Thatcher's removal from office. We were in a recession that never seemed to end. And both the press and certain people inside the party were sniping at us constantly.'

While the majority of the press still supported the Conservatives, an editorial in the *Financial Times* in June 1991 summed up the feeling that the Tory campaign was floundering while Labour's flourished:

> The complacency of 1987–89 has been replaced by a nervous anxiety, a sense of fevered amateurishness, that is all the more striking for the political professionalism of Labour . . . the Tories, bruised and perhaps exhausted by the events of the past two years, appear to be adrift, without an overall strategy, with not a clue as to how to bring these policies into a coherent form and convince the public that they are right . . . What is required is proper Generalship. In short, Labour gives the impression that it knows exactly what it is doing. John Major and his team look lost.

Patten set out to find a new director of communications to devise a plan of attack on the resurgent opposition. In keeping with the new, low-key regime, the appointment would not be high-profile or showbiz. The party was not about to hire another Gordon Reece character. Patten wanted someone with experience of popular journalism and TV, with an ability to write in the sort of tabloid style that would connect with the average voter. Soon, he found him.

'I had been working with Esther Rantzen on *That's Life!* when I got the call,' Shaun Woodward tells me. When I went to meet the man who is now a Labour MP at his Millbank offices in 2013, he had just announced that he would be standing down at the 2015 election. His has been a unique political career: from left-leaning journalist to Major's spin doctor, Conservative MP and, eventually, New Labour cabinet minister. When he was appointed Conservative communications boss in 1990, he was unknown to most within the party and written off by many as incapable of running what was destined to be the party's toughest electoral challenge in years. Many derided Chris Patten for making such a left-field appointment, but Woodward would become a central figure in the momentous campaign that lay ahead.

By 2013 he might have been a Labour MP but he remained proud of his efforts on behalf of the Tories twenty-one years earlier. '1992 was no tea party. Labour had shown us that in the run-up with all sorts of personal and untrue attacks on John Major's character,' he says. 'Peter Mandelson had masterminded their by-election victory in Monmouth the year before by claiming that Major planned to privatise the NHS. Anyone who knew John Major for more than three seconds would know that was impossible. But that didn't stop them saying it. They showed us that they were street fighters. And so I realised early on that I'd need a team of street fighters around me too.'

The show Woodward had previously edited, *That's Life!*, was famous for silly news stories about comedy-shaped vegetables, but Woodward had fused the fun with a popular campaigning element. 'We'd taken on the case of a young boy called Ben Hardwick, who needed a liver transplant,' he says. 'It turned into a full-blown campaign that ended up saving hundreds of lives.' His quiet tenacity and drive, combined with a solid political background working on *Panorama* and *Newsnight*, prompted a mutual friend at the BBC to recommend him to Chris Patten.

'I met Chris and he told me he was looking for someone to bring a fresh eye to how you might sell someone like John Major. Now I was by no means a Thatcherite and was, if anything, left of centre. But I met Major and he said he wanted to be at the centre of Europe, which I liked. And he said he wanted to find a solution in Northern Ireland, which I liked too. I'd been a journalist covering the troubles in Ulster and had seen how many lives they'd ruined. But, above all, John and Chris both struck me as thoroughly decent blokes. Chris offered me the job and it took me about three seconds to say yes.'

Aged just thirty-two, it was a bold and dramatic career move for Woodward. 'Most of my friends thought I was insane,' he says. 'How could someone left-wing work for the Conservatives? And, besides, everyone thought it would be impossible for the Tories to win the election. So I was basically committing career suicide.'

But Woodward, like Patten, was convinced that the party had a trump card in Major. 'People were writing him off as dull and boring,' says Woodward. 'But while we were often behind in the polls as a party, Major's personal ratings were always high, particularly when it came to trustworthiness. We were convinced that we could fight the battle on that basis and win.'

The strategy was broadened out in January 1991, when Chris Patten called a meeting of key campaign figures at Hever Castle in Kent. The plan was to come away with a basic campaign strategy. Guest of honour was Richard 'Dick' Worthing, an American pollster and political consultant who was credited with masterminding Ronald Reagan's two presidential election victories in 1980 and 1984. He presented a poll that demonstrated that while 45 per cent of voters believed Labour had genuinely changed, another 45 per cent thought it remained an old-fashioned party of high taxes and union control. The trick, said Worthing, was to increase the latter figure to 70 per cent by the time the election came around.

In the audience at Hever Castle was Andrew Lansley, the director of the Conservative research department. Lansley would go on to become secretary of state for health and then leader of the House of Commons in David Cameron's government, but his proudest achievement, he says, remains the election victory of 1992 and the role he played in it. When I arrived at his office in the Commons he asked me for a pencil, then proceeded to draw a diagram which he said explained 'how you win elections'. He sketched a cross and began to label it. 'You'll have to forgive me, it's been a while since I drew one of these,' he said. 'At the top you put positive rating, at the bottom you put negative rating. On the right you put high salience, on the left you write low salience. And this is how you win elections. What you want are the policy areas on which you have a positive rating to be high salience. And the politics that your opposition are strong on to be low salience. If the policies your opposition are very weak on are also high salience, then even better. That's what Dick

Worthing taught us at Hever. And that's what we shaped our strategy around.'

Later, Worthing would elaborate on his theory to Shaun Woodward. 'He told me, "Look, when it comes to the NHS, the Tories are perceived as dreadful. So you just shut up. Don't talk about it." And I said, "But hang on, what if Labour say we're going to privatise it?" And he said, "You really don't understand. Don't be provoked. Don't say anything. Let me take this to an extreme. I'm not advocating this but, for right-of-centre parties, defence is normally perceived as a strong issue. Nobody has ever taken my advice, but of course what you should do is start a war. Because you'd make defence high salience."'

Worthing warned Woodward that the Conservatives were losing credibility on economic management. 'It was a problem because it was a high-salience issue. People were losing their jobs and their homes,' says Woodward. 'We had to identify some sort of economic issue that we were still stronger than Labour on.'

To help him do so, Woodward set about hiring a new advertising agency. 'I got a PR firm to send a letter out to all of London's major ad agencies saying, "We have a C2 brand that needs to reinvent itself in the mind of the consumer. Kindly show us the best examples of your television and press advertising work." The party had given me one rule: under no circumstances should I speak to Saatchi & Saatchi. They were seen as divisive, egomaniacs and destructive.'

A few weeks later, Woodward met Chris Patten to update him on his search for a new agency. 'It was one of the hardest things I ever had to do,' he says. 'I told him that while I had met a lot of agencies who I thought could do a great job, the people who were the smartest, most creative and most passionate about helping us win were Saatchi & Saatchi. [Patten] told me, "There is no way I can take that to the prime minister." And I said, "Well, that's as may be. But if you want to know the answer to who I think might actually be able to help us turn the impossible into the possible at the next election, these people at Saatchis are the only ones who can do it."'

After the conflict and chaos of 1987, Saatchis had little desire to work with the Conservatives either. But the likes of Maurice Saatchi and Jeremy Sinclair had earned Chris Patten's respect during the 1979 campaign. And, as Sinclair says, the agency felt 'inextricably linked' with the Conservative Party.

In 1991 Saatchis' new managing director Bill Muirhead received a call in his car from a friend at Brunswick PR. 'He said he wanted to talk to me in secret about a client but couldn't tell me who it was,' Muirhead says. 'I told him I couldn't pitch to a client if I didn't know who they were. So he told me that he played tennis with Shaun Woodward every week and that he'd been struggling to find a new ad agency. Would we be interested? I told him to set up a meeting right away.'

Woodward and Muirhead approached each other cautiously. 'Shaun asked me to his offices on a Friday evening at nine,' says Muirhead. 'I was meeting friends for dinner and thought that this must be a test to see how keen we really were. So I went to central office and he kept me waiting for half an hour. Eventually he got me in there and told me that they didn't want any of the people from the previous campaign involved. I said that I was in charge of the agency now, I hadn't worked on any previous campaigns and, if he wanted, I could get a whole new team together to show him the next day. He agreed, then gave me a lift to Notting Hill to meet my friends.'

It was two days later, on the Sunday evening, that Woodward arrived at Saatchi & Saatchi's offices on Charlotte Street. There to meet him were Muirhead, Maurice Saatchi and Jeremy Sinclair. 'Jeremy was the genius who had really led the previous campaign, so we let him do most of the talking,' says Muirhead. Woodward was blown away by what he heard: 'First of all, they predicted exactly what every other agency had been telling me: that John Major was a nice guy and that we could win on the basis of his appeal alone. But Jeremy said, "They say he's nice now. But in six months' time, at best they'll be saying he's too nice to be decisive. And at worst they'll be saying he's awful. You need something more than that."'

Then Sinclair delivered the line that would change Woodward's attitude to campaigning for ever: 'He turned to me and said, "It's very simple in this game: you either kill or you get killed."'

The young director of communications was hooked immediately. 'There was a real aggression to what they were saying,' he says. 'I can't say I liked it, but they were so serious. Jeremy said, "We're not playing games. If Major doesn't win, he loses. There is no halfway house." None of the other agencies I had met were talking in those terms.'

Sinclair pointed to the seminal posters of previous campaigns – 'Labour isn't working', 'Like your manifesto, comrade', 'Labour's policy on arms'. 'Negative campaigning works,' he told Woodward.

'I told him that John didn't really want to run that sort

of campaign,' says Woodward, 'and he said, "Yeah, well, are you prepared to lose?" And I said, "Obviously not." And he replied, "Well then. Kill or get killed." I told him I thought that was putting it a bit harshly, and he just said, "Well, if you don't mind losing, it's fine." I started to realise exactly what I had got myself involved with.'

Sinclair went on to tell Woodward that the party had shown extraordinary survival instincts by removing their own leader. 'Why recoil now?' he asked. 'I was shocked by the brutal animalism of the whole thing,' says Woodward. 'But I realised that we were entering into a vicious fight and that we would need some creative street thugs like them by our side. So I went to speak with Chris.'

A few days later, Muirhead found himself in a secret meeting with Patten in a private suite at Claridge's hotel in Mayfair. 'Patten told me, "We've been round the houses and we've ended up back in the same room,"' says Muirhead. 'He said they would need high security to prevent any leaks, huge resources and a fresh team with none of the main players from 1987. I told him that we would set up a campaign bunker at our corporate headquarters in Berkeley Square, that we were the biggest agency in the world and that I would personally run the account myself. Maurice would have to take a bit of a backstage role, which he found a little bruising – but he understood why.'

Patten was convinced and took the proposal to Major. 'Ad people were not necessarily the sort of people John felt comfortable around,' says Patten. 'You know, with their oversized cuffs and different-coloured shirt collars. And John was obviously cautious about using the old guard's agency. But he was a listener and he understood why Shaun and I had chosen them.'

Patten and Woodward wanted to begin a preliminary campaign in the autumn of 1991. Still in search of a high-salience issue to focus on, Andrew Lansley and the research department conducted a simple questionnaire. 'We asked people two questions,' says Lansley. 'What are the issues that are most affecting you and your family right now? And which party has the strongest policies on that issue? Again and again we heard people concerned about the future of the economy.'

The campaign team remained cautious of focusing on the economy during a recession. Then Labour presented them with a gift by rolling out a slew of policy commitments in the second half of 1991, including an increase in child benefit, pensions and health spending. Sinclair asked Lansley's research department to calculate the cost of Labour's pledges. Their estimate was £35 billion. 'The public will very often like the sound of a £35 billion spending spree on services, so we had to find a way of turning that around,' says Lansley. 'We kept pushing John Smith [the shadow chancellor] on how he planned to raise this money. First he denied he'd raise VAT. Then he denied he'd raise National Insurance. So that led us to suppose that he would raise it out of income tax. We had our high-salience issue.'

Sinclair took the £35 billion figure and, he says, 'basically divided it by the number of tax payers in Britain'. The mathematics might not have been the most rigorous but it allowed the Saatchi team to produce the most iconic poster of the campaign, one that would define the entire agenda leading up to polling day. In January 1992 sites around Britain displayed a bold, ominous image of 'Labour's tax bombshell', accompanied by the headline

'You'd pay £1,250 more tax a year under Labour.' It was classic Saatchi advertising: it played fast and loose with the facts to deliver a simple, direct message that tapped into existing preconceptions. They had found a way of attacking Labour on the economy that would not backfire. The public trusted the Tories on taxation, and a relentless and co-ordinated onslaught of messages throughout the start of 1992 began to raise its importance in the public consciousness. The poster launch was quickly followed by a broadcast about how much worse off the average voter would be under Labour. Next came a newspaper campaign with ads stating how much extra tax the reader of each paper would pay under Labour (£1,350 for the average *Daily Mail* reader, £1,025 for the *Daily Star*, and so on).

Labour attempted to hit back, denying the accuracy of the sums and presenting conflicting versions of how they might fund their spending. This only served to keep the issue firmly on the agenda. 'We would not be budged on the issue of tax,' says Woodward. 'We kept talking about it at the expense of any other subject. We were relentless.'

Labour were doing just the opposite: furiously denying the spending figures the Tory campaign had conjured but failing to co-ordinate the details of their response. 'What was strange was, we knew that they expected us to attack them on the tax and spending issue,' says Lansley. 'We'd seen leaked strategy documents from Labour. We thought they'd have a plan. But they didn't. They didn't hit back at us on tax, so we just carried on with it.'

In late January Bill Muirhead received a call from Labour's Shadow Communications Agency boss, Chris Powell. 'He came on the phone and said to me, "Congratulations!"' says Muirhead. 'I said, "What for?" And Chris said, "You've won the election. You've hit us on tax and we haven't responded properly. You've won and I'd like to take you for a very expensive meal to congratulate you." And he did, he took me to Alastair Little for dinner. And this was three months before the election!'

Saatchis continued to produce similarly impactful posters, doggedly clinging to the sole subject of taxation. 'Voters kept saying that they welcomed more spending on public services and that they'd happily pay a bit more tax for them,' says Muirhead. 'But our job was to show them what that would actually mean for their lives.' One poster featured the Labour manifesto, under the headline 'Oh no, another tax bill!' Lansley's research team dissected Labour policies on a daily basis and sent their analysis to the Saatchi & Saatchi bunker, where Sinclair's team would use it as ammo for the next attack ad. 'When Jeremy had to go away for a couple of days he left us with a motto which I had framed on the wall,' says Muirhead: '"Hold fast to the main idea. Do not give in to the pressures of the moment."'

Private polling from the research department found that increased taxes combined with the potential for inflation and higher mortgage rates were a major concern for thousands of families. Sinclair and the team at Saatchis developed the idea into a poster featuring two gigantic boxing gloves, one with the words 'More taxes' printed on it, the other with 'Higher prices'. The headline read: 'Labour's double whammy'. Much of the press reacted with derision at the peculiar phrase. But as the newspapers debated what exactly a double whammy was, the phrase – and its message – was repeated again and again, and the poster was featured on editorial pages repeatedly.

While Labour's campaign was continually praised for

its slickness and glamour, the news media bemoaned the Conservative campaign as one-note and unimaginative. But Chris Patten and his team remained determined. 'I'd learnt three things from the 1987 campaign,' he says. 'One was stick to your guns. Have a message and don't get knocked off course. The other was keep a tight relationship between prime minister and chairman, which we managed. And thirdly, don't believe anything you read in the papers.'

The party chairman was frustrated by the cynical response to his campaign in the press. 'My view was that they were punishing us for refusing to place ads with them,' he says. 'I thought press ads made no impact at all and were just a very good way of burning money. But I ended up running some ads with them in the final weeks just as an appeasement gesture.'

When Labour ran the Jennifer's ear broadcast two weeks before polling day, the Conservative team was ready for them. 'We knew that was their bid to move the debate away from tax and back onto their own territory,' says Lansley. 'But we'd also known for six months the truth about the case study because the little girl's grandfather was a Tory member and had tipped us off. What was interesting was that once the whole thing blew up in their face, Labour completely avoided health, even though it was their strongest issue. We couldn't believe it.'

Meanwhile, John Major was successfully presenting himself as a trustworthy man of the people. He toured the country, addressing crowds through a loudhailer while standing on a soapbox. 'The soapbox was his idea,' says Patten. 'He felt comfortable being himself in those sorts of situations.' But when it came to making broadcasts, he was less enthusiastic.

Saatchi & Saatchi hired Hollywood film director John Schlesinger (who had won an Oscar in 1969 for *Midnight Cowboy*, his film about a male prostitute in New York) to shoot a biographical documentary of Major. In it, Major was filmed returning to his the site of his old home in Brixton, south London, and reminiscing about his working-class youth, which underscored his humble background. 'He was uncomfortable talking about his childhood and playing on the "boy from Brixton" thing,' says Patten. 'He preferred being on his soapbox talking about issues.'

Nevertheless, the prime minister was cajoled into delivering a sincere and at times emotional performance by the film director. At one point, as they drive past his old family home, he jumps from his seat in excitement, exclaiming, 'It's still there!' 'I travelled around with him for a few days shooting the film with Schlesinger,' says Muirhead, 'and I got a sense of how honest and down to earth he was. When I turned up at Downing Street for a meeting on a Sunday night, he was very relaxed and said, "Do you want a beer?" I didn't know what to say. I said, "I don't know." And he said, "Well, I'm going to have a beer, so why don't you have a beer too?" He would put you at ease like that.'

On the road, Muirhead and the Saatchi team strove to freshen his much-mocked grey image. 'John [Schlesinger] had this extremely attractive Polish assistant,' says Muirhead. 'It was her job to get him into better clothes. None of us would have the balls to criticise the way the prime minister looked, so she'd produce these brand-new shirts we'd just bought from Thomas Pink and say, "Prime Minister, I think you'd look much better in something like this." Then they would both disappear upstairs and he would come down looking very presentable.'

Schlesinger's film was the most memorable of the entire campaign. But Patten was unsure about the money they had spent on it. 'It was a glossy film by a fashionable director that I thought was very good,' he says. 'But did it make a difference to the turnout or the result? I don't think it did. I think that sort of thing has an impact on the chattering classes and not much more. You waste about three weeks discussing what sort of jumper the prime minister should wear.'

Major was not always so obliging. When the Saatchi team proposed an election broadcast featuring an array of world leaders delivering eulogies to Major's leadership qualities, he refused to sanction it. 'He was a consistently fair guy,' says Shaun Woodward. 'And he said, "Look, we might not win. And if Kinnock's in Number 10 and they've all publicly supported me, that won't be good for the country." We were having breakfast at Downing Street, and Jeremy Sinclair said to him, "Forgive me, Prime Minister, but I wouldn't be doing my job if I didn't say that this was a very, very good idea and I think it would be something of a very, very big mistake if you don't do this." And Major said, "Yes, but I can't do it."'

As the campaign neared its conclusion, campaign funds began to run low. 'We had lost a brilliant fundraiser in Margaret Thatcher,' says Chris Patten. 'And we had much less of a financial advantage over Labour than we'd always enjoyed previously.' Woodward claims that the budget for the entire campaign was £5 million (the party had spent £3 million on press ads alone in the final week of the 1987 campaign). Such was the prolific output of Saatchi & Saatchi's creative team, Muirhead found himself with a surplus of

 posters, slogans and ads that they could not afford to run

in the final week of the campaign. He decided instead to take them to *Sun* editor Kelvin MacKenzie as a gift. 'I had a whole stack of fantastic advertising,' says Muirhead. 'I thought, "There's some brilliant headlines here, and some great ideas." So I go down to Kelvin's office in Wapping. I say, "Look, Kelvin, you can steal any of this you want." He went, "You fucking cunt, you've fucked up! Now I'm going to have to leave the country. You've messed up this campaign." I'm like, "What? What do you mean?" He said, "I've just got the latest opinion poll and you're behind in it! You're going to lose!"'

Despondent, Muirhead went back to the Saatchi campaign bunker and delivered the bad news to his team. They resolved that it was time for a final throw of the dice. 'We devised this thing called the tax calculator,' Muirhead says. 'You slid the marker along to whatever your salary was and it told you how much more tax you'd pay under Labour. Then we took a bunch of them down to a Labour press conference the next morning and handed them out to journalists. That gave them their story for the day.'

Right to the last, Patten, Muirhead, Sinclair, Woodward and Lansley refused to be swayed. When senior Conservatives urged them to broaden the campaign to make sure of victory, they stuck to their number-one issue. 'Our attitude was, "We will talk about tax, then we will talk about tax again and, once we're done, we'll talk about tax some more,"' says Woodward.

In the final week of the campaign almost every opinion poll predicted a hung parliament, with Labour receiving the majority of the votes. In the final forty-eight hours some polls suggested a slim Labour majority. In the event, the Conservatives received the most votes any political party has ever received in a UK general election, securing a majority of twenty-one seats in the House of Commons. Within a week Neil Kinnock had resigned as leader of the Labour Party. Many suggested that his hubris in the final stages of the campaign, and last-minute nerves on the part of floating voters, swayed the results. But in an exit poll conducted by Harris on voting day, only 21 per cent of voters said they had made their minds up in the last week and, of those, only 9 per cent had made their decision on the final day. In 1987 the figures were almost identical.

I still remember staying up to watch the results in 1992 and being astonished by the relative ease with which the Conservatives cruised to a seemingly impossible win. The press, the pundits and the average voter in the street had assumed Labour would ride to glory on the crest of a wave. In fact, it might have been only Patten, Woodward and the Saatchi team who remained confident that victory was in the bag for them all along.

Since 1979 every election result had been so clear-cut that it was very difficult to gauge the impact of advertising on either side. Might the Conservatives have won by a smaller margin had they not advertised in 1983 or 1987? Possibly, but they would have won either way. If any election campaign can ever stand as evidence of the positive impact of political advertising, it was that of the Tories in 1992. Not only were they behind in the polls prior to Saatchis being reappointed, they were struggling for a convincing strategy. The input of Sinclair, Muirhead and their team helped the party identify and execute a single-minded and determined attack that Labour was simply unable to cope with.

As Chris Patten puts it, 'There's quite a lot of pseudo-scientific babble about election campaigns. You have to find two or three simple arguments that are important to the electorate and then bash away at them until the public think they are their ideas. That's what Saatchi & Saatchi helped us do. Plus, they were good at keeping us on track. Politicians have a tendency to follow the issues and respond to whatever the story is that day. The Saatchi team had a discipline that stopped us from doing that.'

It was a high point for advertising in politics, but it also marked the end of an era. 1979 had seen the birth of modern political advertising, and the eighties had seen it flourish, with the Saatchis building the world's biggest ad agency on the back of their relationship with the Conservatives. The Labour Party had belatedly embraced a similar brand of flashy and fashionable advertising to underpin its campaigns. But although the two parties had thrown money and resources at their admen, neither was ever certain what difference it actually made at the polls. By the nineties a new generation of admen would often struggle to identify the powerful characteristics that separated one political party from another, and a new generation of image-conscious, controlling politicians would struggle to delegate the same amount of power to their admen as Thatcher and Kinnock had once done. The Conservatives had proved in 1992 that advertising might just help to win elections. Strangely, neither party would ever try the same trick again.

10

IT MUST BE WORKING

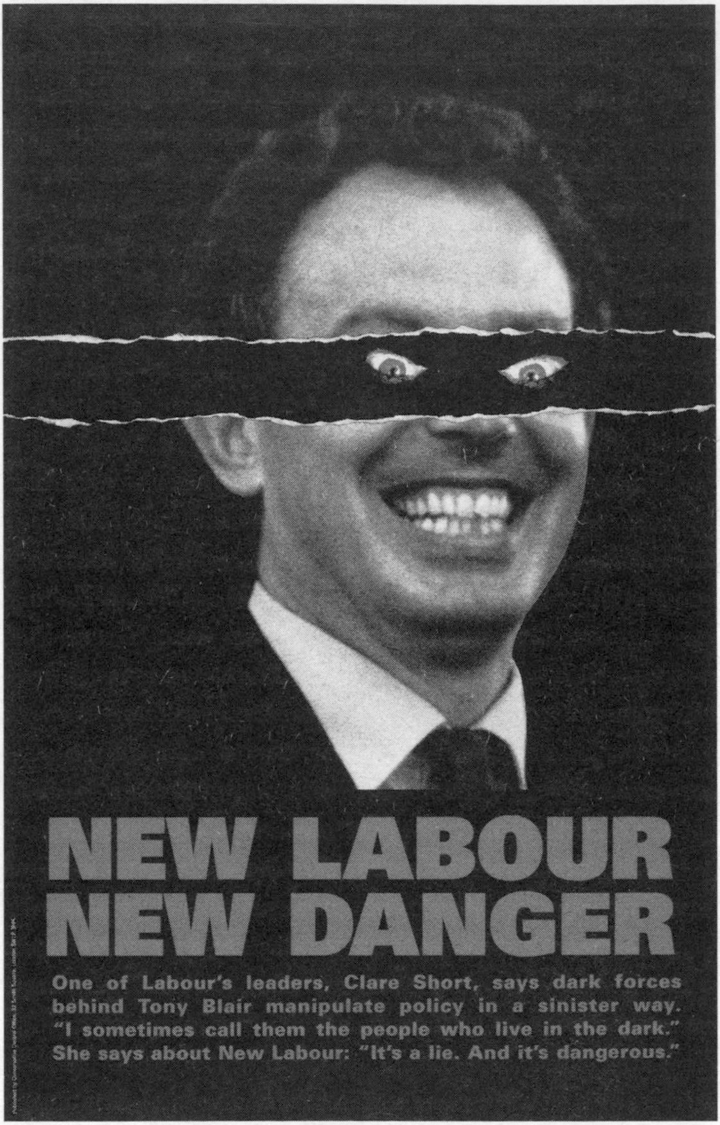
NEW LABOUR
NEW DANGER
One of Labour's leaders, Clare Short, says dark forces behind Tony Blair manipulate policy in a sinister way. "I sometimes call them the people who live in the dark." She says about New Labour: "It's a lie. And it's dangerous."

There's a joke about an old man in France who used to get up every morning at 5 a.m. and sprinkle white powder on the roads in his village. When asked what he was sprinkling, he told passers-by that it was elephant powder. 'But everybody knows there are no elephants around here,' they said. 'Well,' replied the old man, 'then it must be working.'

'That's what political advertising is,' says Chris Powell. 'Elephant powder.' Calm, considered and short on hype and hyperbole, the man who served as Labour's ad advisor across three decades was never completely sure that his industry had anything useful to offer to politics. 'Politicians use people like me because, you never know, the election could finish up close and it could be just that one seat that makes all the difference. So they might as well throw money at the advertising, just in case.'

So why did he bother doing all that work? During the entire period he worked for Labour, he ran one of the world's most successful advertising agencies, but Powell (whose older brother Charles was a foreign-policy advisor to Margaret Thatcher and whose younger brother Jonathan was Tony Blair's chief of staff at Number 10) was a conviction socialist who, through good times and bad, had stuck with the party he had supported all his life.

'I'm a Labour man. I always have been and always will be,' he says. 'I think the other lot are a bunch of people who just want to get their taxes down. They've got no more vision than to pay a little less tax. I think that Labour are the only ones with their heart in the right place and on the side of people who are struggling.'

Powell was never in it for the glory. He struggled throughout the eighties at the helm of the Shadow Communications Agency, fighting a noble but futile battle against a Conservative outfit who, as Powell describes it, always left his side 'feeling outgunned'. And then, after all those years of toil and frustration, and just as the party he loved overhauled their communications, renovated their policies and finally returned to government, he would walk away. But not before he had helped them across the finishing line in 1997.

The bitter battles of 1992 had informed both the main parties' attitudes towards advertising. The Conservatives had learnt that even the worst circumstances could sometimes be remedied by the right ad strategy, while Labour had successfully snatched defeat from the jaws of victory courtesy of an unfocused, inconsistent campaign that was riddled with mishaps; the twin fiascos of Jennifer's ear and the Sheffield rally were still vivid in the party's consciousness. 1992 was the year when communications had proved decisive.

There could be no mistakes this time. Tony Blair's Labour Party finally had the resources to match Tory spending and it was ready to hand a large chunk of that money to its admen. In 1987 the combined expenditure on ads had been just over £5 million; in 1992 it had been £6.5 million. In 1997 Labour and the Tories (together with the Referendum Party) spent £27 million between them, making it the most extravagant advertising campaign in British political history. The stakes had never been higher.

But the two parties would learn that just spending money on advertising wasn't always enough.

Maurice Saatchi was said to have advised John Major that his agency would help him spend his way to victory. But Labour's adman, Chris Powell, was about the only political campaigner in 1997 who was less than certain about the role advertising had to play. 'Going into that campaign, Labour had something like a 20–22 per cent lead in the polls,' he says. 'So what was the point of having any advertising at all? The answer is that there is none, actually.'

In the five years that separated the 1992 and 1997 elections, seismic changes had occurred in the fortunes, image and popularity of both the main political parties. In 1992 the Conservatives had received more votes than any other party in British electoral history as they won their fourth consecutive general election. They were beginning to look unbeatable and people were wondering whether the UK had become a one-party system: if Labour couldn't win while the Tories were overseeing one of the most severe and prolonged recessions of all time, then could they ever win? But less than six months after John Major's surprise victory, the Conservatives were trailing Labour by twenty points in most opinion polls.

On 16 September 1992 the UK had withdrawn from the European Exchange Rate Mechanism after failing to keep the pound above its agreed lower limit, and what became known as Black Wednesday would have a lasting impact on the government's credibility. Labour had led the Tories in the polls many times before, but now the polls were saying something new: that Labour – for so many years the party least trusted on tax or inflation – was considered to be more economically competent than the Tories. Opinion polls that reflect people's stated voted intentions can be misleading, but no party with a low rating on economic competence had ever won a UK general election. Finally, Labour was shedding its image of financial irresponsibility.

John Smith, Labour's new leader, provided a sober contrast to his predecessor, Neil Kinnock. An eloquent Scotsman and former solicitor, he had served both in James Callaghan's cabinet and as a high-profile shadow chancellor under Kinnock. His steady hand was considered by many to be enough to finally allow Labour to win power. But his attitude towards advertising and communications was far less enthusiastic than Kinnock's, and the men who had done so much to modernise Labour's campaign machine over the past ten years found themselves sidelined under Smith's regime.

'I can't tell what would've happened had John Smith remained leader in 1997,' says Peter Mandelson. 'All I know was that John Smith had a disdain for advertising, marketing people and focus groups and polling. His subtle view was that all the Labour Party needed to become electable was to change the face at the top. John thought the reason they didn't elect us in 1992 was because of Neil Kinnock's inability or strength to be a prime minister. He didn't believe in advertising; he thought the people would just make their mind up about him.'

Charles Clarke, who had overseen much of the modernisation of the party's communications under Neil Kinnock, was astonished by Smith's dismissive attitude. 'He hated Peter [Mandelson], who felt very outside of things at that time. As did Tony [Blair],' says Clarke. 'I felt that John was basically completely adherent to what we used to call the "one more heave" school of politics. He thought that if we just hung on in there for one more election, people would eventually say, "Okay, it's time to try the alternative." And I felt politics was much more contested than that.'

The progress made in the eighties seemed to be unravelling. Deborah Mattinson, Philip Gould's business partner and Labour's key focus group strategist from the Kinnock to the Brown eras, recounts in her book *Talking to a Brick Wall* a session she arranged with potential swing voters in Billericay, Essex. Smith had asked her to run the focus groups and went along to observe their discussions from behind a one-way mirror. These were the sort of men and women in key marginals who had voted Conservative in 1992 but whom Labour had to attract in order to win at the next election. Mattinson reports:

> There was short gap between the end of the first group and the start of the second . . . I popped next door to where John Smith and his team were watching to check if they had anything to add to the next discussion. The team looked worried and John was purse lipped, sitting back in his chair with his arms folded high on his chest.
>
> 'Who were those people?' he demanded.
>
> 'They were recruited as C1C2 swing voters to our usual spec . . .' I began.
>
> He cut across me. 'They were awful!' Spluttering with rage, he could hardly bring himself to voice the ultimate insult: 'They were all Tories!'

While Labour had accumulated a gigantic mid-term opinion-poll lead, concern was growing that Smith's rejection of the communications strategy Kinnock had spent ten years establishing would cost them dearly in an actual election campaign.

Meanwhile, Philip Gould, blamed by many traditional Labour figures for a 1992 campaign that had delivered more sizzle than substance, had retreated from the scene. He had travelled to Washington to observe Bill Clinton's campaign team at work. Clinton was in the process of trying to broaden his appeal to middle America by proving that a Democratic president could support aspiration, law and order, and economic prudence. Gould was enthused by the successful execution of a strategy that he had been proposing to Labour for many years. He reported back to Tony Blair, Gordon Brown and Peter Mandelson in London, and soon they also visited the Clinton campaign headquarters. Shadow home secretary Blair returned with a particular fixation on Clinton's attitude to crime. Rather than focus on the social roots of criminality, Blair now espoused a Clintonesque mantra of 'Tough on crime, tough on the causes of crime'.

On 12 May 1994 John Smith died suddenly of a heart attack. By late July Tony Blair had been elected the Labour Party's new leader. In his acceptance speech, he recorded a special note of thanks for a mysterious figure named 'Bobby'. Bobby was, in fact, Peter Mandelson, the man who had meticulously managed Blair's leadership campaign and was now clearly back at the heart of the party's campaign machine. Labour's advertising and communications strategy was about to be revived by the man who had invented it almost ten years earlier. Only this time he'd have a leader and a manifesto that he could actually sell.

John Major's government had experienced a series of disasters since its re-election. After Black Wednesday destroyed its reputation for economic competence, it was plagued by a series of scandals that gained the party a reputation for

 sleaze and undermined their marquee 'back to basics' pledge

to restore family values. Several cabinet ministers, including David Mellor and Tim Yeo, had extramarital affairs exposed in lurid detail by the tabloid press; chief secretary to the treasury Jonathan Aitken became embroiled in a damaging libel case with a newspaper; and a number of other prominent Tories, including Neil Hamilton, were caught up in a 'cash for questions' scandal involving Harrods owner Mohammed Al Fayed. The impression was that of a government that had become complacent and corrupt.

Labour, on the other hand, was finally able to present a fresh and convincing image to the voting public. John Smith had reduced the influence of powerful trade union bosses by introducing a 'one member, one vote' policy into the party's constitution in 1993, while one of Tony Blair's first acts as leader was to reword the party's Clause IV, which prescribed the renationalisation of all major industries. New Labour, as it was now called, claimed to embrace the free-market principles of Thatcherism, with Peter Mandelson later declaring that they were 'intensely relaxed about people getting filthy rich'. This was a party that was delivering on the aspirational, middle-class-friendly policies that Mandelson and Gould had been preaching since the mid-eighties.

But when a general election was announced by John Major on Monday 17 March 1997, both campaign teams faced a new problem: in the perception of the public, there was little difference between Labour and the Conservatives. Steve Hilton, who had been recruited by Saatchi & Saatchi after serving as their liaison at Conservative central office in 1992, would later note: 'We could not argue that Labour had not changed: this was not credible. We could not argue that while Tony Blair might have changed, the Labour

Party would revert to its old ways if elected. This was neither clear nor, we discovered in research, credible. And, most importantly, we could not argue that Labour were copying the Conservatives: this was no deterrent to voting Labour . . . this argument had the opposite effect, serving to confirm that it was safe to vote Labour.'

Saatchi & Saatchi had never found itself in such a position before. The Tories were drastically behind in the polls and there was no obvious angle from which to attack Labour with the agency's trusted 'Hit first, hit hard and keep on hitting' strategy.

'In previous elections we had always been able to base our work on facts,' says Jeremy Sinclair. 'We were able to say that every Conservative government had cut tax, every Conservative government had cut unemployment, every Conservative government had cut inflation. But that was no longer the case in 1997, after Black Wednesday. So, we had to go with a broader, less specific approach. "Labour might have changed, but they're still dangerous. Watch out."'

Sinclair devised a series of posters that would deliver the iconic image of the 1997 campaign. 'I had this idea of two demon eyes staring out of various everyday things to demonstrate the danger of New Labour in all areas of life,' he says. 'We had a pair of them staring out of a purse, under the headline "New Labour, new taxes". The plan was to alert people with these posters and then, in the final week of the campaign, apply them to Tony Blair in our final election broadcast. But midway through the campaign I had to go to America to do some teaching. While I was there someone at the agency got hold of some juicy quotes from some Labour people claiming that there was something "dark" about New Labour.'

In Sinclair's absence, his creative team back in London hurriedly pounced on the quotes from shadow cabinet spokesperson Clare Short and produced what became an infamous campaign poster. A pair of red, demonic eyes were placed over an image of Tony Blair's gleefully smiling face, above the headline 'New Labour, new danger'. Beneath that the copy ran: 'One of Labour's leaders, Clare Short, says dark forces behind Tony Blair manipulate policy in a sinister way. "I sometimes call them the people who live in the dark." She says about New Labour: "It's a lie. And it's dangerous."'

The big idea for a campaign crescendo was blown. But Sinclair understood that events had forced a departure from strategy. 'It made sense for them to do it, I suppose,' he says. 'They were cashing in on the comments. It got loads of attention and PR. But you have to admit it was one of the most famous and ineffective things we ever did.'

Nevertheless, the poster provoked the sort of controversy Saatchis always courted, and Labour was concerned enough to go on the attack. 'I was on holiday at the time and a few of us jumped onto a conference call,' says Alastair Campbell, Tony Blair's director of communications and strategy. 'I think it was Peter [Mandelson] who said, "We need to get hold of a bishop to speak out about this!" And a few hours later we had the Bishop of Oxford condemning it. The whole thing backfired for the Tories.'

Campbell had been a Fleet Street political editor with strong Labour connections. It was he who had sat off-camera and fired the questions at Neil Kinnock for Hugh Hudson's famous election broadcast in 1987. Blair had convinced him to leave journalism and act as his communications chief in 1994, but Campbell's role would quickly transcend press relations. 'Tony [Blair] had no big interest in visual and design things but he was wise enough to delegate that sort of stuff to myself, Peter [Mandelson] and Philip [Gould],' says Campbell. 'But Chris Powell will tell you, we were the clients from hell.'

The Shadow Communications Agency no longer existed and Boase Massimi Pollitt, Powell's agency, now officially held the Labour Party account. But Powell was beginning to regret it. 'In the past, we had been the experts telling them how they should advertise,' he says. 'In 1987 we could have done whatever we liked, to be honest. But by '97 they considered themselves the experts and were telling us what to do. Mandelson and Campbell became quite frustrating.'

Labour had always been unwilling to hand over control of its communications to an agency. And while Powell no longer had to jump through hoops in committee meetings at Labour HQ, he was dealing with campaign chiefs who were determined to avoid the mistakes of the past. In 1992 Labour had failed to co-ordinate its messages on health and taxation. Campbell had arrived to remedy such problems. 'We were control freaks,' he says. 'That's why we never entrusted BMP to play a wider role in the campaign. We were so paranoid that we wouldn't get the message right. For two years we had been running ads designed to reassure people that we had changed and that we weren't about to squander their money.'

Party research suggested that while Labour enjoyed a substantial lead in the polls, 70 per cent of switchers – those who had previously voted Tory but were suggesting they would now vote Labour – were unreliable. In other words, they admitted that they might still be persuaded to vote Tory at the last minute. Powell suggested that the most reliable way of retaining their votes was to constantly remind them of the Conservatives' broken promises. 'A lot of the swing voters in marginal seats were closer to the Conservatives in most of their beliefs,' he says. 'But they were angry at Major for increasing taxes, which is the cardinal sin for a Conservative prime minister. We decided the best strategy was to attack him personally.'

After years of combat with Saatchis, Powell and his team at BMP were learning the power of negative advertising. They devised a poster portraying John Major with two faces, pointing in opposite directions. One pledged to cut tax, while the other announced twenty-two tax rises since 1992. Conservative dishonesty and economic incompetence emerged as Labour's key themes in early 1997. 'People were feeling worse off but didn't understand how the government were responsible for that,' says Powell. 'We decided that we could re-educate the public about taxation and explain how the government had burdened them with indirect taxes like VAT.'

The theme became 'Twenty-two tax rises since 1992'. It was a simple, factually correct line that reminded former Tory voters why they had decided to switch in the first place. BMP was warming to a decidedly Saatchi brand of attack ads. One poster depicted John Major and his chancellor, Ken Clarke, as Laurel and Hardy; a headline ran: 'Britain has dropped to twenty-first in the world prosperity league. Another fine mess.' Next came a parody of the *Mr Men* children's books, in which government ministers were portrayed as cartoon characters and given unkind monikers. John Major was 'Mr Feeble'. 'We were very pleased with those ads but they were banned because of copyright issues,' says Powell. 'But Alastair did a clever thing and leaked the fact that they'd been banned. The press ended up running them on their editorial pages.'

Campbell embraced BMP's combative approach initially. 'The public always say that they don't like negative ads, but I suspected they had a greater impact,' he says. 'Tony [Blair] was always a bit queasy about using those sort of tactics. But I used to tell him, "Don't think that by being more positive you're going to stop them from trying to kill you."'

The Conservative campaign team was struggling to find an effective response. While some senior figures felt they should deny that Labour had really changed, Saatchis deemed it wiser to attack New Labour on the basis of their new image. As Jeremy Sinclair put it, 'We were out to convince people that New Labour were as dangerous as Old Labour.'

The Conservatives set out to convince the public that the word 'new' stood for risky, experimental and dangerous, not fresh and innovative. As Steve Hilton noted: 'Labour's version of "new" was winning. This could either have been because the electorate simply didn't believe what we were saying or that they believed it but didn't care. Our research suggested that it was the latter.'

Tony Blair became the embodiment of New Labour. BMP commissioned a film from Ridley Scott Associates, a company that had found fame producing everything from the cobbled-street, nostalgia-drenched seventies commercials for Hovis bread to blockbusting Hollywood sci-fi movies such as *Alien* and *Blade Runner*. For Labour, they would spend hours shooting a bulldog called Fritz as a means of demonstrating the renewal of British pride. The dog was depicted in black and white, shuffling through the gutter looking downtrodden and tired, before transforming into colour and trotting triumphantly through the streets to the accompaniment of Tony Blair's rousing speech on his new vision for Britain: 'The Tories say Britain's good enough. We say Britain can be better!' the leader declared.

Powell took the completed film to Labour's Millbank HQ and presented it to Campbell and Mandelson. 'Mandelson objected to the bulldog's bollocks,' says Powell. 'He found the sight of them offensive. Especially while Blair's voice provided the soundtrack. He was probably right, so we removed them in post-production.'

Next came a more low-key broadcast. 'There was a concern that he [Blair] was a bit style over substance,' says Powell. 'So we thought it was very important for voters to get to know him. John Webster suggested we make something in a very raw documentary style that got rid of all the gloss.'

John Webster was BMP's creative chief. He had made his name as Britain's top ad creative by devising campaigns that were populist, funny and warm. What he'd done for Sugar Puffs with the Honey Monster and Hofmeister with George the Bear he now sought to do for Labour with Tony Blair. But rather than contrive a documentary style, he wanted the real thing: a warts-and-all film that captured Blair in authentic fly-on-the-wall style. 'We went to speak about the idea with [the director] Richard Eyre, who was at the National Theatre at the time,' says Powell. 'He told us, "You should really use Molly Dineen for this," and we immediately agreed.'

Dineen was a thirty-eight-year-old BAFTA award-winning documentary maker who had won acclaim for *Home from the Hill*, her film about retired soldier Colonel

Hilary Hook. She was renowned for her human touch and ability to get under the skin of her subjects. Powell and Webster commissioned her to shadow Blair over a period of months, during which she chatted with him on a variety of subjects in a series of unguarded moments.

The film's look was almost wilfully low-fi – the perfect riposte to widespread accusations that Blair was a leader surrounded by spin and artful choreography. It opened with the Labour leader in the back of a car, telling Dineen (who sat off-camera) that while growing up he wanted to be 'anything but a politician'. He spoke of his childhood ambition to be a professional footballer for Newcastle United. Footage showed him playing football with kids in a park, every bit the young, thrusting and down-to-earth leader. But the key moments were inside the Blair family home in Islington.

'Like all leaders, he was reluctant about giving access to his home and family,' says Powell. 'But John [Webster] really thought it was key for people to feel like they knew him and his family. And Molly managed to get about twenty minutes of him having dinner with Cherie and the kids that were the crucial moments of the film.'

In 1979, when Saatchi & Saatchi had first attempted to apply a modern ad style to political broadcasts, they had to find ways of minimising the amount of time politicians spent on camera. They were stuffy and formal, uncomfortable in front of the lens and incapable of speaking without a script. Blair was a whole new breed of politician. With an ordinary, modest-looking kitchen as his backdrop, he riffed casually with Dineen about his relationship with his dad, the evolution of his political values and his life as a father. He was relaxed, thoughtful and seemingly sincere.

'Homework!' he said, glancing over his son's shoulder at the kitchen table. 'You'll have more of that under Labour. Just you wait until [education secretary] David Blunkett gets hold of you!'

Blair had an effortlessly relaxed manner; his language was informal and bright, and it all seemed underpinned by a genuine conviction. His laid-back style would become a Blair cliché – the subject of much parody in the years that followed. But at the time his performance was a revelation.

Dineen had taken forty hours of raw footage and edited it into a ten-minute film that portrayed a new type of leader who combined seriousness with warmth, intelligence with humour. Philip Gould wrote in his memoir: 'Its honest, glitz-free, fly-on-the-wall approach broke through the scepticism of the electorate, at a time when they were fed up with the whole campaign, making it probably our most effective broadcast.'

For Chris Powell, it was a campaign turning point. 'Those who had become Labour-inclined but still weren't sure if they could actually vote Labour suddenly felt really good about Tony Blair. It firmed up their votes for us. It was crucial,' he says.

Powell was convinced that broadcasts had more power than politicians acknowledged. 'I don't think [politicians] really like doing them and they think that posters and press ads have more impact,' he says. 'The money spent on posters dwarfs that spent on broadcasts. But our analysis showed that the big moments, where people really decided who they were going to vote for, followed the broadcasts.'

With the election approaching and Labour maintaining its lead in the polls, the campaign team grew in confidence.

In an un-Labour-like show of largesse, Powell suggested that their 'Twenty-two Tory tax rises' poster be displayed across the iconic electronic billboard in Piccadilly Circus. The press had become more reluctant to give coverage to poster launches, but when Labour unveiled their Piccadilly stunt the London *Evening Standard* splashed it across two pages. 'Doing big-scale advertising like that really sends out a message to the public that Labour are getting their act together,' says Alastair Campbell. 'And it impresses the rest of the media too.'

But soon the sentiment of Labour's ads began to change. 'My feeling was always that the public claimed not to like negative advertising but that they actually absorbed it,' says Campbell. 'We'd been attacking the Tories on tax and sleaze for a long time and it got to the stage where we wanted to start telling people what we could actually offer.'

Powell was less convinced about the change of direction, having seen the success that the Conservatives had enjoyed in 1992 with their relentless attacks on Labour tax plans. But in Campbell, Gould and Mandelson, Labour had a trio of formidable communication chiefs who were not easily swayed. 'Peter and Philip and I were almost always in agreement, and it was hard for Chris Powell and his team to convince us of things,' says Campbell. 'Chris knows about politics, and we were a nightmare for him at times. Plus, there was Gordon Brown, John Prescott and numerous others wanting to have a say on everything too. I think BMP must have been thinking, "Who are we supposed to listen to here?"'

Campbell took matters into his own hands, teaming up with BMP creative Pete Gately to produce a series of colourful campaign posters that splashed the succinct headline 'New Labour. New Britain'. Campbell and Mandelson loved the bright positivity. 'They made a promise of a bright new future which I think tapped into a national mood,' says Campbell. The line was later changed to 'Britain deserves better'. According to Gould's memoir, adman Gately objected to the alteration, claiming that the negative sentiment clashed with the bright aesthetic, and quit. 'I didn't want to be clever, I wanted to win,' wrote Gould.

Campbell had become immersed in the ad campaign and was determined to force through his own vision. 'I became obsessed with launching the posters in a field,' he says. 'I called it my "Field of Dreams". I thought it set the tone of optimism that we wanted to capture at the end of the campaign. I think everyone around me was thinking, "What the fuck is he on about now?"'

On Easter Monday 1997 Tony Blair stood before a gigantic, brightly coloured billboard poster in a field in Kent. He delivered a speech and referenced the poster's headline: 'Britain deserves better'. A formerly hostile press was impressed. Even its most pessimistic members could see that the finishing line was in sight.

The Conservative Party knew it too. 'The truth is, Blair was always going to win the election from the start,' reflects Jeremy Sinclair. 'We struggled to find an angle of attack. But on top of that, the [Conservative] party itself had internal problems. I told John Major after the result, "Everyone did everything they could to hand Blair victory."'

The all-important relationship between Tory central office, Number 10 and M&C Saatchi, the breakaway agency formed by Charles and Maurice in 1995, was never as strong as it had been in 1992. Meanwhile, scandal and conflict had beset the campaign's efforts at every turn. As Steve Hilton wrote after the result: 'When unplanned events come to dominate, political advertising struggles to be heard. So our advertising messages, powerful though we believed them to be, were often simply drowned out by the daily diet of sometimes real, sometimes invented – but always exaggerated – splits, rows and gaffes. I cannot recall more than one or two periods with consecutive days of respite.'

On 1 May 1997 Labour won a landslide victory, gaining a majority of 179 parliamentary seats, the largest in their history. On the BBC's election-night programme, Professor Anthony King described the result of the exit poll, which accurately predicted a Labour landslide, as being akin to 'an asteroid hitting the planet and destroying practically all life on Earth'.

After years of trying, the party had finally convinced the British public that it was ready to govern. It had changed, the leader had changed, the policies had changed and even the name had changed. Campbell and Blair had successfully won over the most influential newspapers and had ensured that their messages were given a fair hearing. But their obsession with control had meant that Chris Powell and his team at BMP had found it difficult to effect their strategy and exert their influence the way they had in previous campaigns. 'There was conflict with the agency at times,' says Campbell. 'We sort of made them fly in the face of received wisdom, which was to keep bashing the enemy right to the end. We took a big risk by deciding to go with a positive line.'

In the final analysis, it probably didn't matter. 'Most

elections are decided by economics,' says Powell. 'The moment the Conservatives started raising taxes they lost their credibility, and their own people decided to punish them. They found Tony Blair acceptable. But our research showed the people who switched to Labour still had views on most issues that were closer to the Tories.'

The truth was that the public were tired after eighteen years of Conservative government and had finally found a Labour leader they could bring themselves to vote for. But Blair's inner circle, often vilified for their preoccupation with marketing techniques, had actually curbed the influence of the admen. Chris Powell, who had begun working for the party in the seventies and provided counsel throughout the subsequent two decades, would never work with the party again. 'There were a lot of opinionated Young Turks in the party by then who had no time for our opinions or experience,' he says.

The end of his relationship with the party came in the early hours of 2 May 1997 at the Royal Festival Hall in London, where Tony Blair stood before the celebrating Labour ranks and announced: 'A new era has dawned, has it not?' Powell allowed himself just a small smile of satisfaction. 'I felt peripheral – because I was,' he says. 'I was always quite aware that our contribution was very slight. But by 1997 it was thought by the party to be even slighter than it actually was.'

11

FUCK OFF AND COVER SOMETHING IMPORTANT

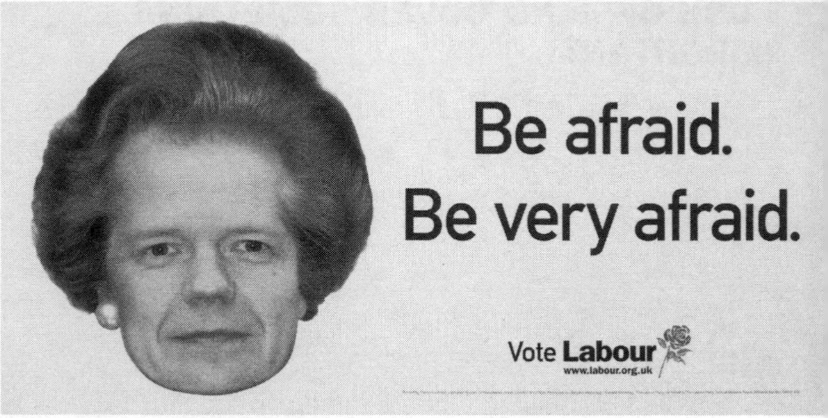
Be afraid.
Be very afraid.
Vote Labour
www.labour.org.uk

Such was the scale of Tony Blair's victory in 1997 that Labour had effectively won two elections in one. Their majority was so huge that the Conservatives would have to achieve the most extravagant swing in electoral history to seize power the next time around. Even moderate Tory gains in consecutive votes would not be enough for them to reclaim power. For that reason, the noughties saw two elections in which the tensions and jeopardy of old had disappeared. Slick young men in suits striving to replicate the Blair magic dominated a new political world. Politics, elections and campaigns got a bit boring.

The golden age of the eighties, with its hellzapoppin election campaigns run by hare-brained admen and gnarly old political operators, was gone. Like so many parts of life in the twenty-first century, politics became more professional. And professional, of course, is just another word for dreary. Certainly, there seemed less fire among the political elite, and it was increasingly difficult to tell any of them apart.

Norman Tebbit had talked passionately about this when I'd gone to see him at the start of my research. It sounded a bit like the grumpy moaning of an old man insisting that the new generation was inferior to his own. Now, on reflection, I realised Norman had a point. Here's some of his rant:

'When I first entered the House of Commons, I'd look across the lobby and see Labour MPs who had come through the TUC, having started out as kids on the shop floor. The Tories were the same. There were people with experience and character. Now all the top politicians on both sides have gone straight from university to a research job in Westminster before getting their seat. They went straight into politics. The consequences are that they don't perceive much of what's going on in the rest of the world.'

'Some of these ministers these days don't talk to their civil servants. They get their special advisor to talk for them. And then they come to me and say, "It's dreadful, my officials won't do what I want!" And I say, "What do you think it was like for me?"'

'When I went into the Department of Employment in 1981, they thought they were sponsored by the TUC! On my first day in charge I got some boys around my desk and said, "Right, first things first – what's happened to the bust of [former Labour Party employment minister] Ernie Bevan? I remember it used to be on the mantelpiece in the ministerial office." And they said, "Oh, we put that down in the basement. We didn't think you'd want it around." And I said, "Why ever not? Look, you have to understand that Ernie Bevin was the greatest minister of labour that this country has ever seen. Go back and read the history of what happened to the labour force during the Second World War. The man was a genius! So put the bust back up today!"'

After being severely injured in the 1984 Brighton bombing, Tebbit spent three months running the Department of Trade and Industry from his hospital bed. Following the successful privatisation of British Telecom, he decided to sneak out of hospital to make a surprise appearance at the celebratory party being held at his office. 'I walked in and said, "So this is what you buggers get up to when I'm away!" he says. 'There were two civil servants, who I happened to know were Labour supporters, who thought privatisation was a terrible idea. I went up to them and said, "Why are you two celebrating? You were against the whole bloody idea!" And they said, "That's right, but people said we couldn't do it. But we did it and we did it bloody well!" I'd hope that would be the ethos under a Labour government too. But you've got to get your officials on side. You have to understand them.'

All of which makes a lot of sense. Tebbit paints a picture of a time when politics was perhaps slightly less about point scoring and more about efficiency and national interest. A time when politicians were rugged, personable and a bit unpredictable. He might have seemed like a heartless, scary bastard back in the old days, but I was beginning to think that Tebbit was, in fact, the embodiment of a more exciting and captivating bygone era.

But then he said this: 'One last comment: gay marriage.'

I hunkered down in my armchair, all ears.

'Whether you're in favour or not, the government discussed it for twenty minutes on the morning of its announcement. They'd done no work on it beforehand. I said to a minister I know, "Have you thought this through? Because you're doing the law of succession too. When we have a queen who is a lesbian and she marries another lady and then decides she would like to have a child and someone donates sperm and she gives birth to a child, is that child heir to the throne?"'

I didn't know what to say, so I just nodded, and eventually he continued. 'It's like one of my colleagues said

– we've got to make these same-sex marriages available to all. It would lift my worries about inheritance tax because maybe I'd be allowed to marry my son. Why not? Why shouldn't a mother marry her daughter? Why shouldn't two elderly sisters living together marry each other?' There was a brief pause, and then Tebbit leaned forward and grinned. 'I quite fancy my brother!'

So, yes, Tebbit still is a bit strange and terrifying after all. Nevertheless, he illustrates an important point: a decidedly blander breed of politician has replaced the fire and know-how of his generation. Could it be that the growing influence of admen, spin doctors and pollsters nurtured this modern creed of overcautious, on-message political clones? Certainly, the high-profile influence of Alastair Campbell, Peter Mandelson and Philip Gould over New Labour's transformation had sent out the message that image and communication were the key to success. The admen – who from time to time had not just lent a bit of colour to election campaigns but had managed to actually influence them too – were reduced to bit-part players. Mandelson had once been so desperate for help that he 'was ready to embrace anything or anyone who came to me with an idea'. But as Chris Powell had found to his frustration in 1997, Mandelson was no longer so willing to take advice. He and Campbell saw themselves as the gatekeepers of the party message. Successive Tory leaders would surround themselves with spin doctors who assumed a similar approach to their work. The days when Margaret Thatcher or Neil Kinnock would simply put their faith in the admen had long gone.

Going into the 2001 general election, Labour enjoyed such a comfortable lead over their rivals that they could well have taken a similar approach to that suggested by Tim Bell in 1987, when, he said, the Conservatives were so nailed on to win that they could have put a poster up in Piccadilly Circus saying 'Fuck off' and still triumphed.

Tony Blair had shifted New Labour so far into the centre ground of politics that voters would increasingly complain that there was little difference between the two main political parties. Neil Kinnock was never likely to be mistaken for a Tory, just as Margaret Thatcher could never have been confused with a socialist. But the noughties generation often seemed interchangeable in the eyes of the British public.

None of this necessarily meant that the new generation were worse at their jobs. All it meant was that they were a less colourful, less distinctive product for the admen to sell. One of the godfathers of modern British advertising, David Abbott, had once told me his key rule of modern creative advertising: 'Find something relevant to say about your product and say it in a way that can't be missed.' That was becoming increasingly hard to do.

Even in the darkest and most hopeless time in Labour's history, when they had entered the 1983 general election campaign like dead men walking, their admen had at least found something unique and engaging to say about them. Michael Foot's Labour Party was radical; it offered a genuine antithesis to the government it sought to depose. It might have been an unelectable shambles, but at least the admen had something unusual to work with.

The ad industry had changed since then too. The type of political advertising that the Saatchis had pioneered in 1979 was born out of a creative revolution that had taken place during the sixties and seventies, when the emphasis on instinctive ideas had elevated maverick admen like Charles Saatchi to the top of the industry. It was a brief moment in which creative types called the shots and clients felt privileged to have them on their side. But by the end of the century the British ad industry had grown so big that corporate boards and faceless shareholders, not renegade ideas men, ran its agencies. An increasing number of firms fought each other over the same number of clients. Gone were the days when privately owned companies could defy clients, ignore research and produce ideas based purely on instinct. Even the Saatchis themselves had been removed from their own agency in 1995 by disgruntled shareholders.

The ad industry had become businesslike. Clients demanded ads that could transcend borders, airing in Sweden, New Zealand and India as easily as in the UK and US. The witty scripts and sophisticated cinematography that had been the trademark of British advertising in the past were replaced by cross-border ads that were devoid of dialogue but rich in pop soundtracks and fast-paced imagery. The mavericks who had built the industry began to leave (Charles Saatchi had, by this stage, devoted himself to his art collection and played only a minor role at M&C Saatchi). British advertising had become so obsessed with respectability that it had ceased to attract the sort of cavalier figures who had built it in the first place.

But there was still the odd one. Trevor Beattie was born into a working-class family in Birmingham. The son of a car mechanic, he was the first of eight siblings to enter higher education, studying graphic design and photography at Wolverhampton University. When he entered the world of London advertising, he didn't fit the slick-suited stereotype:

with his mess of curly hair, he was the scruff-bag outsider in an industry that became dominated by yuppies in the eighties. He was also a lifelong Labour supporter and a conviction socialist. 'I was brought to politics by Margaret Thatcher. I watched the injustice of the miners' strike when I was a kid and it politicised me,' he says. 'When I hear people on radio phone-ins the day before an election saying that they haven't made their minds up who to vote for yet and that they have to work out whose policies will be best for them, I always think, "What about what's best for the country, you selfish bastard?"'

Beattie's political instincts were more tribal and confrontational than those of his predecessors in the Shadow Communications Agency. 'You know when someone leaves a polling station and they get asked who they voted for?' he says. 'The ones who say "Oh, that's between me and the ballot box" are the Tories. But if a Labour voter gets asked, they'll always proudly say they voted Labour. In fact, I always answer, "I voted Labour because I believe in a better Britain."'

Beattie was working in a small advertising agency called Ayer Barker in the mid-eighties, where he was one of the few openly left-wing employees. 'They all told me that they were on my side but they wouldn't admit to voting Labour because there was such a big stigma in those days.' But he would soon meet a genuine ally. 'I was in the pub after work one night, a bit pissed, ranting about Thatcher, and people were saying, "Please, Trev, not politics again." But as I left Deborah Mattinson came over and said, "There's some people you need to meet."'

Mattinson was a planner at the same agency and an active Labour campaigner in her spare time. Together with

Philip Gould, she was beginning to introduce Labour to the sort of modern research practices that were common in advertising. The SCA was in its infancy and Mattinson was keen to involve Beattie. 'We felt like the French Resistance, having covert meetings in the agency,' says Beattie. 'The bosses knew and didn't approve. But we were passionate about it.'

He was first used in a 1986 by-election in Fulham, south-west London. Mattinson asked him to spend a weekend devising a poster campaign for the Labour candidate, Nick Raynsford. 'I told her I was busy and could only spend a day thinking about it,' says Beattie. 'She told me she'd rather have a day of me thinking than a week of anyone else. I was very flattered. She had me then.'

Beattie quickly established that Raynsford was resident in Fulham, whereas the Conservative candidate had been parachuted in from elsewhere. He mocked up a simple poster that read: 'Nick Raynsford lives here'. 'People stuck it in their windows and it was quite funny,' says Beattie. 'It was like an "I am Spartacus" moment.'

Raynsford won the seat and Beattie was in demand. Next, Mandelson and Gould asked him to devise the campaign for their 'Freedom and Fairness' policy document later that year. They briefed him to create something that Gould hoped would be revolutionary in political advertising. As he wrote in his memoirs: 'I demanded a campaign that was bright, modern and distinctive, a consumer not a political campaign, using normal consumer language and not political terms. I wanted language that would be heard and understood in southern suburbs, with a visual identity that was so different it stunned people.'

Beattie rose to the challenge. 'That was the real turning

point for Labour advertising, when Philip [Gould] started giving out proper briefs,' he says. 'He was a planner so he knew what sort of information I needed in order to come up with ideas. He introduced that professionalism to it.'

Beattie took the line 'Labour, Putting People First' and emblazoned it on distinctive metal badges in black, grey and silver. It was edgy and modern, completely different to the usual stickers and pamphlets that made up Labour's campaign materials. In his memoir, Gould recalls a lukewarm reception to the badges when Mandelson and Beattie presented them to the shadow cabinet. 'Are you sure this is what we're looking for, given that it's so harsh and dark?' asked shadow minister Harriet Harman. 'Well, yes, it's ballsy, and that's why it's going to work,' replied Beattie. 'There was a drawing in of breath at the word "ballsy",' recounts Gould.

'The traditionalists in the party had a hostility towards ad people,' says Beattie. 'They thought it was the stockbroker class trying to hijack their party. But they could see I wasn't like that. Peter [Mandelson] invited me to a conference one year to talk to delegates. He said they'd like me more once they met me. So I gave this talk in which I explained that ad slogans weren't a threat to the party's values. They were just ways of communicating to ordinary people. "Coal not dole", "V for Victory", "The lady's not for turning": none of those were created by admen. But they were slogans that had a big impact on people. They seemed won over. I was scruffy, working-class, not like the impression they had of advertising people.'

Beattie continued to work with the SCA throughout the eighties and nineties while his own career began to skyrocket. In 1994 he created the iconic 'Hello boys' billboard campaign for Wonderbra, featuring the prominent cleavage of supermodel Eva Herzigova. Later, he delivered a similarly eye-catching campaign for French Connection, by introducing their 'FCUK' branding. His work helped earn him a reputation as an advertising bad boy: he created simple, striking and brazen ads, often infused with the sort of cheeky laddishness that dominated nineties culture. He was one of the few admen since the Saatchi brothers to develop a profile that transcended the narrow confines of the industry. In short, he was New Labour's perfect adman.

When Labour asked TBWA to take on its 2001 election campaign, Beattie, now the agency's chairman, described it as 'the call I had been waiting for all my life'.

Labour went into the election campaign with a consistent poll lead of almost 20 per cent. But Tony Blair and Alastair Campbell remained cautious, not least about the potential for apathy among their core support. 'We were flying to an event in a helicopter midway through the campaign,' says Campbell. 'And Tony was looking out of the window at all the houses, saying, "What are they thinking?"' Campbell's own interest in the party's advertising had grown. He and Blair would take diversions during car journeys in order to seek out Labour posters, just to boost their morale. 'I came back from holiday at the start of 2001 and kept seeing Conservative posters everywhere on the drive from the airport,' he says. 'I was spooked. I didn't see a single Labour one. I thought, "Something's not right here." What the agency did was get one of ours put up on a billboard at the end of my road to make sure I arrived at work in a good mood every morning.'

Beattie adopted the same approach that the Saatchis had

started out with in 1979: to apply the exact same creative principles to his political ads as he would to his commercial ones. But his style was even more bold and brash than the Saatchis'. He and Campbell clicked immediately. 'What was great about Trevor was that he'd just come up with ideas and do them without bothering us with the thought process,' says Campbell. 'Most admen do a long explanation of their ideas before actually presenting them. But with top-level politicians it's a waste of time. They can understand the thought process very quickly and don't need all the preamble.'

TBWA's election broadcasts were quintessentially New Labour. One celebrated the achievements of New Labour's first term by featuring a series of images of smiling schoolchildren and nurses, set to the strains of 'Lifted' by inoffensive nineties pop act the Lighthouse Family. Next came another rose-tinted vignette of New Labour's Jerusalem, featuring peculiar cameos from Spice Girl Geri Halliwell and cricket umpire Dickie Bird. It was in keeping with New Labour's fixation with celebrity and pop culture: Blair had thrown an infamous party at Number 10 shortly after his 1997 victory, attended by the great and the good of Cool Britannia. Finally, they produced a disaster-movie pastiche featuring terrified voters running scared from Tory economic policies.

In the spring of 2001 Beattie opened a desk drawer in his office at TBWA and produced a mocked-up poster of Conservative leader William Hague wearing Margaret Thatcher's hairstyle. The headline read: 'Vote on Thursday or this gets back in'. Campbell loved the idea but knew that Blair might find it too flippant.

Beattie was invited to Downing Street to present the

poster to the prime minister. 'It was probably the single greatest moment of my career,' says Beattie. 'I'm stood in the prime minister's office, he's flanked by Gould, Mandelson and Campbell, and I've got this poster out of William Hague in a wig. And I've gone, "Right, Tony, this will be the most iconic image of the year."'

Blair frowned and said, 'Oh no, no, no.' Then he laughed.

'I said, "You've just shown why it works,"' says Campbell. 'Because if it's funny, it's fine. People look at it and smile, but it makes a really powerful negative point.' However, the party baulked at the use of the word 'this' in the headline in reference to Hague. It was eventually changed to the rather more cryptic but much funnier 'Be afraid. Be very afraid'.

The Conservative Party was still to recover from the crushing defeat of 1997. Many senior front-bench MPs had lost their seats and the shadow cabinet lacked the nous that had helped guide the party through previous election campaigns. New leader William Hague had been plagued by a series of PR gaffes, allowing himself to be photographed looking gormless on a waterslide with his fiancée and, later, making an uncomfortable-looking appearance in a baseball cap at London's Notting Hill Carnival. Labour's shift to the centre ground had encouraged Hague to take his party further to the right, a move that pleased core supporters but did little to win over floating voters. In keeping with the 'new-broom' policy, the party also employed a brand-new advertising agency. For the first time in over twenty years, the Conservatives would fight a campaign without the Saatchis by their side.

In May 2000 Tory chairman Michael Ancram revealed

the identity of the party's new admen: 'More than twenty years ago a hungry young agency helped Margaret Thatcher to power and became a household name overnight,' he told the press. 'I believe that Yellow M has the drive, talent and nerve to become the Saatchi & Saatchi of the twenty-first century.'

But who were Yellow M? Few in the ad business had heard of them. Based in Edinburgh, hundreds of miles from advertising's heartland, they were only two years old and their existing client list comprised the likes of Strathclyde Passenger Transport and Dunfermline Building Society. The contrast with the Saatchis could not have been any greater. A spokesperson for Conservative central office claimed that the appointment symbolised William Hague's 'determination to break out of the political and media hot-house of London'.

The agency had caught the party's attention the year before, when it had produced the ad campaign for the Scottish Conservatives in the inaugural elections for the new Scottish parliament. Scotland was traditionally dominated by Labour and the Scottish Nationalist Party, and at the time the Conservatives held no Scottish seats at Westminster. But Yellow M proved itself more than capable of handling the role of plucky underdog. Its eye-catching work included a portrayal of Donald Dewar, leader of the Scottish Labour Party, as Tony Blair's puppet. Other posters included Gordon Brown holding a petrol pump like a shotgun, with the headline 'Labour's highway robbery'. Most memorable of all was its conception of the term 'BLIAR', which it printed on stickers for students protesting against the prime minister's tuition-fees U-turn. The Scottish Tories wound up winning a remarkable eighteen seats in a country where they had never enjoyed electoral success of any sort.

'We were small, ambitious, hungry and straight-talking,' says Ronnie Duncan, the Yellow M executive who handled the account. 'William Hague knew they were going into the 2001 election as underdogs and had seen what we could do in a situation like that. We had a reputation for shaking things up.'

They were invited to pitch their ideas to Hague, his chief of staff Sebastian Coe and party chairman Michael Ancram. 'We went to meet them at the Hilton Hotel at Edinburgh airport,' says David Isaac, Yellow M's creative director. 'We were in our early thirties and had only started the agency two years previously. We couldn't believe we were sat there eating chips with Seb Coe.'

To their own surprise they were quickly handed the account, beating two major London agencies that had also pitched for the business. Their appointment astonished the wider ad industry. Advertising magazine *The Drum* pointed out: 'There are bigger accounts out there but in prestige terms [the Conservative Party] is the biggest.' 'I'm not sure why they chose us,' says Isaac. 'They were a bit of a toxic brand at the time so maybe some agencies wanted to stay away. But we were brash and ambitious, which is what they needed in that campaign.'

The party hierarchy were extremely clear about what they wanted from their new agency. 'I'd heard the Saatchis had been heavily involved in the whole electoral strategy,' says Ronnie Duncan. 'But what Hague's team wanted was simply a creative agency to provide their ads. They were less interested in us telling them what to do, just showing them how to do it. Which was something we were fine with.'

Unlike the Saatchis, Yellow M's team had no personal affiliations with the party. 'My partner, Kevin, was an ex-striking miner from Newcastle,' says Isaac. 'Initially, he'd said, "There's no way I can do this." We convinced him it was a great opportunity. Ironically, it was losing his job after the strike in 1984 that had got him into advertising in the first place.'

The Conservatives seemed uninterested in the personal politics of their admen. 'A minister asked me just once who I supported,' says Ronnie Duncan. 'I admitted that I'd voted Labour in 1997, and he said, "Oh, that's all right. That means you're exactly the sort of person we're trying to convince."'

The agency found the Tories to be convivial and charming clients. 'They had to be,' says Duncan. 'We were a tiny company who put everything into their campaign. They understood that and treated us with total respect. The fact we'd stepped into the shoes of the Saatchis never crossed our minds. No one ever mentioned them or the previous campaigns.'

Their first work for the party was a poster at the 2000 conference in Bournemouth. In keeping with their controversial approach, it featured an elderly woman, under the headline 'In 1997 I was mugged. I voted Labour.'

Soon after, Duncan and Isaac were invited to the Commons to outline their plans for the general election. 'We were stood at the reception in Parliament, a couple of scruffs from up north, thinking, "Flippin' 'eck, what are we doing here?"' says Isaac. 'We found them snooty until we said we were there to meet William Hague, when suddenly they changed their tune.'

Again, they were presenting to Hague and Coe, plus

campaign boss Andrew Lansley. 'They were charming, very informal,' says Isaac. 'William Hague offered us a beer and brought out a load of cans of Budweiser which we all started drinking.' Isaac had devised a number of creative options for Hague's team to choose from. His favourite centred on the government's failure to deliver on public services since 1997. Duncan was a planner by trade, and he had provided Isaac with a damning set of statistics on the length of NHS waiting lists, the state of transport services and police funding. 'They'd promised all this public spending and things were still in a terrible state,' says Isaac. His posters featured a disgruntled-looking commuter, beneath the headline 'You paid the tax – so where are the trains?' Another showed an elderly hospital patient, beside the words 'You paid the tax – so where is your operation?' 'We laid all of the ideas in front of them, and Hague just asked me, "So, which one do you think we should go with?" I pointed to the "You paid the tax" posters and told him straight, "This is definitely the campaign you should use." And he said, "Right, we'll go with that then." The looks on his team's faces said it all. They all wanted their say, but he just put his trust in us.' The theme of the campaign would be 'Is this what you paid for?', focusing on Blair's broken promises.

Ronnie Duncan was instructed to set up a temporary office in London. 'They told me that they needed me to be ten minutes away from central office at all times,' he says. 'So I told my wife I had to move to London for a while. We found a place and hired twelve staff. The creative directors stayed in Edinburgh, but we were all up and down the entire time.'

For the previous twenty years, the Conservatives had

worked with the world's biggest agency, which had ploughed the full weight of its immense resources, numerous offices and thousands of staff into managing their campaign. Now, in the biggest uphill electoral battle in Tory history, they were relying on twelve people in a temporary office.

On 16 May, deep into the campaign, Labour suffered a double PR disaster. First, Tony Blair was accosted outside a hospital by a raging woman called Sharon Storer, who was protesting about how long her partner had been waiting for treatment. News cameras captured the whole exchange. Meanwhile, in Rhyl, a farmer had thrown eggs at deputy prime minister John Prescott, who had responded by punching him in the face. It was easily the most memorable and entertaining moment of an otherwise pedestrian campaign. But it was not enough to knock Labour off course. 'John is John,' grinned Blair at a press conference the next morning when asked about the punch. The controversy ended and Prescott's popularity rating shot up. It seemed that Labour, now supported by every national paper other than the *Telegraph* and the *Mail*, could do no wrong.

Yellow M produced an election broadcast on law and order, attacking Labour for the early release of convicts who went on to commit more crimes. Actors, lying in wait to mug a woman, portrayed the criminals. The film made specific reference to two convicts who had committed rape shortly after their release. It was strong stuff. Even the *Telegraph* described the broadcast as 'too extreme', while the *Mail* said it was 'in the gutter'. With a little under a month until election day, the Tories remained nineteen points behind in the polls.

On 20 May the *Sunday Telegraph* splashed its front page

with the headline 'Tories in rift over Hague strategy as polls fail to shift'. The story claimed: 'William Hague's election campaign was in crisis last night as a bitter rift opened in the Conservative Party high command over advertising strategy.' Ronnie Duncan of Yellow M was described as being 'dismayed' by the leadership's decision to move away from their public-services message and focus on the core Tory vote, with a slew of new posters on Europe and taxation. An unnamed senior Conservative was quoted as saying the rift between party and agency was threatening a campaign 'meltdown'. Duncan was astonished. 'It was my *House of Cards* moment,' he says. 'I had no idea who had used my voice for the story or why. But I'd never heard anything about a rift over strategy.' He went directly to Conservative central office that Sunday morning to offer his side of the story to chairman Michael Ancram. 'He just listened to what I had to say and then said, "Okay,"' says Duncan. 'I assume he went and reported it back to someone else. I heard nothing more about it.'

David Isaac had sensed there was trouble brewing behind the scenes. 'I had the idea that some people in the party wanted Hague to fail,' he says. 'There had already been a leak of our work the week before. We'd mocked up an ad of a mosquito draining the blood from the country. The next thing we knew, the exact same idea had been used as a cartoon in the *Independent*. Why? It felt like people inside the party were trying to destabilise the campaign.'

Specific creative ideas regarding Europe were now being passed directly from the Conservative research department to Yellow M's creative team in London. 'We felt strongly it was the wrong way to go,' says Isaac. 'Europe was not an issue that was on people's minds. With ads you're always trying to tap into something that already exists in the public mind, and Europe wasn't it.' Posters leaked to the *Telegraph* included a map showing southern England connected to northern France. Another showed the words 'In Europe' in Labour red and 'Not controlled by Europe' in Tory blue. Isaac distanced himself from the ideas. 'They were handed down to us by the party and we were obliged to produce them under duress,' he says. 'They were pretty poor, wallpaper-type ads that nobody would notice. We felt it was far too late in the campaign to start trying to raise the salience of new issues.'

With Hague increasingly beleaguered and another election whitewash looking inevitable, Isaac suggests that certain senior Conservatives inside the campaign team were already jockeying for position as the new leader. 'The Scottish Conservatives had given us a lot of freedom in 1999, which is how we delivered such great ideas,' he says. 'But the central office team turned out to be so much more controlling. It was a case of being hired to do something, then not being allowed to actually do it.'

On the day Tony Blair had announced the election, the *Daily Express* had splashed 'Blair by 250' on their front page. Hague's campaign team was fighting a losing battle from that point onwards. In the event, Labour gained 62 per cent of the vote, losing only four of their parliamentary seats. Tellingly, the voter turnout dropped below 60 per cent for the first time in British history. The Labour Party had delivered a memorable ad campaign featuring one of its most iconic posters. But it was easy to take risks in 2001 with a majority of over a hundred and an opposition in disarray.

'We were always going to lose that election, and the next one too,' says Jeremy Sinclair. 'It was partly because the Conservatives weren't ready to win, but mostly because Labour weren't yet ready to lose.' M&C Saatchi had not pitched for the Conservative account in 2001. 'I would never turn them down if they asked,' says Sinclair. 'But they didn't – and we could all see how that election would turn out.'

Four years later Immediate Sales, a subsidiary of M&C Saatchi, would take on the Conservative campaign. By now Maurice Saatchi was co-chairman of the party, but the chief campaign strategist was Lynton Crosby, an uncompromising Australian pollster who had successfully masterminded election victories for Australian prime minister John Howard in 1998 and 2001.

'They wanted to do their own thing, although I contributed one ad that I was pleased with,' says Sinclair. 'It was about "the real Michael Howard", which Lynton's team managed to leave 90 per cent unmolested.' It seemed peculiar that Howard would appoint an adman like Saatchi as his co-chairman, then not consult him on ad strategy. 'You have to ask [Howard] why,' says Sinclair. 'I think it was a nightmare for Maurice.'

Michael Howard had been chosen by the Conservatives to lead them into the 2005 campaign on the basis of his experience. But the former home secretary was plagued by an image problem: Tory frontbencher Ann Widdecombe had suggested he had 'something of the night about him' – an accusation that Labour's campaign team was happy to cash in on. Trevor Beattie, again at the helm of Labour's ad campaign, produced a poster portraying Howard as Dracula, swinging a hypnotist's pocket watch and declaring,

'I can spend the same money twice!' Labour, again entering the campaign with a gigantic majority, focused on a 'steady as she goes' message. Beattie's team created simple posters featuring Tony Blair and Michael Howard that confidently asked voters 'Who do you want to run the country?'

But Labour's popularity had been hit badly by Blair's decision to go to war in Iraq. Controversy had raged around the government's justification for armed invasion. One million people had marched through London in protest and Blair's popularity had plummeted. Chancellor Gordon Brown remained popular by comparison but speculation about his frosty relationship with Blair beset the campaign. A broadcast was produced to counter the idea that the two friends were at war. Ridley Scott Associates were commissioned to shoot the film and Anthony Minghella, who had won an Oscar for his film *The English Patient*, would direct. It showed Blair and Brown in chummy conversation over mugs of tea, discussing the nature of their working relationship. Confusingly, the backgrounds often changed, as did their outfits, suggesting that the supposedly casual, unguarded chat had been filmed over a series of separate shoots. To loosen them up, Minghella had asked Blair and Brown to write down something they admired in the other on a piece of paper before filming began. According to Andrew Rawnsley's definitive book on New Labour, *The End of the Party*, Blair (who right up until the commencement of the campaign had been contemplating sacking Brown) wrote 'a strong economy'. Brown also wrote 'a strong economy', as if he were completely unable to write something positive about Blair and therefore chose one of his own achievements.

Meanwhile, Labour's poster campaign continued its

strategy of attack. But not all the ideas were coming from Beattie. 'We were skint and so we decided to announce a stunt where we got Labour members to come up with poster ideas,' says Alastair Campbell. 'The winner was an image of Michael Howard and Oliver Letwin [shadow chancellor] as flying pigs, with the headline "The day Tory sums add up". We stuck it on the side of a truck and called a press conference.'

But the stunt backfired. A Conservative blogger suggested that the poster was anti-Semitic (both Howard and Letwin were Jews). 'It had never crossed my mind, of course,' says Campbell. 'But people assumed it was Trevor who had made it, so suddenly he was under attack for being anti-Semitic!'

Beattie was surprised to find a camera crew camped outside his house demanding an explanation for a poster he had no part in creating. 'Trevor emailed me saying, "I've got fucking newsmen on my doorstep. What am I supposed to say to them?"' says Campbell. 'So I emailed back saying, "Just tell them, 'Fuck off and cover something important, you twats.'" But I accidentally sent the email to the editor of *Newsnight*! The next day all the headlines were "Campbell loses rag after poster gaffe!"'

The Conservative campaign had none of the lighthearted tone of Labour's. Lynton Crosby had instructed Immediate Sales to focus on five key policy areas: tax, immigration, education, the NHS and the trustworthiness of Tony Blair. One particularly impactful poster featured Blair's face, beside the headline 'If he's prepared to lie to take us to war, he's prepared to lie to win an election.'

But Crosby's key strategy was to use so-called 'dog-whistle' ads. These were messages that seemed to mean one thing to the general public but carried a more specific meaning for a targeted subgroup. Huge posters with headlines written in child-like felt-tip pen that read 'It's not racist to impose limits on immigration' and 'It's time to put a limit on immigration' were put up around the UK. The Tories were hoping to appeal to hard-right groups without appearing racist or intolerant to the wider electorate. But the press pounced on the messages immediately, accusing the Conservatives of chasing votes from the far-right British National Party.

Jeremy Sinclair, who watched the campaign from the sidelines, was unimpressed. 'Personally I don't believe in this dog-whistle stuff,' he says. 'I'm not anti-immigrant. And I thought it was in bad taste.' But wasn't it in keeping with the aggressive campaigning tactics his own agency had employed in the past? 'Yes. But we tried to have a touch of humour about them somewhere. I personally would not be involved in something that involved stirring up hatred of people. I think politicians are fair game. If they stand up and you want to chuck a tomato, that's fair. But to start making people hate their neighbours, I would not do it. It's wrong. Michael Howard himself was from immigrant parents. And two of my partners here in the agency are Jewish.'

The two general elections of the noughties were certainly not without incident, but the strategic lessons of the eighties and nineties had been forgotten. While the likes of Saatchi & Saatchi and BMP had helped bring discipline and substance to previous campaigns, in 2001 and 2005 the stakes were low: rarely had two parties entered into combat with such a wide gap in popularity. But strangely, as digital media spread and the public's exposure to marketing messages increased, the parties were reducing their investment in advertising. This was due to reduced party funds and a lack of faith in the effectiveness of traditional advertising. But the next election would be quite different: a contest so close that advertising agencies would once again be put to the test.

12

THE SADDEST THING IS THAT THESE ADS ACTUALLY WORK

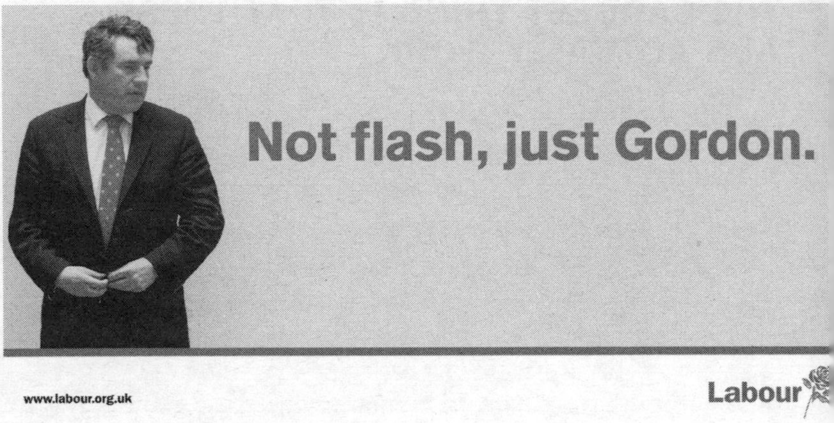
Not flash, just Gordon.
www.labour.org.uk
Labour

It was 6 April 2010. The Conservative Party had invited the media to the unveiling of its new election campaign poster. Polling day was just a few weeks away and the lead that David Cameron's newer, nicer, greener and seemingly rehabilitated Tories had built up in the polls over the past five years was narrowing rapidly. They needed a big idea, something to get their campaign back on track and halt the momentum that Gordon Brown's Labour government seemed to be gaining.

It was fresh-faced shadow chancellor George Osborne who whipped away the curtain and unveiled the giant billboard to an expectant press: an image of two enormous hobnailed boots thundering through a post-apocalyptic tundra, one with 'Job tax' emblazoned across the toecap, the other with 'More debt'. The boot on the left was about to crush a tiny green shoot emerging from the barren landscape. 'Vote for change, vote Conservative', implored the headline in the bottom-right corner. As the assembled hacks tried to make sense of the visual analogy that towered before them, two Conservative aides emerged in Gordon Brown and Alistair Darling face masks, wearing the same boots as in the poster, and started to dance on an actual green shoot, to the strains of Nancy Sinatra's 'These Boots Were Made for Walking'.

Which was all very strange but undeniably compelling. It represented a change of tone too: up to this point, the Tory campaign had focused on warm appeals to floating voters, while projecting David Cameron as a down-to-earth but dynamic young leader. This new effort was bolder, more confrontational and just weird enough to have the wider media talking about it for days afterwards. It was little surprise to find out who was responsible. After a decade of semi-detachment from the party who helped make their name, the Saatchis were back. And, as always, they were spoiling for a fight.

Since being elected leader in 2005, David Cameron had worked hard to soften the image of his party. Like Labour in the eighties, they had even decided to change their logo: the powerful blue torch became the scribbled green tree. Cameron portrayed himself as an environmentally aware family man who cycled to work and spoke about 'hugging hoodies'. The Tories, he seemed to be saying, weren't as nasty as they used to be.

The electorate seemed to be buying the idea, as opinion polls gradually improved over Cameron's subsequent five years in charge. But members of the Conservative old guard were less impressed. One of them was Maurice Saatchi, who had commented in 2007: 'When the Conservative Party moves along the dimension from nasty to nice, nothing happens. It follows that nothing will happen until the Conservative Party has something compelling to say about the subject that matters – economics.'

Like his predecessors as party leader, Cameron was reluctant to rely on Margaret Thatcher's favourite admen to project a new image for his party, and in 2007 he hired Euro RSCG to handle the Conservative account. Cameron's new director of communications, Andy Coulson, had employed the same agency while he had been editor of the

News of the World. The previous year Euro RSCG had become the first-ever ad firm to be named global agency of the year by both of the industry's top periodicals, New York's *Advertising Age* and London's *Campaign*.

As early as 2009 they had showed their hand. Two hundred and sixty billboards across the UK were used to display Conservative posters that featured a newborn baby, beside the headline 'Dad's nose. Mum's eyes. Gordon Brown's debt'. The Tory strategy was clear: they would pin the blame for the country's precarious economic circumstances directly on Prime Minister (and former chancellor) Gordon Brown. The strategy echoed that of 1992: an incessant and uncompromising attack on the economic incompetence of the Labour Party. This was underlined in December 2009 with a poster that featured a child writing figures on a whiteboard, beside the headline 'Gordon Brown's debt. Hasn't it grown?' Here was a clear, uncompromising message that the Conservatives' campaign team had the foresight to instil in the public consciousness well in advance of polling day.

But behind the scenes at Tory HQ there were rumours of a rift among the campaign managers. Former Fleet Street editor Andy Coulson favoured a negative campaign that attacked Brown's record, but Steve Hilton, the former Saatchi executive who was now David Cameron's director of strategy, favoured a more positive approach. Hilton had been the key architect in the party's 'nice' makeover, pushing their green credentials and the much-lauded 'Big Society' initiative, which encouraged individuals to play a more active role in their community. His vision for the party was delivered by Euro RSCG on posters that appeared on 1,500 sites across the UK in February 2010, featuring single mothers, ethnic minorities and blue-collar workers, under the headline 'I've never voted Tory before but . . .'

The posters were an echo of the 1959 Tory campaign which had sought to broaden the party's electoral appeal with the slogan 'What does a Conservative look like?' But switching to a positive message was about to backfire. Euro RSCG produced a poster designed to promote David Cameron as a caring but determined prime-minister-in-waiting. An image of Cameron dressed informally in an open-necked shirt and exuding conviction appeared beside the headline 'We can't go on like this. I'll cut the deficit, not the NHS.'

The strategy might have been sound (emphasising to wavering voters that public services would be safe in Conservative hands) but the execution would prove fatal for Euro RSCG. No sooner had the posters appeared than Tory opponents had vandalised them in a variety of imaginative ways. On 22 January 2010 the *Daily Mail* ran photos of a Cameron poster in Hereford that had been spray-painted to depict the Tory leader wearing Elvis-style sideburns and a quiff. The headline had been adapted to mirror the lyrics of an Elvis classic: 'We can't go on like this – with suspicious minds.'

It didn't end there. A website entitled mydavidcameron.com allowed anyone to upload their own heavily Photoshopped renditions of the poster, attracting 90,000 views in its first two weeks. Distorted versions of Cameron's poster circulated on social media, carrying headlines such as 'I'm a progressive Conservative, please stop laughing', 'Some of my best friends are poor' and 'Vote Conservative or I'll kill this kitten'. After six weeks the website had received 252,641 hits and had gained wide coverage in the mainstream media. And it wasn't just the headlines that were being mocked: David Cameron's face and hair, unnaturally neat and flawless, were also subjected to parody. As Peter Mandelson put it: 'The Tory high command would be better advised to turn their hand to new policy rather than bring in another ad agency to help them with their new posters. As if David Cameron needed more airbrushing! Doesn't he realise that is his problem? He is too much PR, and not enough PM.'

With election day looming, Euro RSCG had accidentally made the elementary mistake of turning their client into a joke.

In March 2010, less than two months before the country went to the polls in what would be one of the closest-run general elections of modern times, Bill Muirhead received a telephone call at the Soho headquarters of M&C Saatchi. The voice on the other end of the line was that of Steve Hilton, the man he had poached from Conservative central office in 1992 and who had since moved back into the political world. Muirhead had been watching the Tory ad campaign unfold with a sense of dismay. 'When I saw that giant super-sized version of Cameron's face, badly airbrushed, with a nice chatty headline about the NHS, I just nearly cried,' he says. 'I said to myself, "This is crappy. Absolute crap."' Muirhead had been half expecting a call, and Hilton got straight to the point: 'Bill, I think it's time we had a coffee.'

Meanwhile, the Labour Party had been quietly preparing its own ad campaign to counter the Tory assault. Kate Stanners was a lifelong Labour supporter who had started out as a creative in the ad industry, 'when I was the only female southerner among a bunch of northern blokes'. She had been at Ayer Barker in 1984, when she had met Deborah Mattinson, who had recruited her to the fledgling Shadow Communications Agency along with Trevor Beattie. 'I'd been raised as a Labour supporter,' says Stanners. 'My mum has never been so proud of my career than when she found out I'd met Peter Mandelson.'

By 2007 Stanners had established herself as one of the industry's top creative figures. As creative chief at Saatchi & Saatchi she had one of the highest-profile jobs in the business and was well aware of her agency's historical associations with the Conservatives. But when Gordon Brown's campaign chief, Douglas Alexander, contacted her with an invitation to pitch for their ad account, she spotted an opportunity. 'I just knew that it would cause a stir,' she says. 'The Conservative agency taking on Labour's account was always going to attract publicity.'

Stanners was asked to produce a number of ideas within twenty-four hours of her initial meeting with Alexander. By the next morning she was able to present fifty posters. 'We made this bunker in the basement of the agency,' she says, 'and we invited anyone who had an interest and a sympathy for Labour to join in. We didn't want to force anyone.'

Shocked by the Saatchi team's prolific output, the Labour chiefs picked out their favourite poster: a powerful image of Gordon Brown, with the headline 'Not flash, just Gordon'. A strategy was agreed between agency and party: Brown would be portrayed as the strong and dependable father of a group of young, dynamic visionaries. The government's popularity had been knocked by the unprecedented scale of a global recession that had begun in 2008, but Stanners and her team would seek to convince the public that Brown was the only man with the experience to navigate the country out of the crisis.

Initially Alexander had briefed the agency to ready itself for a 2007 election. Brown had become prime minister that summer, after Tony Blair had stepped down. He was enjoying the traditional honeymoon period in the polls, his no-nonsense style proving popular at first among a British public fatigued by ten years of Blair's pzazz. But following the party's autumn conference Brown nervously decided to postpone the election, despite a promising lead in the opinion polls.

'We were absolutely gutted,' says Stanners. 'We would have won had we gone ahead as planned in 2007. As it was, we had to throw out all the ideas we had lined up for the campaign and wait. But over the next couple of years the cracks started to show.'

Barack Obama's successful campaign to become US president in 2008 had utilised the might of social media. Many believed that the UK election of 2010 would be decided in the same way. Both parties were operating with vastly reduced campaign budgets and might have hoped that the free marketing provided by the Internet could prove decisive, but Stanners and her Saatchi team were under no illusions about the enduring impact of the poster. 'The poster helps to boil down the political feeling to a simple line,' she says. 'We help to distil and simplify ideas into a form that ordinary people can engage with.' Unlike his predecessor, Brown was known for his love of detail and forensic engagement with policy formulation. Engaging him in the succinct and punchy thinking of the ad industry was not going to be easy. 'He had this integrity whereby he wanted everything to be about policy, not personality,' says Stanners. 'We had two years to work closely with him and the cabinet on simplifying the way they communicated with the public. Gordon had incredible intelligence and insight but he sometimes over-thought things, which could paralyse his decision-making.'

During an early presentation at Downing Street Stanners casually remarked that the prime minister's use of political jargon while explaining a particular policy initiative was 'a bit wanky'. This might have been the sort of informality that was bandied about during Tony Blair and Alastair Campbell's reign but, says Stanners, her flippancy prompted an intake of breath among Brown's inner circle. 'After the meeting Philip Gould wandered up and said, "Congratulations, you're the first person to call the prime minister 'wanky' to his face."'

While Euro RSCG plastered the streets with gigantic images of David Cameron's face, Stanners and her team saw the counter-strategy as obvious. 'We wanted to make it a heavyweight versus lightweight battle,' she says. 'Gordon was the wise old head, Cameron was an upstart PR man.' The online mockery of the Tory campaign was a gift to Labour, but some commentators questioned the actual impact of sites such as mydavidcameron.com. Posters mocking Cameron were shared on social media among people who were already opponents of the Tories, not among the sort of floating voters who were more valuable to campaigners. Saatchi & Saatchi therefore applied the sentiment of the online parodies to a real-life poster, which compared a flattering picture of Gordon Brown to the allegedly airbrushed image of Cameron. 'Building a foundation', read the caption beside Brown. Beside Cameron it said, 'Wearing one'.

But there was only so much that posters could achieve on Labour's tiny budget. 'We didn't buy any poster sites in the whole campaign,' says Stanners. 'We had to launch our posters for the media and rely on them gaining PR.'

In March 2010 the leading blog LabourList ran a contest for members to submit their own poster ideas. The winning entry came from a twenty-four-year-old Labour supporter called Jacob Quagliozzi from St Albans. It featured Cameron mocked up as the brash TV detective Gene Hunt from eighties-set cop drama *Ashes to Ashes*. He was slouched arrogantly on a lurid orange sports car, next to the headline 'Don't let him take Britain back to the 1980s'. But it was easy prey for the online community, who swiftly parodied the poster with their own scathing headlines. The Tories themselves quickly used the same image with a swaggering new headline: 'Fire up the Quattro, it's time for a change'. This was becoming a whole new sort of election campaign: the ad teams were locked in a battle that changed by the second depending on what was happening online. In many ways, it pushed the levels of creativity further than ever before.

But behind the scenes the most experienced figure in political advertising was now pulling the Tory strings. Jeremy Sinclair was delighted when Bill Muirhead informed him of Steve Hilton's invitation for coffee. 'They'd been with another agency who couldn't hack it,' he says. 'So we were invited back to the card table. Nothing feels better than that.'

Within hours of the call Muirhead and Sinclair had strolled to the fashionable members club Soho House to meet Hilton. It was mid-February, with the election set for May. Ordinarily, the agency would have been working up a campaign for at least a year. 'Luckily, Jeremy seemed to have had a bunch of ideas tucked away in his sock drawer just in case,' says Muirhead. 'He immediately produced one for Steve which blew him away. It was right up there with "Labour isn't working".' Hilton asked them about their availability. The meeting was over within half an hour, Muirhead leaving Hilton with the words: 'You know where we are whenever you need us.'

By the following day M&C Saatchi had been re-appointed by the Conservative Party. While central office insisted publicly that Euro RSCG remained their 'lead agency', it was Muirhead and Sinclair who would now lead the charge. It was clear to them both where the campaign was going wrong. 'Strategically, they were jumping around too much from the NHS to the debt to Cameron,' says Muirhead. 'We had just a short period to build one core message in the public's mind and we had to be consistent with it. Tonally, Jeremy said it was time to drop the nice stuff and go on the attack.' The Saatchi team pulled their gloves back on and had one target in their sights: Gordon Brown. Within weeks 850 posters sprung up around the country with typically brutal execution: Gordon Brown's face, locked in his trademark awkward smile, beside a variety of headlines that varied between 'I let 80,000 criminals out early, vote for me' and 'I doubled the national debt, vote for me'. Underneath, the tag line read: 'Or vote for change. Vote Conservative'.

While Hilton had previously favoured a more positive message, he was a Saatchi alumnus who had implicit belief in Sinclair's ideas. 'Jeremy is a genius,' he says. In the final throes of such a closely fought campaign, he realised that a strategy of attack was the only option. 'My feeling was that

Andy Coulson was responsible for switching the campaign message so often,' says Muirhead. 'He had been a tabloid editor, where the job is to follow the different stories. One week you might have a front page about lesbian porn, the next week it's about dogs being eaten. Our style is to keep consistent and keep banging away on a single message.' A few weeks later, as the astonished media found themselves watching a young intern in a Gordon Brown mask dancing to Nancy Sinatra while a grinning George Osborne stood beside them, it was clear that M&C Saatchi had already made its mark.

Over at Sinclair and Muirhead's old Saatchi & Saatchi offices on Charlotte Street, Kate Stanners and her team prepared for the battle to intensify. 'We were back and forth to Downing Street constantly,' she says. 'We all loved getting to eat our lunch in the cabinet room, but their team preferred coming to us because we had nicer tea,' she says. 'They'd say, "Can we meet at your place? You have such nice biscuits."' Down in the Charlotte Street campaign bunker Mandelson rallied the team for the final weeks of battle. 'We're used to most clients being terrified of sticking their necks out,' says Stanners. 'But in politics the reverse is true. Mandelson kept telling us, "Don't hold back. Attack them. Stick the boot in and don't go on the defensive."'

The rhetoric was intensifying by the day. The *Guardian* ran a story claiming that Labour was gearing up to present Brown as a bare-knuckled street fighter who was ready to crush a callow David Cameron. They ran a poster featuring a grim-faced Brown shrouded in shadow and the headline 'Step outside, posh boy'. It might well have fitted into the increasingly bloody campaign, but it turned out to be an April Fool by the newspaper. A few weeks later Brown slipped up at a public appearance in Rochdale, Greater Manchester, when confronted by Gillian Duffy, a sixty-five-year-old lifelong Labour supporter. She ranted at the prime minister about Eastern European immigrants who, she suggested, were flocking to Britain to claim benefits. After discussing the matter politely, Brown was caught by a Sky News microphone angrily describing her as a bigot to his press advisor. The stolen remarks were broadcast widely and Brown was forced into an embarrassing apology. But Labour's ad team would not be deterred from their portrayal of Brown as a tough and dependable leader. Trying to turn what became known as 'Bigotgate' to their advantage, they parodied an iconic Irn-Bru slogan by devising a poster that showed Brown beside the headline 'Made in Scotland with girders'. Allegations of his bullying managerial style had plagued Brown during his time in office, and Stanners and her team believed this reputation wasn't necessarily a bad thing. But Labour's senior advisors decided to drop the poster at the last minute.

Nor would the party endorse any class-based attacks. Much was made of the social background of Cameron's shadow cabinet, which contained a disproportionate number of Eton-educated upper-class white males. 'They didn't want us to use those sort of stereotypes to attack the Tories,' says Stanners. 'They thought it would make us look cheap. Besides, they knew that job would be done by the wider media and the online community.'

A spoof of the Pulp single 'Common People' was released online, with an accompanying video that featured an animated David Cameron demonstrating his patronising attitude towards the working class. Supposedly created by an anonymous bedroom blogger, it became a viral hit. It later transpired that key figures at another Labour-supporting ad agency had come up with the idea.

Labour could ill afford to lose its nerve; the M&C Saatchi team were characteristically uncompromising in their approach. Cameron was portrayed in a series of posters addressing an animated crowd of supporters in an open-necked shirt, sleeves rolled up and ready for action, beside bold declarations of intent: 'Let's cut benefits for those who refuse work', 'Let's stop Labour's jobs tax' and 'Let's scrap ID cards'. It was simple, loud and populist, with the sort of easily digestible messages that were likely to resonate with ordinary undecided voters on the street.

Labour had already blinked in the midst of battle by reacting to a Tory poster that claimed that Labour planned to tax people after their death in order to pay for the treatment they received in old age. The headline ran: 'R.I.P. off. Now Gordon wants £20,000 when you die.' The poster only ran on eighteen sites around Britain but it attracted a huge amount of coverage in the wider media, thanks to the angry response from Labour. Health secretary Andy Burnham said: 'If the Conservative Party had a shred of decency they would withdraw this flippant, distasteful poster. Posters with gravestones are grubby and desperate. This is a craven attempt to frighten the most vulnerable in society. David Cameron should be ashamed of such black propaganda.'

This outspoken response made the poster a centre of media discussion for days afterwards. As Sinclair notes: 'Your top priority with any political ad is to provoke the other side into a response.' Just as they had successfully goaded Denis Healey in 1979, now they were doing the same with Burnham thirty-one years later. Labour once again found themselves hamstrung by a preoccupation with the ethics of the debate. The Tories, always happier to follow their gut instinct and worry about the details later, were concerned with nothing other than winning.

What was unusual about 2010 was that both parties agreed on the battleground. In previous years Labour and the Tories had competed to control the agenda, with one side traditionally favouring a debate on public services, the other preferring tax and the economy. This time round they both wanted the discussion to centre on Gordon Brown. The only question was, whose version of the prime minister would convince the public? Was he tough, honest and competent, or grumpy, inefficient and charmless? In the end, the respective ad teams lost control of the message when the three main parties agreed to televised leaders' debates. Over the course of April, Brown, Cameron and Liberal Democrat leader Nick Clegg competed in a trio of live discussions on different themes: first domestic policy, then foreign affairs, and finally the economy. The people would now be able to judge the prime minister's character for themselves, without any filtering, spin or gloss from his ad team. Brown was generally thought to be a less capable media performer than Clegg or Cameron, but with a better grasp of policy. 'It was completely new ground for Gordon,' says Peter Mandelson. 'The debates were an entirely fresh idea and the two younger leaders found them easier to adapt to.'

In the event, Nick Clegg was widely regarded as the surprise winner of the debates but, crucially, Cameron came out on top in the final debate on the key issue of economics.

Immediately after the show ended the Conservatives had a 5 per cent lead over Labour.

At 9.41 a.m. on 7 May 2010 the BBC announced a hung parliament. No party had managed to achieve an overall majority in the Commons, but Cameron's Tories held the largest number of seats. After four days of frantic negotiations between the parties, Gordon Brown resigned as prime minister on 11 May and David Cameron was invited to form a government by the Queen. The following day the Conservatives struck a coalition deal with the Liberal Democrats and thirteen years of Labour government came to an end.

Many commentators, not least disgruntled traditionalists within the Conservative Party, criticised Cameron's failure to win outright against an unpopular prime minister and tired government in the midst of the worst recession ever. Despite gaining power, the accusation would plague him for the next five years. But, on closer analysis, his achievement was greater than some supposed. In 2009 the party had published an internal report entitled 'Uphill Challenge' that explained the scale of victory they would require. To earn a working majority, they would need to win 117 seats with a 6.9 per cent swing, larger than any swing the party had enjoyed since 1931. In the event, they achieved a 5 per cent swing, which was almost exactly the same as that achieved by Margaret Thatcher in her epochal 1979 victory. Their net gain of ninety-seven seats was the biggest in the party's history. In the closest-run election of modern times, the Conservatives had somehow managed to break their own electoral records to scrape over the finishing line.

But how? As always, it was difficult to properly assess the

impact of the ads themselves, but by switching agencies so close to the election, the Conservatives displayed a ruthless commitment to winning that gave them an edge over their opponents. By recruiting the often heartless but relentlessly creative and persistently focused men from M&C Saatchi, they gave a previously confused campaign much-needed focus. If Gordon Brown's character was the principal battleground, the masters of attack advertising were always likely to win. That they triumphed over their former agency, which had unceremoniously pushed them out fifteen years previously, no doubt made it all the sweeter.

Politics, the advertising industry and the media landscape itself had changed immeasurably between 1979 and 2010. The latter election had been fought online using technologies that weren't even conceived of when Margaret Thatcher first gained office. Live TV debates removed control from the admen who had gained so much influence over political messages throughout the eighties and nineties. But some things, it seemed, never changed. Three decades after Andrew Rutherford produced 'Labour isn't working' for Thatcher, the Saatchi old guard were still at the centre of the battle. Old-fashioned posters were still able to boil convoluted campaigns down to one powerful message. And now, perhaps more than ever, negativity worked.

In 2011 the excellent blog politicaladvertising.co.uk unearthed an unaccredited quote regarding the Canadian election of the same year. It could just as easily have applied to elements of any British election of the past thirty years. 'Political advertising is a sad business. The saddest part isn't the sneering tone, the obsession with irrelevant attacks on character or even the high-school-level production value. The saddest thing is that these ads actually work.'

Epilogue

PEOPLE AREN'T IDIOTS

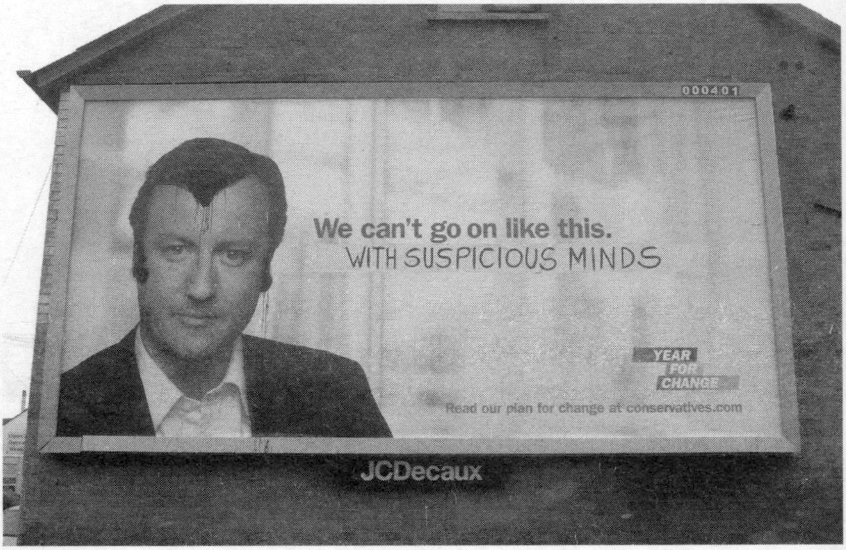
000401
We can't go on like this.
WITH SUSPICIOUS MINDS
YEAR
FOR
CHANGE
Read our plan for change at conservatives.com
JCDecaux

There was still no word from Maurice Saatchi. What was his problem? Well, whatever, I went back for another chat with the creative overlord of his agency, Jeremy Sinclair. Ask anyone and they will tell you Sinclair was the real brains behind the Saatchi operation. Certainly, he was the man who wrote the ads that helped make the Saatchi brothers rich, Tim Bell famous and Margaret Thatcher powerful. I asked Sinclair why Maurice had gone on *Channel 4 News* after Thatcher's death and denied that the agency had played any significant role in her success. Sinclair smiled broadly and said, 'Because Maurice is clever.' I asked him what he meant by that, and he told me to go back to the clip and listen to what Jon Snow said at the interview's conclusion (you can easily find the clip if you google it). While Saatchi was banging on about the seductive allure of what he called 'Thatcher's philosophy', steadfastly refusing to be drawn on how the agency had helped package and promote that philosophy, Snow interrupted, saying, 'Well, I'll tell you what, I've learnt something, and that is that the adman doesn't want to waste time talking about how he does it, all he wants to do is sell the content – and you've done it.' Saatchi actually giggled with excitement, slapping his thigh flamboyantly like a pantomime Dick Whittington. Snow had rumbled him, but the interview was over and it was all too late.

Saatchi is an influential Conservative peer nowadays and

his agency is still thriving. Why would he need to talk to Jon Snow, let alone me, about how terrific and significant his role in Thatcher's success was? 'Because, you see, it's not the job of the agency to become famous,' says Sinclair. But the Saatchis really did become famous, I say. 'Yes, we did,' he says. 'But we guessed that might happen. Without Mrs Thatcher we could not have become the agency we've become. That is a fact. It's a coincidence of forces coming together at the same time. There's a film about the Beatles where someone says, "They weren't going to become famous until Ringo arrived." It's true that Ringo is not the best drummer in the world. But until the four of them got together they weren't going to take off. That was like us managing to get involved with the Conservatives.'

Sinclair's work for the Tories has been a labour of love. 'There have been some who have said, "Why didn't you go into politics and become a Tory MP?" And I did think about it. I was offered an opportunity to stand in the early eighties. But I asked someone for advice and they told me that I could probably have more effect on the outside.'

And besides, he might not have been that keen on switching agency for church-hall meetings with constituents, right? 'I don't think I would have been very patient listening to people worrying about their benefits,' he says. 'But I also think that working in advertising can help you shape politics more effectively. Making ads forces you to sieve your thoughts and concentrate, to get the essence of your argument. All the waffle and detail that a politician can get away with in a speech isn't allowed. Get to know your brand. Keep things simple. These are the disciplines that anyone in advertising understands. People say that's boiling things down to superficialities, but it is not.

Advertising disciplines force politicians to get to the heart of the policy, to deliver the key argument succinctly in a way people can understand. We helped politicians understand how to speak to people in a way they could hear. If you shout at people, they will switch off. You've got to be normal. I think Tony Blair's greatest strength was that he appeared to be normal. When he first came along, he came across like someone who would feel more or less the same as you and I would feel about anything. A regular bloke you could have a drink with.'

Towards the end of 2014 I was invited along to a meeting among a small group of journalists, politicians and think-tank types to discuss ideas for a new type of politics. The people in attendance (there were fewer than a dozen of us) felt sure that the public were exasperated with parties of all political hues and that there was an opportunity to conjure something new, inspirational and popular that would transcend tribalism and reinvigorate people's faith in the ability of politics to change lives. Which all sounded fantastic to me.

It was all very fascinating to listen to but I did wonder what the hell I'd been invited for. And, boy, did they talk! Round and round and round they went, discussing the intricacies of tax policy and the ethics of immigration laws. Maybe they thought that I, with my background in mostly knockabout, popular journalism, might have some ideas on how to help them take their new brand of politics and communicate it to ordinary idiots in the street like me, people who might not spend much time reading leaders in *The Times* and usually prefer listening to talkSPORT over the *Today* programme in the morning, but nonetheless have certain values and beliefs about how society should be run.

I realised that I would probably be of more use to them once they had a better handle on exactly what their new brand of politics actually was. They all seemed clever, compassionate and determined enough to work out something marvellous eventually, but they were still very much at the working-out stage. That's when I appreciated how valuable people like Sinclair were to political types. The men and women in that little meeting I attended were hamstrung by their own intelligence. The detail and the intellectual rigour is all very well when you're working out what you want to say but, when it comes to working out how to say it, you need an aggressive clarity, the sort of expert grasp of simplicity that great admen specialise in and great politicians are usually rubbish at.

As Sinclair puts it: 'Posters have always been and always will be the battleground. Because if you can't sum up your message in five to six words, then your message isn't right. Mediums might change, they might be electronic posters, but posters will be with us in some form for ever.'

I had certain assumptions about advertising and politics when I started out. First, I knew them both to be particularly introspective worlds. I could sort of understand how political types in Westminster had come to perceive their own work as the most important thing in the world. After all, they were trying to work out how best to run it. When your day job is making decisions that affect millions of lives, it must be easy to get carried away with yourself now and then. For all their talk of wanting to understand life outside of the Westminster bubble (an ever-louder proclamation from panicky politicians in the UKIP era) I always assumed they were paying lip service to the news cameras.

They knew how important it was to appear to be humble, but it was all just a self-serving pretence. In their minds, they were the Masters of the Universe, pulling the strings of our ridiculous little lives from on high. On the news they were all about understanding normal lives, ordinary people and real issues, but I'd spent time behind the scenes with these people and all they talked about was internal party politics and Westminster gossip. I felt they were all patronising us.

As for advertising, that can be even worse. Admen are very good at dismissing the importance of their craft when the microphones are switched on. But once they think there are no normals listening and that they are surrounded by their own creed, some of them will harp on about the merits and importance of their work with dizzying self-indulgence. Like Westminster, adland is a bubble. But it is an even smaller bubble that can, at times, have an even more inflated sense of self-importance. Mind you, I happen to think that's no bad thing. Regardless of any outsider's objective assessment of their work, it's nice for people to believe in the importance of what they do for a living. Most of us seem to drift through our careers, our attitudes to work veering between abject misery and existential malaise. We've all got a living to earn, and if you can go to the office convinced that the world revolves around what you're about to do, then what's the harm in that?

But here's what I suspected when I started to write this book: that political advertising really is pointless. I knew Maurice Saatchi had been bullshitting Jon Snow: I could see that twinkle in his eye that seemed to say, 'Of course, we were as integral to the political history of this country as Oliver Cromwell, William Gladstone and Margaret

Thatcher combined, but I am way too smart to say that out loud on the news, you imbecile!' I figured that's what a bunch of admen thought about how their snappy slogans, fancy films and ludicrous PR stunts had shaped the political landscape. But I believed there would be plenty of evidence to the contrary. That if I looked closely enough at the election campaigns of the modern era there would be all the proof we needed that the daft frippery of advertising had been nothing but a mildly distracting sideshow. But I was wrong.

In March 2013 Trevor Beattie announced to the Advertising Week Europe conference that he had 'decided to embrace impatience'. New Labour's adman explained: 'I'm announcing the death of the thirty-second TV ad – it is too long, it is bullshit. Five seconds is the right length. One of the ways of getting noticed is to change the standard unit of consumption. That unit is thirty seconds and it is boring.' It fitted in with something Beattie had been telling politicians for years: boil it down to a succinct headline and you'll have people noticing your ideas.

'"Women of Britain say – 'Go'" is one of my favourite ever lines,' says Beattie. 'When Cameron said, "We're in this together", it didn't half have some power, even if you didn't agree with the sentiment. "No Child Left Behind". "Back to Basics". There is such a power to language if you use it in the right way. And imagery. I put a wig on William Hague in 2001 and it sent a message more powerfully than a 10,000-word article ever could. People instantly got what we were saying within two seconds.'

Researchers say that there is no statistical evidence to show that exposure to advertising influences people's voting choices. But that's not really the point. Admen, the good ones anyway, help politicians to put their complicated ideas into succinct packages. They help them to focus their strategy, and the ads they make can help signpost elaborate, multifaceted political debates for the press and the public. That's what Sinclair and Beattie seemed to be saying, anyway. And I agreed.

Chris Powell concurs: 'I would argue that in politics the real effect of advertising has been to get the parties to develop decent strategy – because that's what you have to do in commerce. You have to work out what the one thing you need to say is and keep on saying it. Advertising has tried to show politicians that you usually only get to talk about one thing, because after that people get bored. Ad people run around boasting about the impact of particular posters or slogans, but they don't work unless the politicians have got something valuable to sell.'

That is what happened in 1992, when the Tories learnt to beat Labour over the head with tax until they could take no more; then again in 1997, when the Labour Party pulled almost the exact same trick in reverse. Maurice Saatchi's favourite way of describing it is 'brutal simplicity of thought'. What admen bring to politics is a tunnel vision based on pragmatism. Politicians, usually more complex in their thinking than admen, will always struggle with that sort of mental discipline. Chris Patten summed it up to me by saying: 'Politicians have a tendency to follow the issues. Admen kept us on course.'

But even he couldn't see just how important this was. 'I think that, if I'd had my way, I'd save the money and not advertise at all,' he said. 'I think most people don't remember the ads. I don't think they raise the turnout. I don't think they even increase the salience of the issues on which we were focusing, and I certainly don't think they increase the share of the vote.

'I think it's part of basic political electoral arithmetic to recognise the average person is a great deal smarter than some people think. People aren't idiots. On the whole, they don't buy crap. And on the whole, they get election results right. With hindsight, they've pretty much always elected the right government regardless of the advertising and campaign strategy.'

And maybe that's true. But what guided the public's decisions? How did they learn about the parties, the policies and the personalities on offer? How can the public make informed decisions without proper communication? It's snooty and unrealistic to expect us to do all the legwork. It is also disingenuous for politicians to assess political advertising on the narrow basis of how many votes it wins.

Cecil Parkinson is still friends with Tim Bell and is a colleague of Maurice Saatchi's in the House of Lords. He doesn't want to upset anyone. But then again: 'What I'm trying to do is to redress what I regard as a colossal imbalance,' he says. 'They [Tim Bell and the Saatchis] made a fortune out of the fact that they ran the 1983 and 1987 campaigns.'

As party chairman, Parkinson had hired Saatchi & Saatchi in 1983 and had paid the company well. But he was never sure what he was actually getting for the money. 'They were the best advertising agency we could have. But the political party that lets an advertising agency run its campaign is just heading for trouble. What did they do? Right, they did the party political broadcasts. We would like to get over, for instance, the mess that Labour had made. And they would come up with Anthony Quayle, who had a wonderful voice, who would say, "Do you remember the winter of 1978, when the dead couldn't be buried, hospitals weren't allowed to operate, dustbins weren't removed?" There were pictures of rats running up and down Knightsbridge. They were very good at that – but we only got about three party broadcasts. What difference did it make?'

I asked Parkinson about all those posters, about the brilliant annihilation delivered by Sinclair's 'Like your manifesto, comrade' headline. 'But how many people look at poster boards?' he says. 'I'm not running down what they did. Some of the posters were excellent. Some of them weren't so good. The real campaign is being done with the prime minister as the central figure. They did the poster boards, they did the press advertising, they did the party politicals, but the manifesto, putting it over and selling the prime minister – they took no part in that.'

Parkinson, like many politicians, was unable to step back and see how advertising had dovetailed with politics in a broader sense. It wasn't just about making posters to win votes; it was about refining the often horrendous and impenetrable thoughts, messages, technicalities and processes of the political world into a palatable form. In studying all of these election campaigns I had, at times, witnessed two very contrasting mindsets working in perfect harmony: the complexity and nuance of politics, and the succinct practicality of advertising.

A good ad is not always a winning ad. Hugh Hudson's Neil Kinnock film in 1987 conveyed the personality, convictions, values and passions of Kinnock with authenticity and depth, in a way that any ordinary viewer could absorb by osmosis in a few short minutes. Anyone could understand who Neil Kinnock was and what he stood for. And, on that basis, most of them decided not to vote for him. Their decision was better informed than it had been before they'd seen the film. All of this stuff plays a vital role in the process.

Despite the advances made since 1979, political communication is probably in a bigger crisis now than it was forty years ago. Modern politicians seem to speak almost entirely in bafflingly wonkish jargon. They have lost all grip on the importance of rhetoric that explains to, and resonates with, ordinary people; they seem terrified that saying anything that makes sense will leave them exposed to attack. And so they fall over themselves to say nothing. The impression we are all left with is of a political creed without any conviction; a set of careerists more interested in keeping their heads down and climbing the slippery pole than standing up for what they actually believe in. Fewer people are voting, and the younger generation is disillusioned with the whole boring business. Politicians need people to help them engage more than ever.

'Gordon [Brown] was notionally in charge of the campaign in 1997 and he refused to see or sign off any part of it,' says Peter Mandelson. 'The grid, the advertising – none of it. It was extremely unhelpful. When John Major called the election, Tony [Blair] called Gordon and myself to a meeting and pleaded with Gordon to look at the campaign grid, with all the timings, phasings and messages that I had drawn up. And he wouldn't. He would not sign it off.'

Mandelson was involved again in 2010, by which time Gordon Brown was in the top job. But things had not changed. 'The problem with 2010 was that we were emerging, we thought, from the worst financial crisis any of us had ever seen. It shook the foundations of the entire global economy, and it happened on our watch. What I couldn't get everyone to agree on – or what I couldn't get Gordon to agree with me and the chancellor on – was what our approach and argument should be and how we should position the government in relation to the crisis. We were therefore running a campaign without the complete personal commitment of the leader of the party to what I thought should be our message.'

Some people hated Gordon Brown; others thought he was one of the smartest leaders we have ever had, who was undone only by a steadfast refusal to compromise. Margaret Thatcher was just the same – and yet while Brown never managed to win a single election as prime minister, Thatcher won more than anyone. How did she manage to overcome the same political flaws that Brown couldn't? I was reminded of one of her sayings: 'If you have a good thing to sell, use every single capacity you can to sell it.'

There are those who think that advertising has a tendency to make politics superficial; others believe that unelected admen influencing politics is undemocratic. But that's looking at things the wrong way round. The politics always come first. Yes, some admen like being seen circulating in powerful circles and hobnobbing with prime ministers. Who can blame them? But I hadn't found anything to suggest that their agenda is to shape policy. These people are advocates, and proud of it. All they really want to do is help make sense of what politicians are trying to explain. And that is a deeply democratic objective.

'I think what happened after 1979 was that politicians

realised more and more that they had to ask people for their vote,' says Tim Bell. 'To look at and understand specific groups of people. Not just publish a manifesto and imagine that people will read it and identify the bits that are relevant to them. The press and the media had already begun to make more of an effort to explain politics before we got involved. Advertising tends to follow close behind these trends, not lead them.'

Here's another thing I learnt: there isn't anything wrong with tapping into the public's fears – as long as those fears already exist. Manufacturing fear (which is something that newspaper editors, rather than ad execs, usually take care of) is another matter. But what's wrong with showing an understanding of what voters are worried about and promising to protect them from it?

As Neil Kinnock reflects: 'Ads that tapped into prejudices or fears about Labour helped distract people from the Tories' own flaws. The "Tax bombshell" poster, the "Labour isn't working" poster – they didn't make people love the Conservatives. But they were powerful enough to make people think they weren't going to bother voting for Labour.'

Bill Muirhead and Jeremy Sinclair have been dishing those body blows out to their opponents for years. Mind you, you couldn't hope to meet a pair of more laid-back blokes. 'A simple thing that I learnt from doing this work is that you never win an election by doing what I call positive campaigning,' says Muirhead. 'You only win by attacking your opponent, because that's what people remember. It's interesting. People say these days, "Oh, we don't know what David Cameron stands for." But I don't know whether that's a bad thing or a good thing. Because instead I find myself thinking, "Okay, what are the weapons you'd use against Ed Miliband in an election campaign?" Well, he stabbed his brother in the back. And, you know, anybody that does that to his brother, I mean, bloody hell. Imagine what he'd do to the country?'

It almost sounds like the makings of a campaign slogan. There is a certain relish on Muirhead's face as he contemplates it. The 2015 election is just around the corner, and I recall Muirhead telling me how they won back the Tory account at the last minute in 2010. He'd mentioned a slogan that Jeremy Sinclair had brought to their meeting with Steve Hilton. I remember how Muirhead had said it was one of the best he'd ever seen. How it had convinced Hilton to reappoint the agency on the spot. I asked him what the slogan was. 'We never released it in the end,' he grinned. 'We're keeping it up our sleeve for next time round.'

Addendum

THE 2015 GENERAL ELECTION CAMPAIGN

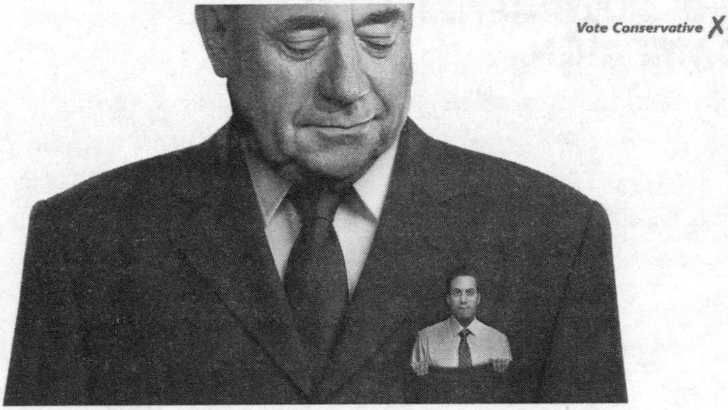
Vote Conservative X

'The trouble with a lot of the coverage of elections these days, with all these polls that have come out, is that it is like a kid sitting in the back seat of a car shouting, "Are we there yet? Are we there yet?"' says Lynton Crosby, the Conservative Party's 2015 election campaign director. 'You just wanna tell them, "Shut up, close your eyes, sleep for half an hour, and we will be at Grandma's soon." But they want to be there now. So there is this absurdity.'

The media coverage of the 2015 general election was particularly frenzied. A relentless cycle of news and speculation, amidst an electoral landscape disrupted by the rise of numerous small parties, changed direction from one moment to the next. Successive opinion polls suggested the country was heading for another coalition government. At the eye of the storm was Crosby, hired by David Cameron to remain calm and deliver the outright election victory that had somehow eluded the Conservatives in 2010. His job was to ignore the voices from the back of the car who told him that his mission was impossible. 'Of course, if everyone keeps shouting at you, you hear the noise,' he says. 'But if you're leading a campaign, your job is to stay calm and make everyone around you believe that if you just keep doing what you're doing, you can win.'

It was this hardened belief in the forensic campaign strategy he had been planning for the past two years that helped Crosby deliver one of the greatest electoral surprises of recent times.

On 9 April 2015, ten days into the election campaign, defence secretary Michael Fallon launched a brutal attack on Labour Party leader Ed Miliband. Suggesting that Miliband would scrap the UK's Trident nuclear deterrent in order to strike an electoral deal with the Scottish Nationalist Party, Fallon told *The Times*: 'Miliband stabbed his own brother in the back to become Labour leader. Now he is willing to stab the United Kingdom in the back to become prime minister.'

Until this point, Labour's campaign had been gaining momentum: some polls had them narrowly ahead of the Tories, and Miliband's pledge to crack down on tax avoidance by non-domiciles was dominating the headlines. Fallon's attack seemed crude and uncalled for. Many commentators suggested that it would backfire on his party. His words caught my eye in particular because they were so similar to the comments made by M&C Saatchi exec Bill Muirhead a year previously when I had interviewed him for the first edition of this book.

You can flick back a few pages and compare them for yourself. It was such an uncanny repetition of Muirhead's words that I took Fallon's outburst to be clear evidence that the dark hand of the Saatchis was once again guiding the Conservative campaign.

But I was wrong. Muirhead and the gang at M&C Saatchi remained the Conservative Party's primary ad agency, but this time around they were answering to Lynton Crosby, a campaign boss more formidable and demanding than any they'd encountered before. His firm, Crosby-Textor, was a veteran of 250 election campaigns across the globe, and his record of election victories had earned him the nickname 'The Wizard of Oz'. He was also known to some as 'the Rottweiler'. His campaigning philosophy was not dissimilar to that of the Saatchi team: it was about simple messages that tapped into what the electorate might already be thinking. But if anything, he was more brutal and relentless than the experienced admen. A story by Tim Montgomerie in *The Times* in early 2015 reported a Downing Street meeting among senior Tories in which they sought to craft more imaginative ways of positioning themselves on the economy. This ranged from cracking down on bankers to building more houses in London to cool the property market and offering more help to the low-paid. According to Montgomerie's source, Crosby's response was characteristically frank: 'All very fascinating, but voters only need to know two things about the economy: it was broken five years ago by the other lot and it's okay again now under us.'

Like Muirhead, Crosby was born and raised in South Australia. The son of a farmer, he had studied economics at university and ran unsuccessfully as a parliamentary candidate before becoming a campaign strategist, most famously for the leader of the Australian Liberal Party, John Howard. Crosby was credited with playing a vital role in Howard's four successive election victories between 1996 and 2004. In 2005 he had been hired by the then Tory leader Michael Howard to run his UK election campaign. Crosby's so-called dog-whistle approach (whereby advertising came with an often unpalatably right-wing subtext) had caused controversy back then, and the Conservatives had been defeated at the polls by Tony Blair's Labour Party.

Crosby had claimed that he had been hired too late in the day to make a proper impact: 'You can't fatten the pig on market day,' he was quoted as saying.

Now, in 2015, he was back at Tory HQ. And he wasn't happy with Bill Muirhead. The Saatchi man's remarks about Miliband had been published in the *Guardian* in February, shortly after this book was first published. But it was the comment that immediately preceded them that angered Crosby most, in which Muirhead had said that the public weren't sure what David Cameron stood for, but he didn't know whether that was 'a bad thing or a good thing'.

'Not helpful,' was how Crosby described the quotes down the phone to Muirhead. In the past, Muirhead and his team had been accustomed to calling the shots during a Conservative election campaign. But this time around it was clear that they would be dancing to the Rottweiler's tune.

Indeed, it was Crosby, not Muirhead, who had been behind Michael Fallon's attack on Miliband. In order to counter the apparent upturn in Labour's campaign, Crosby had deployed his signature 'dead cat' manoeuvre, a strategy that Boris Johnson, who employed Crosby as his campaign manager during the 2008 and 2012 London mayoral elections, once described like this: 'There is one thing that is absolutely certain about throwing a dead cat on the dining room table – and I don't mean that people will be outraged, alarmed, disgusted. That is true, but irrelevant. The key point, says my Australian friend, is that everyone will shout, "Jeez, mate, there's a dead cat on the table!" In other words, they will be talking about the dead cat – the thing you want them to talk about – and they will not be talking about the issue that has been causing you so much grief.'

And that is exactly what happened. For the next twenty-four hours, media attention switched away from Labour's clampdown on tax loopholes and towards Fallon's outburst. The veterans at Saatchis were increasingly impressed by their new campaign boss.

'He lent a tremendous discipline and focus to the campaign,' says Jeremy Sinclair. 'He could be blunt but he kept everyone on track.' Many within the Conservative Party had perceived the 2010 election campaign as a shambles. The party had flip-flopped over their strategy. They had switched ad agency halfway through the campaign. And there had been confusion over who was in charge, with both Andy Coulson and Steve Hilton playing senior, but often conflicting, roles.

David Cameron would not make the same mistake twice. Crosby had been appointed as the Conservatives' full-time campaign chief in 2013, for a reported fee of £500,000. His first instruction was for the party to 'scrape the barnacles off the boat' by shedding extraneous policies in favour of a ruthless focus on core issues such as welfare and immigration.

It sounded like something that the Saatchi team themselves might advise. But while the perennial Tory admen admired Crosby's abilities, the feeling wasn't mutual. 'He had his own in-house advertising team. I'm not sure he wanted to hire any agency at first,' says Muirhead. 'And particularly not us, because he likes control and may have thought there might be a risk we would use the back door to go straight to the prime minister or the chancellor. That never happened. He was always there when we presented our work.'

Certainly, a bond had been formed between Cameron and the Saatchi team after the events of 2010. Cameron had sent a note to the agency after the election which read, simply, 'What can I say? You've done it again.' He and his chancellor George Osborne assumed that the admen would be returning to the fold in 2015, but Crosby would first take some convincing. 'He doesn't believe in magic,' says Jeremy Sinclair. 'He is very focused on strategy and is not easily excited about the way in which you execute it.' In other words, it would take more than a funny headline and some glossy images to impress the hard-nosed Australian.

I met Crosby for the first time in September 2015, at his offices in Mayfair. The boardroom where we spoke was adorned with mementoes of his successes: framed press articles proclaiming him the mastermind behind Cameron's victory; signed pictures of the prime minister; a (life-sized) cardboard cut-out of Boris Johnson, with a handwritten message from the mayor which gushes: 'Thanks for running the most amazing campaign!' All of which belies Crosby's reputation as unflashy, blunt and hard to impress. Certainly, he remains far from convinced about the power of traditional advertising in modern politics: 'It is one in a number of tools in a campaign,' he says, before listing direct mail and phone calls as equally important components of the armoury. 'The most effective advertising is that which takes an existing perception and leverages it. So there is a view already held, and the advertising, you hope, will find a powerful way to leverage that view. So advertising is, of itself, not a very persuasive medium or a mind-changing tool. But it is a key part of communications strategy. Its purpose is really to reinforce and trigger existing perceptions.'

The defining theme of the Conservative campaign came as a surprise to some. Midway through, the Saatchi team would unveil a poster depicting Ed Miliband tucked into the breast pocket of former SNP leader Alex Salmond. It was a classic Saatchi execution: simple, powerful, funny and brutal. With a minimum of fuss it made a significant political point seem entirely self-evident. Later, with characteristic self-congratulation, M&C Saatchi would take out a double-page ad in *Campaign*, demonstrating the relationship between the advent of the poster and increased press coverage of a potential Labour/SNP pact. But, as Sinclair suggests, Crosby does not believe in magic. Public fears about the prospect of a so-called 'coalition of chaos' were, Crosby says, prevalent long before the Saatchi poster. 'It was part of our strategy to target Miliband's perceived weakness,' he says. 'We knew a whole year before the campaign started that people were concerned that he would succumb too easily to powerful interest groups. The poster was just an expression of that popularly held perception. It didn't create it; it just drew attention to it.'

Crosby is personable but a vaguely disdainful curl hovers on his lips as he recites this measured assessment of advertising's influence. 'It used to be a twenty-four-hour news cycle, now it is literally a few seconds news cycle,' he says. 'So the days of hiring an agency, getting them in for discussions, sending them away to work on ideas for a few weeks, then getting them back for a presentation and yet more discussions – they're gone. It's just not an appropriate response to most things that happen in a campaign.'

Crosby acknowledges the impact the best political advertising can have on what he calls 'earned media'. 'A great poster, like the Salmond/Miliband one, can get conversations started in the press and on the TV because journalists get excited by it,' he says. But, for him, exciting the media was very much a secondary concern. His priority was to speak directly to voters themselves. In a particularly close electoral fight, with several minor parties muddying the waters of the usually straightforward three-party race for parliamentary seats, Crosby knew it was crucial to identify the small groups of voters in marginal seats who could influence the overall result. And a new media landscape allowed him to communicate with those individuals directly. Social media, he says, 'has increased the intimacy and speed' of communications. Gigantic posters plastered on British high streets now seem a blunt tool by comparison.

In 2013, around the time that Crosby returned to the Tory fold, so too did a lesser-known figure who would play a major role in their campaign. Tom Edmonds had started out as an ad agency copywriter before becoming an in-house creative at Conservative HQ during the 2010 campaign. He had found it a frustrating experience, with the digital work he had produced continually playing second fiddle to the headline-grabbing posters and press ads produced by expensive ad agencies. 'Digital stuff was just an afterthought in 2010,' he says. 'Millions were being spent on posters, many of which backfired. It was a frustrating experience and I decided soon after the election to go back to agency work.'

Edmonds is not a typical Tory advisor. A thirty-something East Midlander, he says he had never been a Tory voter before joining their campaign team. Back in 2010 he had been attracted by the opportunity to work with the likes of Andy Coulson and Steve Hilton rather than by any political convictions. But even after he went back to working in agencies, something bugged him about the events of 2010. He knew that the campaign could have been so much more effective if it had embraced digital media with more enthusiasm. Then one night in 2013 a former colleague from the 2010 election – Craig Elder, then director of digital at communications firm Blue Rubicon – came over to Edmonds's house for dinner and the two began to plan their return to politics. 'We got incredibly pissed on red wine and talked about what we'd do differently if we got a chance to do an election again,' says Edmonds. 'And we both agreed we'd build an in-house agency so that we had the speed and flexibility we needed, as well as being able to produce the volume of content we needed to run incredibly micro-targeted campaigns, taking advantage of all the advances in digital tools that had taken place over the last few years. Plus everything we did would be measurable and quantifiable, and aimed at the voters we needed to win the election – no more gimmicks just for the media.'

The ideas dovetailed perfectly with those of Crosby. There was a sense at Tory HQ that their journey to government in 2010 was far more bumpy than it might have been. There was an appetite for radical change inside the campaign machine – and radical change was what Edmonds and Elder were offering. Their first task was to identify the exact people the party needed to communicate with. 'The first two years was a case of building our database of Tory voters – and potential Tory voters,' he says. 'We grew our mailing list from 300,000 to 1.5 million. That doesn't happen overnight, and it took money. We did some stuff on change.org and other petition sites to find people who were interested in causes that chimed with Conservative values. We sought out like-minded people on YouTube and

Facebook. Once you have these people on your mailing list, you can start communicating with them on a regular basis. Email becomes your most powerful driver.'

As the election drew closer, Edmonds and his team – under the stewardship of Crosby – began producing bespoke content for specific voting groups around the country. Rather than the 'one-size-fits-all' approach of traditional political ads, Edmonds and his team could craft specific content for each type of voter. There were those who perceived the Conservative campaign to be low-key by comparison to the theatrical broadcasts and poster unveilings of the past, but Edmonds insists this was a view generated by a London-based media that was not the target of their carefully planned digital campaign. He showed me a selection of messages sent out to different types of potential Tory voter. One Facebook post, which came with a short video attachment about the economic recovery, was designed specifically with female UKIP waverers in mind. 'We're building a brighter, more secure future for our children and grandchildren,' it read. 'A vote for UKIP, or any party other than the Conservatives, would let in Labour and the SNP – and risk everything we've achieved together over the last five years.' 'We knew they would lean Conservative when the choice was about the economy and their family's future,' explains Edmonds. Another sponsored tweet, aimed squarely at Lib Dem waverers in the south-west, declared: 'This general election is not like last time. By voting Lib Dem you could end up with a chaotic coalition of Ed Miliband and who-knows-what other parties that could put the economy, jobs and public services at risk.' The accompanying image showed a swingometer with David Cameron looking decidedly prime ministerial on one side and a confused-looking Miliband, flanked by Alex Salmond and new SNP leader Nicola Sturgeon, on the other. An arrow pointed to a small amount of white space dividing them, beneath the headline 'Yours is one of 23 seats that will decide this election.'

It was a graphic and immediate way of spoon-feeding key people the notion of tactical voting. It was a quietly relentless campaign that went largely unnoticed by London journalists covering the election, but it proved decisive in the marginal seats. 'In terms of how we communicated with the public, it was a complete turnaround from 2010,' says Edmonds. 'We could put together ideas quickly in-house, get a quick approval from Lynton, who would be sat beside us in the office, then send it out immediately. We could also track its impact. If it seemed to be working, we would press on. If people weren't engaging, we tried something else. It was so much more trackable than a poster.' The amount of online activity by the Conservatives was immense: in April the press reported that the party was spending £100,000 per month on Facebook advertising alone (a figure which Edmonds confirms was 'roughly accurate').

Meanwhile, the press were paying closer attention to the more visible ads being created by M&C Saatchi. These, says Edmonds, were 'great for the morale of party workers because of the bullish tone and visibility', but were regarded by party HQ as far less important to the electoral battle. As far back as 2014 Jeremy Sinclair and Bill Muirhead had been pitching their ideas for the campaign ahead. 'We produced an image of a bucket of manure and a shovel,' says Sinclair. 'The headline read: "We're sorry it's taking us so long to clear up Labour's mess." We presented it to the leadership at party headquarters and everyone seemed to like it.

The prime minister is very receptive to advertising and so is George Osborne. They laughed.' There was an enthusiasm among key members of the campaign team to run the poster right away and set the tone for the following year's battle. But one figure – a woman whom Muirhead and Sinclair refuse to name – argued against the idea, saying: 'I don't think people find manure particularly attractive.'

The first prominent poster produced by the Conservatives in 2015 showed a sunny road alongside the headline 'Let's stay on the road to a stronger economy.' The subhead read: '1.75 million more people in work. 760,000 more businesses. The deficit halved.' It didn't appear to fit in with the usual Saatchi approach: the image of a road merging into a Union Jack was muddled; the headline was long and fact heavy; most tellingly of all, it was positive. Jeremy Sinclair was dismayed when he saw it: 'It wasn't us, and anyone who knew our work would have been able to see that,' he says. 'As a Conservative I was disappointed because I didn't think it did its job very well.' Edmonds agreed: 'It was trying to be positive, and people don't tend to remember positive posters,' he says. 'They remember the ones that take the piss out of the other side. Also, in the old days the media would have simply run a story saying that the Conservatives have a new poster out. Nowadays, they wait for the spoofs and parodies to take off online and run a story on that instead. There is so much expense and risk involved in that sort of ad.'

Indeed, it took the papers less than twenty-four hours after the poster's unveiling to establish that the road in the ad ('It's a British picture, a British road,' George Osborne had said at the launch) was in fact a library image of a German road. The posters that followed would be put safely back in the hands of M&C Saatchi. At the beginning of March, billboards across the UK were plastered with a gigantic wrecking ball smashing into a headline that read: 'A recovering economy. Don't let Labour wreck it.' It was as blunt and confrontational as one would expect from an M&C Saatchi poster, and in its wanton simplicity it was straight out of the Lynton Crosby playbook. 'Labour will wreck the economy, that was the perception that our research proved was already out there,' says Crosby. 'And that was all we really wanted to say. In any campaign you have limited resources. You cannot talk about fifty different things because people don't have time to think about them all. They are not thinking about political issues every day. In fact, Jim Messina [the former Barack Obama pollster who worked alongside Crosby for the Conservatives] said that studies during the US presidential election showed that people thought about politics for just four minutes a week. So you really have to talk about one or two things that are important or emblematic and keep focusing on that, otherwise you are going to have no impact.'

Danny Brooke-Taylor, founder of ad agency Lucky Generals, puts it more simplistically: 'Politicians can forget how to communicate their message to people who don't give a shit.' Two years before the election Brooke-Taylor had found himself having lunch with celebrity cook Delia Smith and shadow chancellor Ed Balls. 'It was a bit like a weird cheese dream,' he recalls. He had met Smith while making a commercial for Waitrose. Knowing that Brooke-Taylor was a Labour supporter, Smith had arranged the lunch with Balls. 'She sat next to Ed at a Norwich City match and said that she had wanted to get us together for a while,' says Brooke-Taylor. 'She was very passionate about

Labour and kept banging on the table, telling us that we needed a massive poster that said something like, "We want all Labour supporters to get out and vote!" She was waving her hands around and saying, "I need a better phrase than that." I was sitting there thinking, "Please say, 'Let's be 'avin' you!' [the phrase Smith had ill-advisedly shouted at Norwich City supporters through a microphone during a match some years previously]."'

It was a strange start to what would prove a troublesome relationship. Brooke-Taylor and his business partner Helen Calcraft were lifelong Labour supporters who let it be known that their new agency (they had founded Lucky Generals in 2013) was at the disposal of the party. 'If you are a new agency and you want to be making work that has a social relevance beyond just flogging stuff, then political advertising is very fulfilling,' says Brooke-Taylor. 'If it meets with your own political sensibilities as well, then the momentum and natural energy that bubbles up from that is quite thrilling.' But once they had made initial contact with Labour's campaign team, the relationship turned out to be rather less inspiring than Brooke-Taylor had hoped. 'We wanted to advise them on how to excite Twitter, to start conversations not just with existing supporters but potential voters too. We wanted to talk to people through social media, get involved with the issues they were interested in and develop the party's personality beyond just telling people to vote Labour or slagging off the Tories. But all they ever asked us was, "What's the poster?" And I personally am sick and tired of seeing some politician with their sweep-over hair pulling back a crappy velvet curtain to unveil some shitty poster that will only stay up for about five minutes.'

Brooke-Taylor's fears were aroused at initial meetings with Labour's campaign chiefs, among them shadow foreign secretary Douglas Alexander, head of strategy and communication Tom Baldwin and campaign director Spencer Livermore. Tellingly, says Brooke-Taylor, they would each arrive separately from different locations, giving the impression that they were not a cohesive unit with a cogent strategy. As an agency, Lucky Generals was unable ever to establish which individual among the throng was in charge – and what the plan was. 'When the wrecking-ball poster came out, they asked us to think up a spoof where it swung back the other way with a different message. My first thought was, "For fuck's sake."'

They had first produced work for the party in May 2014, when they were asked to make a broadcast in response to George Osborne's budget. Brooke-Taylor was keen to investigate the positive message Labour could put out, positioning the party as a viable alternative to the coalition government. 'When we work with commercial clients we are always looking for ways to talk about the positive contributions they can make so people feel good about their brand,' says Brooke-Taylor. 'But when we pitched that approach to Labour we were basically told, "Yeah, fuck that, let's nail Clegg."' Calculating that the easiest way to achieve power would be to undermine deputy prime minister Nick Clegg and inherit wavering Liberal Democrat voters, Labour insisted on a negative ad. Lucky Generals came up with a spoof of the popular archaeological TV show *Time Team*, hosted by the Labour-supporting actor Tony Robinson. The idea would see Robinson digging up a relic of Nick Clegg's backbone – a reference to the Lib Dem leader's apparent capitulation to Tory demands. The idea was rejected. So too was a later idea for a broadcast featuring actors portraying David Cameron and George Osborne as slippery estate agents trying to sell a house that, like the UK economy, appeared in good condition but was rotten and dilapidated on the inside. But even these ideas were conceived with some reluctance, says Brooke-Taylor. 'We rolled over on strategy because we were new to politics and thought that they might know best,' he says. 'But we felt that all the Tory-bashing made us look like the snide bloke in the pub who couldn't stop having a pop about the other bloke.'

Negativity and fear-mongering were working for the Tories. They were applying the principle best summarised by Tim Bell: 'People vote out of fear.' But in opposition things are more complicated. The public could see what David Cameron had done in government and were capable of making their own minds up. What Tony Blair had emphasised in 1997 was the positive changes he would make if he were elected. So, while attacking John Major's government for its record, he offered a specific outline of the improvement he could make. His campaign was infused with a message of hope and optimism, as encapsulated by the pledge card, which detailed five simple policy promises that would make an immediate impact on people's lives. In 2015 the Labour team tried and failed to create an equally neat campaign tool. 'There was an obsession with finding the new pledge card,' says Brooke-Taylor. 'At one point we had the idea of it being someone's hand held up, each finger representing a pledge. But then they dreamt up a sixth pledge, so we would have had to have found a politician with six fingers on one hand to make that work.' Instead, they returned to the comfort zone of negative campaigning.

Eventually, the May 2014 broadcast was entitled *The Un-Credible Shrinking Man*, a spoof on a fifties B-movie trailer, in which Nick Clegg was portrayed as the pathetic object of Tory bullying. It was cleverly written, nicely performed and a refreshing change from traditionally sober and dull political broadcasts. But Brooke-Taylor was convinced it backfired on the party. 'Nobody saw it because the party couldn't afford to do a promoted tweet about it,' he says. 'Most people just read about it in a hostile press, who said, "Look at all the money the Labour Party spent on getting some advertising wankers to make a bitter, snide attack on Nick Clegg." It just added to this sense that we had nothing positive to say.'

Nevertheless, the relationship between the agency and the party continued into election year. Despite announcements that Lucky Generals had been appointed as Labour's lead agency, Brooke-Taylor says they never felt central to the campaign. 'We were not involved in any strategic thinking. We were just receiving muddled briefs from various people and colouring in the gaps,' he says. 'Other agencies were involved, which was difficult because it made everyone feel as if they were pitching against each other the whole time. It was the sort of situation that we wouldn't have tolerated from another client. I confess I naively assumed that we could do some work that somebody on the street might think was interesting, forgetting that it had to go through a complex spaghetti junction of other people before it got made.' The fundamental problem, says Brooke-Taylor, was that the party leadership were preoccupied with internal politics. As he puts it, 'They liked the smell of their own farts.' The obsessive navel-gazing, the machinations of internal politics, the tangled web of party management and confused leadership structure sounds uncannily, almost implausibly like the situation faced by admen like Chris Powell and Johnny Wright in the early eighties, before the likes of Peter Mandelson undertook the long, arduous process of modernising Labour's communications. It is remarkable to hear Brooke-Taylor's account of how easily and quickly things seemed to have slipped back to the same shambolic state they had been in three decades previously. Tellingly, none of those who had fought to change the party were prepared to speak about the sorry events that surrounded Labour's 2015 campaign. One of the party's most experienced communications advisors told me that the experience had convinced him to 'retire from politics'.

Some of the Conservative campaign team were incredulous at Labour's approach. 'All we saw was them attacking our record,' says Tom Edmonds. 'But they never seemed to convince people that they could do anything better if they were in government. We couldn't understand why they didn't work harder at that.' But the team at M&C Saatchi were less surprised by Labour's inadequacies. 'We were called at the last minute for the "No" campaign during the Scottish referendum,' says Jeremy Sinclair. 'It was run by Douglas Alexander, who we knew would be in charge of Labour's campaign the following year also. There was a sense that his team couldn't leave any of our ideas alone. There was interference and over-analysis. It was annoying at the time but encouraging for us knowing that they would struggle with their own election campaign in 2015.'

The experience of the Scottish referendum would inform much of the Conservative campaign the following year. Lynton Crosby continually fed Saatchis evidence that Ed Miliband was perceived as dangerously weak by large parts of the public. In early 2015 Sinclair and Bill Muirhead had presented a poster depicting the Labour leader stood beside the deep end of a swimming pool and wearing goggles, a rubber ring and inflatable armbands. There was no headline; the image said it all. But focus groups suggested that the poster was perhaps too mean. The Saatchi team created a second draft of the poster, in which Miliband was joined by Alex Salmond, dressed in a lifeguard's uniform, with a speech bubble that read: 'I'll save you!' Salmond was no longer leader of the SNP but his public profile had been boosted by the referendum, and the Saatchi team used it to their advantage. The poster was received positively by focus groups, but the Saatchi team refined it further, depicting a gormless-looking Miliband peeping out of Salmond's top pocket. Discussion of a possible Labour/SNP coalition rocketed across the wider media as soon as it was unveiled. The poster convinced floating voters in England that a vote for any party other than the Conservatives would deliver a 'coalition of chaos', while those in Scotland were further persuaded that a vote for the SNP would deliver serious influence for the party in Westminster. The poster now sits prominently in reception at M&C Saatchi's offices in Soho. In an election year when the influence of traditional advertising was generally seen to be in decline, the Saatchi team still managed to deliver the most memorable piece of communication.

'They got their famous poster out of it,' says Tom Edmonds. 'But no ad agency in their right mind would take on the sort of campaign that we were running out of party headquarters. There were dozens of messages going out every day. This was quick turnaround stuff that was approved by Lynton across the desk at short notice before going up online. Ad agencies just aren't set up to do that weight of work. They have other clients to service. Plus, they like every piece of work they produce to be a ten out of ten because their name depends on it. I've worked in agencies and sat through many three-hour meetings on what ampersand to use on a poster. There is just no time for that level of analysis in an election campaign. Sometimes we had to be just as happy with an eight-out-of-ten idea.'

On 9 April, just as *The Times* was reporting Michael Fallon's attack on Ed Miliband, the *Guardian* splashed their front page with the headline 'Labour Moves Ahead of Tories on the Day the Polls Turned'. The newspaper's political editor, Patrick Wintour, wrote underneath: 'The strongest, if still tentative, sign that the Conservatives' narrow and negative campaign is misfiring emerged on Thursday when three polls showed Labour moving ahead and, for the first time, one poll found that Ed Miliband had more positive personal approval ratings than David Cameron.'

By this stage, says Danny Brooke-Taylor, Labour had 'gone quiet' on his agency. Some posters attacking the Tory record on the NHS had appeared online but nobody knew who had created them. It seemed that the encouraging movement in the opinion polls had convinced Ed Miliband and his team that they were on course for a narrow victory, with or without extra campaign advice. Meanwhile, at Lynton Crosby's campaign nerve centre, there was a great deal more scepticism towards the polls. 'All of the polls they referred to were well within the margin of error,' says Crosby. 'There is laziness to political discourse. Commentators sit in their offices and think, "I'll go and write a column." They have not gone out there and talked to a voter. They would not know a bloody voter if they fell over one. Then they look at a poll and assume that a poll is a proxy for what is really going on.'

The polls continuously pointed towards a hung parliament, with the Conservatives as the slightly larger party. The eventual result, in which David Cameron was able to form a government with an overall majority of twelve seats, proved the biggest shock since the 1992 election. Crosby and pollster-in-chief Jim Messina were perhaps the only people in the country who were not surprised, having ignored the public opinion polls throughout the campaign. 'Ask my wife and she will tell you that I was the most relaxed I have ever been during a campaign,' says Crosby. 'That does not mean that there weren't some highly stressful nights. But when you looked at the numbers and put them into our model I always believed that David Cameron would be prime minister.'

Even large parts of the Tory-supporting press had been critical of Crosby's campaign. And as his party failed to improve its standing in the polls, the clamour for a more aggressive approach had increased. But the Australian had remained unmoved.

'The problem with polling now is that it has become a commodity,' he says. 'So most of these polling companies use polls to get coverage in newspapers to build their brand. That is what they do, which is fair enough, and an understandable strategy. But they are therefore inevitably somewhat simplistic in their approach. I am not dismissing it, but they tend to ask very binary questions. So, unlike going to the doctor, a public poll will tell you that your temperature is thirty-eight-and-a-half or forty-one or forty-two degrees. It does not tell you whether it is that temperature because you have cancer or because you have got a cold or because you have just been wearing too many clothes. It is not a criticism in a sense, but the truth is [public polls] are somewhat superficial.'

Crosby insists that the polls overestimated the turnout among groups more likely to vote Labour, such as young people and ethnic minorities. 'Newspapers are not interested in reporting statistical dead heats,' he says. 'There is no drama in that. They want to speculate about who is going to win. We were using polling differently. We look at polls and think, "Well, shit, we are down with women! Why are we down with women? And what can we do about it?"

'All pollsters and polls make assumptions. Any pollster will tell you that a poll with a margin of error of plus or minus 3 per cent means the numbers could be 3 per cent higher or 3 per cent lower, 95 per cent of the time. Five per cent of the time they could be completely out of queue with what is going on. But the media just grab the top line and focus on that.'

Danny Brooke-Taylor had spent much of the run-up to the election co-writing a Labour Party broadcast with Paul Greengrass, the director of such Hollywood blockbusters as *The Bourne Ultimatum* and *Captain Phillips*. 'It was supposed to be a gritty and emotional depiction of Ed Miliband in a car on his way to Parliament. But they dropped it at the last minute because somebody panicked and said the public just wasn't buying Ed.' Brooke-Taylor was deeply frustrated by his experiences with Labour but maintains he'd do it again. 'I think we would insist on being more involved at the strategic level,' he says. 'We were probably a bit flattered to be involved, but to make a difference we'd have to be given more responsibility.'

Labour's final campaign debacle was the unveiling of Ed Miliband's so-called 'Ed Stone', a 2.6-metre-high, two-tonne stone with Labour's key election pledges chiselled into it. Miliband declared that, once elected, he would erect the stone in the Downing Street rose garden to remind him of his goals. Immediately, it became the object of online ridicule. Brooke-Taylor had watched its unveiling on the news, aghast. 'I was initially worried that it might have been somehow based on one of our ideas, which it wasn't,' he says. 'But at least it was offering something positive, not just bashing the Tories like everything else.' Having cost an estimated £30,000 to make, just days after the election the stone was found dumped in a skip on an industrial estate in Woolwich, south-east London.

But for many it was symbolic of a vague and complacent Labour campaign strategy that would ultimately doom them to one of their worst ever election defeats. 'Labour thought that because the Conservatives did not win in 2010, when Labour had Gordon Brown as their leader and the economy was in the toilet, the Tories would be unable to win [in 2015], and all they had to do was sit on the horse and hang on and they would win,' says Crosby. 'So that is the mistake they made. They never said sorry for their mishaps, they never really did an honest review of their policies, they never had a story about the future for the British people. Elections are about the future. David Cameron had a story about the future, about how he had a plan for a better future, about what that future might look like, and that is why he won. They just did not do the work. They were intellectually lazy and thought themselves intellectually superior. They convinced themselves that they just had to sit on the horse and they would get there.'

The 2015 election might have seen influence slip further from the hands of traditional ad agencies, but the principles that Crosby successfully applied to the Conservative campaign – brevity, relentlessness, focus on and leverage of the public's preconceptions – were the same ones that ad agencies – not least the Saatchis – had been espousing for decades. It was not the strategy that Crosby changed but the execution. Digital media has increased both the possibilities and the demands of political communication. Tom Edmonds's ten-man team at Tory HQ was better able to keep pace with the fast-turnaround world of digital content. Suddenly, traditional ad agencies seemed flat-footed by comparison.

For Jeremy Sinclair and Bill Muirhead, the campaign had been like no other they had worked on before. 'People in the London/Westminster media "bubble" didn't see the real picture because there were not as many forty-eight-sheet posters as usual,' says Muirhead. 'It was based upon micro-targeting very specific groups of voters in marginal seats. That is how accurately campaigns can be organised now.' Sinclair is nevertheless convinced that the bigger, national message still played a crucial role in the result. 'The whole thing was based on a very simple message: only one of two people could be prime minister. One of them is weak, the other is David Cameron. Cameron won the election because he was the more convincing prime minister. And we are at our best when we have a good product to work with.'

It might be that they never get the chance to do so again. 'It is interesting because there are a lot of countries in the world that do not use advertising agencies any more,' says Crosby. 'In Australia, the Liberal Party has not used an advertising agency as such since the mid-nineties. It has tended to bring together people from advertising agencies, so people with creative or production experience, but it has not got an agency. It has effectively built a virtual agency, and in some ways that is the direction things are going.'

The 2015 general election campaign might have felt like the beginning of the end for the traditional ad agency model. But it can simultaneously be seen as its greatest vindication. Lynton Crosby triumphed in one of the closest electoral battles of modern times by employing the same key principles that ad agencies – particularly the Saatchi team – had been espousing for decades. He ran a campaign which took simple messages about leadership and economic management and repeated them ad nauseam. Admen had been using the same techniques in commercial campaigns for over a century, and had been trying to do the same for political campaigns since the seventies. It is ironic that now, just as those ideas seem to have been fully embraced by the political class (or at least the Conservative Party), the ad agencies themselves have started to look slightly outdated. The mystique and ceremony that agencies apply to their creative processes were an integral part of their industry's growth, but in the digital age the ad business no longer has a stranglehold on creative magic. Communications can be produced to a similar standard, with seemingly less fuss and fanfare, by those outside the traditional agency system. It is hard to see why or to what end political parties will ever employ ad agencies again. But, however election campaigns are executed in the future, the strategic foundations established in the late twentieth century by the likes of Tim Bell, Trevor Beattie, Jeremy Sinclair and Chris Powell will always remain. And if the history of British electioneering has taught us anything, it's that we should never rule out a comeback by the Saatchis.

ACKNOWLEDGEMENTS

First of all, thanks to everyone who agreed to be interviewed for this book. You definitely had better things to do. I owe you all.

Some thanks to the people who helped me out with invaluable contacts when I started on this project: Lucy Owen, Rosie Brown née Seed, Matt Nikson, John Plunkett and Julia Hobsbawm. I am sure I have been a pain in the neck to the various PAs who have helped facilitate interviews over the past couple of years, particularly Maree Glass, Jackie Francis, Tahlia Dolan and Teresa Woodley. Thank you all for being helpful and patient.

Thanks to Jay Pond-Jones for support and interest throughout; to Deborah Mattinson for the background input and contacts you put my way; to Frank Lowe for the support, contacts, insight and friendship; and to Professor Ivor Crewe for his time and help.

Nick Canham at the Richard Stone Partnership: thanks for all the hard work and support.

Alan M. Watson for the diligent, efficient and invaluable transcribing – many thanks.

Thanks to Antonia Jennings for all the background research, notes and bibliography. Top marks for intelligence, efficiency and niceness.

Adam Gordon, you went above and beyond the call of duty on the old picture research. You did so without complaint, managing to maintain your stunning looks and poise throughout.

Jeremy Monblat made a brilliant documentary called *Selling Power* a few years ago, which was one of the inspirations for this book. Benedict Pringle runs a brilliant blog called Politicaladvertising.co.uk, which was a great resource throughout my research. Many thanks to you both.

Matthew Hamilton at Aitken Alexander, my agent, is a great man. Thanks for everything, mate.

Julian Loose at Faber & Faber: thank you for buying into this idea. I mean that both metaphorically and literally. I hope you like it. You're stuck with it now.

Kate Murray-Browne, your insights and advice have been invaluable. And your patience has been greatly appreciated.

Ian Bahrami, thanks so much for your skill and diligence in the editing process. You have helped mould this manuscript into shape with supreme deftness.

John Grindrod, I've always said you were a genius, and you proved it once and for all by pushing Faber to buy this book and advising me on how to write the bastard thing.

Thank you, Sophie Portas. You are almost certainly the best publicist at Faber. You're certainly the best publicist I've worked with.

Here are all the family and friends who helped me out while I was trying to finish this book amidst the busiest and most chaotic year of my life: Chris Payne, you are a rock, an unflinching heroine in our family's life. Thanks for everything, always. Sue and Caspar, thanks for letting us live at your house and allowing me to use it to write while you were at work. Sorry about losing the dog. I was stuck on Chapter 2 at the time.

Sophie Wright, what would any of us do without you? Thanks for everything.

Bren, you're the best mum in the world. Obviously. Thanks for everything you've done to stop me going mad and eating the manuscript. And thanks for bringing me up. You taught me pretty much everything.

Baz, this book is dedicated to you because you're a great dad and inspired my interest in all this stuff. I hope you like it. Imagine if I wrote 'I love you'. That would be a bit embarrassing for both of us, wouldn't it? Don't worry, I'm not going to do that.

Lenny, this book is also dedicated to you because you're the best son a man could ever wish for. I am immensely proud of you. You're the funniest bloke I know. When I was trying to finish this book in my office and you kept banging on the door and screaming, 'Daddy, Daddy, what are you doing?' I found it very soothing and helpful. You're the best.

Coco, you are a wonderful girl and I am so proud of you. Sorry that this book took up so much of my time. I owe you about a billion weekends. You are kind, clever, funny and brilliant, and I am touched by how much interest you've taken in this book. Don't ever read it, it's boring. Sorry we couldn't use your cover in the end.

Anna, however difficult this book made 2014 for me, it made it twice as difficult for you. As ever, you have been patient, kind, understanding and unflinching in your support. You are the most brilliant, wise, smart, funny, beautiful and brilliant wife a man could hope for. Love you always and for ever, even on Sunday mornings when I'm a bit grumpy.

And, finally, Tom 'Pilau' Pallai. Thanks for absolutely nothing, ever.

SOURCES

INTRODUCTION

xxiv 'Tim Bell had been ushered through the security gates', Tyler, 1987.

CHAPTER 1

3 '"I feel neither depraved nor uplifted"', *A Short History of British Television Advertising*, National Media Museum files, p. 1.

4 '"Persil washes whiter. That means cleaner"', ibid.

5 '"The only criterion that mattered in the industry"', Delaney, (2007), p. 23.

5 '"Bob suggested that once you'd worked out"', ibid., p. 9.

12 '"I was a rare thing in that I was politically motivated"', *Selling Power: Admen and Number 10*, BBC Four documentary (2008).

CHAPTER 3

38 '"[Reece] jollied me along"', Hollingsworth (1997), pp. 51–2.

38 '"If you have a good thing to sell"', ibid., p. 53.

41 '"I've always thought a committee approach"', Fallon (1998), p. 187.

41 '"God, we could get really famous"', ibid.

42 '"There was a dynamism about the place"', ibid., p. 188.

43 '"We had to explain"', Hollingsworth (1997), p. 58.

45 '"Get a lot of trouble"', ibid.

53 '"no theme, no passion and no relation"', ibid., p. 68.

54 '"The Conservatives could therefore present themselves"', ibid., p. 69.

CHAPTER 5

78 '"I was immensely confident"', Hollingsworth (1997), p. 81.
81 'In reality, Lawson had no intention of dropping the agency', ibid., p. 93.
82 '"It's better to be a bankrupt party in power"', ibid., p. 92.
82 'a casually racist little Englander', ibid., p. 81.
82 '"one of the greatest mistakes of his life"', ibid., p. 82.
88 '"Tim had a more sensitive set of antennae"', ibid., pp. 93–4.

CHAPTER 6

102 'The next day he saw a GP', Mandelson (2010), p. 85.
104 '"This was the situation I found in 1985"', Gould (2011), p. 51.
106 'Back at Walworth Road, Mandelson sat', ibid., p. 41.
109 'He was unable to stop the singing', Mandelson (2010), p. 89.
109 'Brent Friends of the Earth to the Rastafarian Society', Gould (2011), p. 68.
111 '"If we lose this election"', ibid., p. 71.
113 '"Tebbit's words bore little relationship"', ibid., p. 76.
113 '"Presenting Labour in a positive light"', ibid., p. 69.
116 '"Some people say that"', ibid., p. 76.
120 '"Can I record that I believe"', Mandelson (2010), p. 103.
120 '"the Machiavelli of Walworth Road"', ibid.

CHAPTER 7

126 '"That's it: she's downhill"', Thatcher (1993), p. 585.
126 '"It was not a happy"', ibid., p. 573.
130 '"[Young] was a businessman"', Hollingsworth (1997), p. 58.
132 '"a ding dong row"', Thatcher (1993), p. 584.
136 '"I said, 'Now look, Maurice'"', Young (1990), p. 54.
137 '"They're a bit amateurish"', ibid., p. 223.
138 '"It really is unseemly"', Bell (2014), p. 119.
139 '"In the meantime, I'm going to invest"', ibid., p. 120.
140 'The Saatchis were so angry', Hollingsworth (1997), p. 183.

CHAPTER 8

146 '"He deserves it but he's left us in the shit"', Mandelson (2010), p. 125.
146 '"I've never known Neil so angry"', ibid.
149 '"In short, Labour has stalled"', Gould (2011), p. 98.
151 'Smith told them angrily', ibid., p. 119.
153 '"Maurice Saatchi told a friend"', ibid., p. 113.
154 'Philip Gould was later told', ibid., p. 127.

CHAPTER 10

186 'In 1987 the combined expenditure on ads', Crewe (1998), p. 32.
189 '"There was short gap between the end"', Mattinson (2011), p. 103.
191 '"intensely relaxed about people getting filthy rich"', *Financial Times*, 23 October 1998.
191 '"We could not argue that Labour had not changed"', Crewe (1998), p. 45.
196 '"Labour's version of 'new' was winning"', ibid., p. 47.
199 '"Its honest, glitz-free"', Gould (2011), p. 320.
201 '"I didn't want to be clever"', ibid., p. 314.
202 '"When unplanned events come to dominate"', Crewe (1998), p. 47.

CHAPTER 11

214 '"I demanded a campaign"', Gould (2011), p. 56.
215 '"There was a drawing in of breath"', ibid.
227 'Blair . . . wrote "a strong economy"', Rawnsley (2010), p. 305.

CHAPTER 12

237 '"The Tory high command would be better advised"', *Independent*, 26 March 2010.

ADDENDUM

268 '"Miliband stabbed his own brother in the back"', *The Times*, 9 April 2015.

269 'All very fascinating, but voters', *The Times*, 19 March 2015.

270 '"You can't fatten the pig on market day"', www.bbc.com/news/uk-politics-20461630.

270 '"There is one thing that is absolutely certain about throwing a dead cat"', *The Spectator*, 9 April 2015.

277 'the party was spending £100,000 per month on Facebook advertising alone', *Guardian*, 6 February 2015.

286 '"The strongest, if still tentative, sign"', *Guardian*, 9 April 2015.

289 'Having cost an estimated £30,000 to make', *Daily Telegraph*, 16 May 2015.

BIBLIOGRAPHY

Bartle, J., Mortimore, R. and Atkinson, S. (eds), *Political Communications: The General Election of 2001*. Routledge (2002).

Bell, T., *Right or Wrong: The Memoirs of Lord Bell*. Bloomsbury (2014).

Campbell, A., *The Blair Years: Extracts from the Alastair Campbell Diaries*. Arrow (2008).

Crewe, I. and Gosschalk, B., *Political Communications: The General Election Campaign of 1992*. Cambridge University Press (1995).

Crewe, I., Gosschalk, B. and Bartle, J., *Political Communications: Why Labour Won the General Election of 1997*. Routledge (1998).

Crewe, I. and Harrop, M., *Political Communications: The General Election Campaign of 1983*. Cambridge University Press (1986).

Crewe, I. and Harrop, M., *Political Communications: The General Election Campaign of 1987*. Cambridge University Press (1989).

Delaney, S., *Get Smashed: The Story of the Men Who Made the Adverts that Changed Our Lives*. Sceptre (2007).

Fallon, I., *The Brothers: The Rise and Rise of Saatchi & Saatchi*. Hutchinson (1988).

Fendley, A., *Saatchi & Saatchi: The Inside Story*. Arcade Publishing (1996).

Gould, P., *The Unfinished Revolution: How New Labour Changed British Politics Forever*. Abacus (2011).

Hollingsworth, M., *The Ultimate Spin Doctor: The Life & Fast Times of Tim Bell*. Coronet Books (1997).

Mandelson, P., *The Third Man: Life at the Heart of New Labour*. HarperPress (2010).

Mattinson, D., *Talking to a Brick Wall: How New Labour Stopped Listening to the Voter and Why We Need a New Politics*. Biteback Publishing (2011).

Rawnsley, A., *Servants of the People: The Inside Story of New Labour*. Penguin (2001).

———, *The End of the Party: The Rise and Fall of New Labour*. Penguin (2010).

Routledge, P., *Mandy: The Unauthorised Biography of Peter Mandelson*. Simon & Schuster Ltd (1999).

Särlvik, B. and Crewe, I., *Decade of Dealignment: The Conservative Victory of 1979 and Electoral Trends in the 1970s*. Cambridge University Press (1983).

Scott, J., *Fast and Louche: Confessions of a Flagrant Sinner*. Profile Books (2010).

Thatcher, M., *The Downing Street Years*. HarperPress (1993).

Tyler, R., *Campaign! The Selling of the Prime Minister*. Grafton (1987).

Wring, D., Mortimore, R. and Atkinson, S. (eds), *Political Communication in Britain: The Leader Debates, the Campaign and the Media in the 2010 General Elections*. Palgrave Macmillan (2011).

Young, D., *The Enterprise Years: A Businessman in the Cabinet*. Headline Book Publishing (1990).

INDEX